Native American Legends

Southeastern Legends: Tales from the Natchez,
Caddo, Biloxi, Chickasaw, and Other Nations

AUGUST HOUSE

AMERICAN
FOLKLORE
SERIES

Native American Legends

Southeastern Legends: Tales from the Natchez, Caddo, Biloxi, Chickasaw, and Other Nations

Compiled and edited by
George E. Lankford

THIS VOLUME IS A PART OF
The American Folklore Series
W.K. McNeil, General Editor

August House / Little Rock
PUBLISHERS

Published 1987 by August House, Inc.,
P.O. Box 3223, Little Rock, Arkansas, 72203,
501-372-5450.

Printed in the United States of America

10 9 8 7 6 5 4 3 2 1   HC
10 9 8 7 6 5   PB

LIBRARY OF CONGRESS CATALOGING-IN-PUBLICATION DATA

Lankford, George E., 1938-
Native American legends.
(American Folklore Series)
Bibliography: p. 258
1. Indians of North America—Southern States—Legends.
2. Indians of North America—Legends.
I. Title. II. Series
E78.S65L36   1987
398.2'0897075   87-1144
ISBN 0-87483-038-9 (hc)
ISBN 0-87483-039-7 (pb)

Cover design by Harvill Ross Studios Ltd.
Production artwork by Ira L. Hocut
Typography by Diversified Graphics, Little Rock, Arkansas
Design direction by Ted Parkhurst
Project direction by Hope Coulter

AUGUST HOUSE, INC.   PUBLISHERS   LITTLE ROCK

To the memory
of the ancient inhabitants
of the Southeast

Contents

List of Texts

List of Figures

Acknowledgments

In the course of producing a volume such as this, an author incurs a great many debts to scholars and friends who share their knowledge and give aid and support to the project. Among the many who have given me such support are the following:

■ the Folklore Institute at Indiana University, where my interest in Southeastern narratives was first quickened.

■ Arkansas College, which granted me a semester's leave in which much of the work was done.

■ the Hall Center for the Humanities at the University of Kansas, which made me a Mellon Fellow and gave me a temporary home for the semester.

■ William K. McNeil, folklorist at the Ozark Folk Center, editor of the series and careful critic.

■ John T. Dahlquist, historian and dean of Arkansas College, who read and commented on the manuscript.

■ V.J. Knight, archaeologist at the University of Alabama, who reviewed the volume from an anthropological and ethnohistorical perspective.

■ T.E. Blythe, legal editor in New York, who gave the manuscript a painstakingly close reading.

To all of these friends go my thanks for their aid and support. In many cases I have followed their advice, but in some I have stubbornly followed my own lead. They, of course, are in no way responsible for the deficiencies of this book.

Map of the Native American Southeast

Introduction

The traditional narratives of the American Indians have been of interest to outsiders since Europeans first discovered this New World. Indeed, on his second voyage to America in 1493, Christopher Columbus brought along Friar Ramon Pané for the express purpose of collecting all the data he could from the natives concerning "their ceremonies and their antiquities."[1] The two years the priest spent among the Taino, a now long extinct tribe living in present-day Haiti, resulted in a slender volume titled *On the Antiquities of the Indians* (1496), a work that has descended to the present in its entirety only in Ferdinand Columbus's life of his father.[2]

Although small in length, the little book's twenty-six brief chapters are filled with information about a variety of customs, beliefs, legends, and myths. Considering his profession it is hardly surprising that Pané viewed the Indians as ignorant savages who were basically believers in erroneous ideas. There was one point, however, on which they agreed with Europeans. The Taino believed in a supreme immortal invisible being "whose dwelling place and habitation is heaven."[3] But this was as much as the missionary would grant, for "with this true and catholic knowledge of the true God they mingled these errors to wit, that God had a mother and her brother Guaca and others of this sort."[4] Pané proceeded to catalogue various Taino beliefs that he considered false or mistaken, illustrating them by examples of their myths. In the missionary's view, these people had no beginning, for according to their tradition even in the beginning "there were a lot of people who were confined to two caves. At night they were watched over by a man named Marocael who determined where the people would be sent. One day he tarried in returning to the door and was carried away by the sun; when the people saw what had happened they closed the door and so he was changed into stone near the door."[5] Other tales told about the origins of trees, birds, women, the sea, the sun and the moon, the making of *cemis* or idols, and various incidents were alleged to have happened to these gods. Undoubtedly Pané could have gathered even more material, but his missionary work hindered his collecting pursuits. Whenever he gave up hope of Christianizing a village he immediately left and attempted to collect no more of its traditions. Although Pané never set foot in the present-day United States, his small volume set the tone for the major thrust of collecting in America prior to the twentieth century, for until then aboriginal lore remained the main area of concentration for Americans interested in oral traditions. Because of this extensive and long-standing collecting one can say that the folklore of the American Indian has been more thoroughly recorded than that of any other ethnic or cultural group in America.

Pané's work was also typical of most American folklore collecting prior to 1900 in several ways. The Indian was viewed as quaint, curious, and exotic, and above all as an inferior in need of conversion to Christianity and thus, by implication, to civilization. Recording myths and legends, and other types of folklore, was in some instances merely by accident, but in many others, such as Pané's case, by plan, because the material was viewed as providing important insights into the makeup of the natives, who to the European-Americans were the most unusual people they knew. Collections of such material have continued unabated almost to the present time, but most of this work has not been done in the Southeast. The sparsity of field materials from this region is attributable to many factors, not the least of which is that several Southeastern tribes disappeared early on in the era of European contact. Many of those that did survive had their society and culture so disrupted and altered that by the time outsiders became interested in recording their traditional narratives there were few people left who could provide the information.

The picture is not totally bleak, though, for there were several persons who recorded myths and other folk materials from the Indians of the Southeast. Prior to the nineteenth century most of these were travelers, traders, or soldiers who, despite their attention to such matters, cannot be called folklorists, because they were primarily curiosity seekers who gathered oral traditions accidentally. Even those who set about finding data systematically had no concept of a scientific discipline based on these materials. Few of those who did note down Southeastern Indian traditions paid attention to their narratives. For example, John Lawson, a British colonist who traveled through the Carolina Piedmont in 1700 and later published *A History of Carolina* (1718), refers to customs of the Catawbas among whom he spent some time, but says nothing about their myths. Thus, while the writings of Le Page du Pratz, a Frenchman who spent several years along the lower Mississippi River in the early eighteenth century; Jean-Bernard Bossu, a French naval officer who traveled through present-day Alabama and in the Mississippi Valley from 1751 to 1762; Henry Timberlake, a British soldier who spent some time with the Cherokees during the French and Indian War; and Bernard Romans, a surveyor who had a brief stay with the Seminoles in the 1760s and 1770s, are useful for some aspects of Indian life, they contain little information about Southeastern narratives.

One other eighteenth-century writer is worthy of mention here because he was the first American to produce a book that used Indian traditions to advance a theoretical viewpoint. In *The History of the American Indians* (1775) James Adair (1709?–1783?) tackled a problem that had long puzzled intellectuals in Europe and America, namely the subject of Indian origins. It was generally agreed that the Indian peoples were not indigenous to the New World, but there was widespread agreement on little else concerning the question of their origins. The most popular solution offered in the sixteenth century postulated that the Indians were descendants of the Ten Lost Tribes of Israel. In 1607 Gregorio Garcia, in *Origen de los Indios de el nuevo mundo* (The Origin of the Indians of the New World), mentioned the theory of Jewish origins for Indians as a current theory concerning the people of the Western Hemisphere. Although Garcia thought the thesis had merit he did not personally adhere to it. Others, however, were far more enthusiastic. Manasseh ben Israel, an erudite member of the Amsterdam Jewish community, strongly defended it in his *Spes Israelis* (The Hope of Israel) (1650). Thomas Thorowgood's *Jewes in America, or probabilities that the Americans are of that race* (also 1650) went one step further than Manasseh and attempted to demonstrate the theory's validity by a comparison of Indian and Jewish culture.

There were, of course, many writers who disagreed with the theory and tried to disprove it. These included Sir Marmon l'Estrange, who in *Americans no Jewes, or improbabilities that the Americans are of that race* (1652) maintained that Thorowgood's list of parallels between Indian and Jewish culture did not advance his argument because the features he pointed out were merely general human customs. L'Estrange also noted that there are far more differences between the two groups than similarities. Others such as Theophilus Spizelius and Georgius Hornius held that the Jewish theory of origins was implausible, but the thesis persisted and was widely accepted in the eighteenth century.[6]

Thus, Adair's was the first extended treatment of the theory of origins by an American, although his main motive was not unique and numerous earlier colonials had espoused the concept.[7] Moreover, Adair was the first subscriber to this school of thought to reinforce his conclusions with extensive data gathered from Indians. A highly educated man who came to the New World from Ireland, Adair engaged in the Indian trade in 1735, at first with the Catawbas and Cherokees and later with the Choctaws and Chickasaws. He became quite intimate with the tribesmen, so much so that he was able to persuade the Choctaws away from the French and into an alliance with the English. This activity involved him in difficulties which, he felt, resulted in his financial ruin. Perhaps because of these problems he returned in 1751 to live with the Cherokees in what is now Laurens County, South Carolina, and remained there until 1759. Then, after a brief period as commander of a Chickasaw scouting band in the Cherokee War, he went to live among the Chickasaw tribes in what is now northern Mississippi, where he remained until 1768 when he visited New York. Evidently, the greater part of the *History* was written during his seven-year stay with the Chickasaws, and his departure was in part motivated by his desire to find a means of publishing his book. In 1769 ads appealing for subscribers to a projected volume on the North American Indians appeared in New York, Charleston, and Savannah, but the proposed work was not published until 1775. Nothing is known of the author after this time, although he is believed to have died in North Carolina shortly after the close of the Revolution.[8]

Without *The History of the American Indians* Adair's name would no longer be known. Although it tells little of how he collected his material, the book abounds in minute descriptions of aboriginal life that could only be supplied by one who had spent considerable time observing the Indians. For this reason, and because Adair held "truth" as his "grand standard," his work remains a valuable source for historians, anthropologists, and folklorists dealing with the Indian tribes of the Southeastern United States. It is not, however, a history of all Indians, as purported in the title, but rather an account of a few tribes with which the author was well acquainted. That he considered them typical of all North American Indians reveals his ignorance of other tribal cultures as well as his stereotyped view that all Indians are alike. Occasionally Adair even parrots the prevailing view of his time about Indian inferiority to white society. For example, in one of his early chapters he speaks of these "rude and uncivilized" people "who rely solely on oral tradition for the support of their ancient usages,"[9] and there are several other sections where he refers to the tribesmen as "rude and uncivilized."[10] But, considering the era in which it was produced, the book is remarkably free of judgments about the manners and customs of the aborigines, and even the ethnocentric statements in favor of the white man's way of life are somewhat mitigated by remarks in which Indian ways are held up as models for white society. In patriotism, equality, and generosity, for example, Native Americans are pictured as superior to most whites.[11]

Basically the *History* is a description rather than an attempt to judge, and Adair's long residence among the Cherokee, Chickasaw, and Choctaw made him an ideal person for this task. As he asserts in his dedication and preface, "[T]ruth hath been my grand standard,"[12] and he does not intentionally distort facts, but even so it seems likely that his conclusions concerning origins were reached a priori. Combining an elementary knowledge of Bible lore with an excellent knowledge of Cherokee, Choctaw, and Chickasaw traditions, Adair amasses several "particulars" and "circumstances" which he then draws on in finding parallels between American Indian and ancient Israelite life. To a limited extent he relies on Indian myths, which in his view indicate a belief in the Deity as immediate head of the State and a belief in the ministration of angels to buttress his argument for a Jewish theory of origins. Indian traditions that the tribes originally "came from a far distant country, where all the people were of one colour; and that in process of time they moved eastward, to their present settlements" are presented as corroborative evidence for the thesis.[13]

Although the Jewish theory of origins is no longer accepted, the *History* remains a valuable work. Few men in eighteenth-century America lived as long as Adair among any Indian tribes or knew their traditions so well, and even fewer wrote down so many detailed observations. Furthermore, the trader generally avoided marring his material with ethnocentric judgments. He even comes close to the principle of cultural relativism in understanding that the Indians prefer their ways to those of whites, a viewpoint with which he is often sympathetic. Important as the volume is, it is not extremely useful as a sourcebook for Southeastern Indian narratives, for only a relatively small number appears in its pages.

Much more substantive work on Southeastern Indian narratives was carried out in the nineteenth century, although the best quality publications came toward the end of those hundred years. Some of the biggest names in the field of Indian studies, however, made little in the way of significant contributions to this particular topic. Henry Rowe Schoolcraft (1793–1864), the father of American folklore studies, was an active collector in the 1820s and published his most significant work, *Algic Researches,* in 1839. Schoolcraft was interested in the lore of some Southeastern tribes and considered tales of utmost importance, as these introductory remarks to *Algic Researches* make clear:

> It was found necessary to examine the mythology of the tribes as a means of acquiring an insight into their mode of thinking and reasoning, the sources of their fears and hopes, and the probable origin of their opinions and institutions. This branch of inquiry connected itself, in a manner which could not have been anticipated, with their mode of conveying instruction, moral, mechanical, and religious to the young, through the intervention of traditionary fictitious tales and legend...Nothing in the whole inquiry has afforded so ample a clue to their opinions and thoughts, in all the great departments of life and nature, as their oral imaginative tales; and it has, therefore, been deemed proper to introduce copious specimens of these collections from a large number of the tribes, embracing three of the generic stocks of language.[14]

Despite his interest, Schoolcraft's only attention to Southeastern materials was an "Indian romance" titled *Alhalla, or the Lord of Talladega: A Tale of the Creek War* (1843). This piece of fiction, which incorporated Creek myths and legends, was written at Sault Ste. Marie in 1826, but for some reason its publication was deferred for seventeen years.[15]

Another important nineteenth-century American student of Indian folk-lore was Daniel Garrison Brinton (1837–1899), who authored *The Myths of the New World* (1868). This comparative study of the origin and creation myths and culture-hero legends of North and South American Indian tribes, however, slights Southeastern myths. His only publication dealing with Southeastern materials is a thirteen-page pamphlet titled *National Legend of the Chahta-Muskokee Tribes* (1870), a minor effort among his numerous articles and books. Brinton was very influential in late nineteenth-century American folklore circles, and his book of myths was revised and reprinted throughout the last three decades of the century. He was a theorist rather than a collector, a fact implied in the epithet "fearless critic of Philadelphia" that was sometimes applied to him.[16] Important as he was, Brinton's contributions in the area of Southeastern narratives were minimal.

Far more substantive was the work carried out under the auspices of the Bureau of American Ethnology. Established in 1879 under the leadership of John Wesley Powell (1834–1902), the new bureau was intended by Congress mainly as a department to carry on research already begun, but it is clear that from the outset Powell intended the agency as something broader. He saw it as the focal point around which all American Indian studies would be centered. Toward this purpose he implemented a research program including detailed bibliographic compilations, new field studies, the development and circulation of new questionnaires, and publications, in the form of *Annual Reports* and *Bulletins*, containing material resulting from these studies. The *Annual Reports* were initiated in 1881 and the *Bulletins* in 1887, and from 1881 to 1893 there was also a series titled *Contributions to North American Ethnology*. Although other matters than folklore were treated in these works, a sizeable number of volumes was devoted to oral traditions, in particular myths. The first planned series, and the one containing the most narratives, was the *Annual Reports*. Although later they became nothing more than accounts of administrative accomplishments,[17] under Powell's leadership they were hefty tomes containing not only the director's report but also accompanying essays by staff members and collaborators on all topics falling within the scope of ethnology as interpreted by the bureau. It was in the nineteenth of these *Annual Reports* that one of the most significant collections of Southeastern narratives appeared—the material having been compiled by a journalist turned fieldworker.

James Mooney (1861–1921) started his career as a schoolteacher and later took a job as a reporter for the *Richmond* (Indiana) *Paladium*. Since childhood his main interest had been the American Indian, and he read everything available on the subject. In 1885 he planned to go to Brazil to study the aborigines there, and to promote this idea he went to Washington, D.C., and met John Wesley Powell, who was so impressed with the young Hoosier's knowledge that he hired him immediately. Mooney remained with the bureau until his death thirty-six years later, dividing his time between library and field researches. Most of his collecting was carried out among the Cherokees and the Sioux and was facilitated by Mooney's insistence on learning the language of his informants. It is appropriate that the two major works for which he is now remembered, *The Ghost-Dance Religion and the Sioux Outbreak of 1890* (1896) and *Myths of the Cherokee* (1900), are evenly divided, with one dealing with the Sioux and the other with the Cherokee.

Mooney's earliest field research was conducted on the Cherokee reservation in North Carolina in 1887 and 1888 and resulted in *Sacred Formulas of the Cherokees* (1891).[18] The book was originally planned as an account of plants used by the Cherokees for food or medicinal purposes and the manner in which they were applied, but Mooney soon came to believe that the cermonies where the medicine was used were more important than the medicine itself. He then proceeded to collect material on these ceremonies by various means; some of his techniques included payment of money or some article of clothing to informants. But with his star informant Ayuini or "Swimmer" (1835?–1899) he found an appeal of another sort worked best:

> He was told that the only object in asking about the songs was to put them on record and preserve them, so that when he and the half dozen old men of the tribe were dead the world might be aware how much the Cherokees had known. This appeal to his professional pride proved effectual, and when he was told that a great many similar songs had been sent to Washington by medicine men of other tribes, he promptly declared that he knew as much as any of them, and that he would give all the information in his possession, so that others might be able to judge for themselves who knew most.[19]

The material collected from Swimmer was used by Mooney in both of his books on the Cherokee.[20]

Myths of the Cherokee, Mooney's most important contribution both to folklore and mythology, was the lead work in the nineteenth *Annual Report.* The 548 pages of material were recorded between 1887 and 1890, most of it taken from Swimmer but with contributions from eight other informants as well. Mooney divided the material into four large categories—sacred myths, animal stories, local legends, and historical traditions, with the animal narratives presented under three subheadings. With the publication of these 126 items, not all of which were myths, Mooney reopened a Pandora's box that had first been unlocked nearly twenty years earlier by Thomas F. Crane, a Cornell University professor and one of the foremost American folk narrative specialists of the nineteenth century. This was the question of origins, specifically whether or not Indians borrowed tales from Negroes. Writing in *Popular Science Monthly,* Crane had discussed parallels between South American

Indian and American Negro narratives and concluded that the Indians heard the stories from African slaves in Brazil, who like American Negroes had brought the tales with them from Africa. In *Nights with Uncle Remus* (1883), Joel Chandler Harris had arrived at a similar conclusion in his consideration of Negro and Creek parallels, asserting dogmatically that there was no question about the Creeks' borrowing from blacks. However, there was indeed question about this and, as Harris notes, John Wesley Powell was one of the doubters.[21]

James Mooney was another. In an early article on Cherokee folk narratives he noted that certain of the Indian tales resembled the Uncle Remus stories and suggested this was due to the Negro's borrowing from Indian traditions.[22] This viewpoint was soon refuted by Adolf Gerber, who used a comparative argument to demonstrate that the majority of Negro folktales—and, in all likelihood, all of them—were of Old World origin. Most were, he argued, African or European and derived from their own heritage and contact with their white masters. Any influence the Indians may have had was, at best, minimal. Gerber's article, however, did not end the controversy; instead it seemed to stoke the fire of argument. In *Myths of the Cherokee* Mooney refers to "ingenious theories" of origin "in the absence of any possibility of proof."[23] He then proceeds to attack those who posit an African origin for the tales on the basis of the prominence of Rabbit in the animal stories. His dogmatic refusal to accept the idea that the Cherokees, or other tribes, borrowed from Afro-American folklore leads him into exaggeration. Thus, he speaks of "the Great White Rabbit" who "is the hero-god, trickster, and wonder worker of all the tribes east of the Mississippi from Hudson Bay to the Gulf."[24] To corroborate this statement he uses an argument about a confusion of languages:

> Among the Algonquian tribes the name, *wabos,* seems to have been confounded with that of the dawn, *waban,* so that the Great White Rabbit is really the incarnation of the eastern dawn that brings light and life and drives away the dark shadows which have held the world in chains. The animal itself seems to be regarded by the Indians as the fitting type of defenseless weakness protected and made safe by constantly alert vigilance, and with a disposition, moreover, for turning up at unexpected moments. The same characteristics would appeal as strongly to the primitive mind of the negro. The very expression which Harris puts into the mouth of Uncle Remus, "In dem days Brer Rabit en his fambly wuz at the head er de gang w'en enny racket was en hand," was paraphrased in the Cherokee language by Suyeta in introducing his first rabbit story: *"Tsi stu wuliga natutun une gutsatu gesei*—the Rabit was the leader of them all in mischief." The expression struck the author so forcibly that the words were recorded as spoken.[25]

If, as Mooney asserted, blacks borrowed from aboriginal folk traditions, then it is necessary to know the circumstances under which this borrowing occurred. To this problem Mooney had a ready answer, but it is one that argues just as well for the opposite viewpoint as for his own. According to this solution the interchange took place as a result of miscegenation and the enforced contact of slavery in many southern colonies where Indians were kept in servitude and worked side by side with blacks to the time of the American Revolution. Apparently it never occurred to Mooney that it would have been just as easy for Indians to borrow from blacks in this situation as vice versa, or that the exchange might have worked both ways. Perhaps this failure was due to a racist bias. Certainly Mooney was guilty of accepting some current stereotypes of blacks, as is shown in this passage that attempt to correct a negative image of Native Americans:

> The Negro, with his genius for imitation and his love for stories, especially of the comic variety, must undoubtedly have absorbed much from the Indian in this way, while on the other hand the Indian, with his pride of conservatism and his contempt for a subject race, would have taken but little from the Negro, and that little could not easily have found its way back to the free tribes. Some of these animal stories are common to widely separated tribes among whom there can be no suspicion of Negro influences. Thus the famous "tar baby" story has variants, not only among the Cherokee, but also in New Mexico, Washington, and southern Alaska—wherever, in fact, the piñon or the pine supplies enough gum to be molded into a ball for Indian uses—while the incident of the Rabbit dining the Bear is found with nearly every tribe from Nova Scotia to the Pacific. The idea that such stories are necessarily of Negro origin is due largely to the common but mistaken notion that the Indian has no sense of humor.[26]

Mooney's arguments can be faulted on at least two counts. First is his erroneous assumption about the rabbit-trickster. Except for the Southeastern tribes, this figure does not appear in American Indian folklore and even in the region where it is common is not found in every tribe. Second, many of the stories in Mooney's collection probably originated neither among Native Americans nor Africans but in Europe, or at least in the Old World.[27] Of course, modern scholarly aids, such as type and motif indexes, make the determination of origins easier.[28] Mooney's subjective guesswork was typical of his time and predictable, since to make meaningful, objective conclusions on sources requires a comprehensive knowledge of world folk traditions, and Mooney made no claim to such authority.[29] His approach was no different from, or worse than, the traditional tendency of collectors to identify with their informants to the point of becoming their advocate. He was interested in and studied American Indians and they became "his" people. Thus, when the occasion presented itself he "defended" them. In this instance the issue he kindled continued to burn long after his day.

Despite his entry into the dispute about origins, Mooney was not primarily a theorist. His forte was collecting and he realized it; his success in fieldwork was facilitated by his ability to see the Indian point of view. His particular skill in presenting it makes his work of enduring value.

Mooney, of course, was not the first Bureau of American Ethnology worker to collect folk narratives in the Southeast. That honor belongs to Albert S. Gatschet (1832–1907), a linguist who worked for Powell in 1877 before the bureau was established and continued in his employ until ill health forced him into retirement in 1905. A native of Switzerland, Gatschet migrated to New York in 1868, by which time he was already a skilled linguist. In 1872 a friend showed him some Indian vocabularies that whetted his interest and started him on a field of study he would pursue for the next thirty-three years. His first work for the bureau was on the Pacific Coast, but between 1882 and 1890 he made several short, frequently fruitless trips through the Southeast seeking out remnant linguistic groups. While gathering these data he recorded some folk narratives, notably among the Creek, Yuchi, and Hitchiti. His book *A Migration Legend of the Creek Indians* (1884) was based on these almost incidentally recorded items.

Another linguist, James Owen Dorsey (1848–1895), is another Bureau of American Ethnology fieldworker who made a small contribution to the collection of Southeastern Indian narratives. Dorsey started his career as an Episcopal missionary, but ill health forced him to return to his native Baltimore where he engaged in parish programs. In 1880 Powell hired him primarily to do work among the Omaha Indians. An expert fieldworker, Dorsey also made several successful forays among various tribes and, at Powell's urging, made a special effort to collect animal myths. Even so, he recorded relatively few narratives, an indication both that his major interests were elsewhere and of the greater difficulty he had in eliciting folk items rather than linguistic ones. He wrote a bureau staff member that he had acquired about two thousand terms peculiar to the Biloxi language from six members of that tribe, but had only the promise of a single text of a myth from an elderly woman. Even there he had problems, for "…the old woman objects to dictate it to me: she says that she will tell her son-in-law."[30] Dorsey was more successful when he ventured among this tribe a year later, in 1893, for he wrote John Wesley Powell that he had gathered some ten texts of animal myths and knew that several more narratives were available that he had not yet recorded.[31] Nevertheless, the body of traditional tales Dorsey unearthed was miniscule in comparison to the linguistic matter he found. His publications using this material are even smaller, for they consist of a single article, a three-page item in the initial 1893 issue of the *Journal of American Folklore*.[32]

Far more prolific in collecting Southeastern Indian narratives was John Reed Swanton (1873–1958), a member of the Bureau of American Ethnology staff from 1900 to 1944. A student of Frederick Ward Putnam and Franz Boas, two of the foremost figures in early twentieth-century American Indian studies, Swanton was the most prolific of the bureau authors. In all he contributed twenty monographs, fifteen for the *Bulletins* and five for the *Annual Reports*. A follower of the philosophy of Emanuel Swedenborg, the Swedish theologian of the eighteenth century, Swanton was overly sensitive to human faults. Yet his general failure to point out the personal flaws of others and his quiet, self-effacing nature made Swanton popular with most of his colleagues. Originally assigned to study Northwest Coast Indians, Swanton initially worked among the Chinooks, the Dakotas, and the Sioux. But it is for his fieldwork among the Southeastern tribes that he is best remembered. He produced *Early History of the Creek Indians and Their Neighbors* (1922) and *Source Material for the Social and Ceremonial Life of the Choctaw Indians* (1931) as preliminary works for *The Indians of the Southeastern United States* (1946) and *The Indian Tribes of North America* (1952). His classic work on Indian folk narratives was *Myths and Tales of the Southeastern Indians* (1929).

The 305 texts in Swanton's folk narrative volume are from the Creek, Hitchiti, Alabama, Koasati, and Natchez tribes, most of them recorded between 1908 and 1914. A majority of the Creek narratives collected by William O. Tuggle, a lawyer who recorded a variety of oral traditions while serving the tribe from 1879 to 1883, was included, as was one text noted by William Bartram, a naturalist who toured the Southeast from 1773 to 1777, and one set down by Albert Gatschet. Everything else was the result of Swanton's own fieldwork. Like several other Bureau of American Ethnology fieldworkers, Swanton obtained the narratives as a bonus while seeking information about linguistics, a fact that may account for the general lack of discussion about informants and collecting situations. Swanton broke down the tales into six broad categories: stories dealing with natural phenomena or the deeds of ancient heroes, stories of the visits to the world of the dead, stories telling of encounters between humans and animals or supernatural beings in animal form, tales dealing with happenings among the animals, stories known to have been borrowed from whites or blacks, and miscellaneous war tales.

In clearly identifying some narratives as being derived from Afro-American folklore, Swanton was taking a position that differed from that advanced by Mooney, Powell, and other bureau staff members. Even so, he essentially agreed with them that the rabbit trickster originated among the aborigines in pre-Columbian times, although he was too knowledgeable about folklore to try to maintain the untenable stance that all of the tales in which the rabbit figured were of Native American origin. This matter of origins was important to Swanton but not one on which he spent great time, for like Mooney he was primarily a collector, not a theorist. To him the amassing of texts was more important than speculations about their ultimate derivation; in gathering such data no one was more skilled or successful.

Beyond Mooney, Swanton, Dorsey, and Gatschet, there is little to discuss concerning Bureau of American Ethnology collections of Southeastern narratives. The only other staff member to make a contribution on this topic was David I. Bushnell, Jr., who was primarily known as an armchair archaeologist because of his extensive library research on tribal migrations. Much of his time was spent traveling throughout the United States and Europe looking for Indian vocabularies, histories, and paintings by artists who knew the early Indians. From 1908 to 1910 he spent some time collecting narratives and other traditions from three Choctaws living at Bayou Lacomb, Louisiana. In 1910 he published "Myths of the Louisiana Choctaw," a ten-page article based on his fieldwork, in the *American Anthropologist,* and his *Choctaw of Bayou Lacomb, St. Tammany Parish, Louisiana* appeared in 1909 as *Bulletin* 48.[33]

There were, of course, some people outside the Bureau of American Ethnology who did significant work in the area of Southeastern narratives. In the nineteenth century the work of Tuggle has already been mentioned; in the twentieth century the most significant name is Frank G. Speck (1881–1950). Beginning in 1904 he collected narrative materials primarily from the Catawba, Chickasaw, Creek, and Tutelo and recorded various types of folklore from various other Southeastern peoples. From the outset of his work his main theoretical concern with narratives was the question of origins. In 1905, in his M.A. thesis "A Comparative Study of the Native Mythology of the South-Eastern United States," he considered the question of possible African origins of American Indian tales. Ultimately he opted against taking a dogmatic stance in this matter, concluding that it was too early to form firm opinions on the subject. Speck's refusal to present speculation as fact is laudable, as is his willingness to admit the possibility of African influence, something several of his colleagues refused to do. His view was that too little in the way of reliable West African collections was available to settle the question, a stance that he echoed in some later writings.[34]

Speck's concern with Southeastern narratives was primarily non-theoretical, most of his publication on this topic consisting of collections. His chief narrative publications are *Catawba Texts* (1934), *The Creek Indians of Taskigi Town* (1907), and *Ethnology of the Yuchi Indians* (1909)—the latter two being works that include narratives, although they are not solely devoted to that aspect of folklore. Despite his early work in the Southeast, Speck is primarily remembered for his studies of northern Indians in volumes such as *Naskapi: The Savage Hunters of the Labrador Peninsula* (1935).

There are several other twentieth-century personalities who contributed publications of Southeastern narratives, ranging from Howard N. Martin, a white man who grew up with Native Americans and published *Folktales of the Alabama-Coushatta Indians* (1946) which appeared in revised form in 1977, to John Witthoft and Wendell S. Hadlock, who published an article in the *Journal of American Folklore* on the "Cherokee-Iroquois Little People."[35] The list of major names is exhausted except for one who, interestingly, produced an influential collection but was not a collector. Stith Thompson (1886–1976) is one of the major names in the history of American folklore studies, founder of the first American graduate program in folklore and, for more than fifty years, one of the leading scholars in the field. His interest in American Indian tales developed at Harvard while he was working on a Ph.D. and he did his dissertation on "European Borrowings and Parallels in North American Indian Tales" (1914). He later revised the dissertation and published it as *European Tales Among the North American Indians* (1919). Ten years later, in 1929, he published *Tales of the North American Indians*, which was both an anthology and an index to American Indian tales as well as a complement to the 1919 volume. The book also represented the culmination of a type of work that had been envisioned as early as 1883 when the Bureau of American Ethnology commissioned Jeremiah Curtin to collect American Indian tales for the purpose of eventually producing a myth concordance. Franz Boas, the famous anthropologist who was also very interested in folklore, was particularly interested in such a work and was one of the people Thompson corresponded with while working on the dissertation that became the foundation for the 1929 book.

Only a handful of Southeastern narratives appears in *Tales of the North American Indians,* but of course the importance of the book is that it shows how regional stories fit into the entirety of the Native American tradition. Perhaps not the ideal narrative concordance, Thompson's volume remains the most successful venture in that direction yet attempted, and even today, over fifty years after its publication, it is still valuable and useful. Although there have been recent collections in the same vein, most notably Richard Erdoes and Alfonso Ortiz's *American Indian Myths and Legends* (1984), Thompson's 1929 compilation has yet to be supplanted.

While the publication and study of Southeastern narratives has lagged behind that from other areas, quality has generally made up for the lack of quantity. Two of the most important works on American Indian tales, that of Mooney and Swanton, are solely concerned with Southeastern material. Most of those who occupied themselves with the stories of Southeastern Indians were collectors rather than theorists, although they were generally aware of theoretical issues of the day and, as in the case of origins, they sometimes entered into the ongoing discussion. But overall they were content to present their texts in the best systemic matter they knew. For that all scholars interested in folk narrative can be grateful, especially since several of the tribes whose tales have thus been preserved are now extinct.

W.K. McNeil
THE OZARK FOLK CENTER

● *NOTES* ●

1. Edward Gaylord Bourne, "Columbus, Ramon Pané and the Beginnings of American Anthropology," *Proceedings of the American Antiquarian Society,* New Series, XVII (April, 1906), 313.

2. Pané's booklet appears on pp. 153–69 of Benjamin Keen, translator and annotator, *The Life of The Admiral Christopher Columbus By His Son Ferdinand* (New Brunswick, New Jersey: Rutgers University Press, 1959). Apparently Columbus was not very pleased with Pané's work, for he remarks, "[I]t contains so many fictions that the only sure thing to be learned from it is that the Indians have a certain natural reverence for the after-life and believe in the immortality of the soul" (p. 153). Bartolome de Las Casas referred to Pané as "a simple-minded man so that what he reported was sometimes confused and of little substance" (p. 299). It is unclear whether Columbus is unhappy about Pané's recording material that he believes fictitious or whether he is suggesting that Pané simply didn't get his facts straight; possibly it is the former.

3. Bourne, p. 318, footnote as translated by Bartolome de Las Casas. The words are slightly rearranged in Keen, p. 153.

4. Bourne, p. 319.

5. Ibid. This narrative contains a number of widely traveled motifs including "Mankind emerges from caves" (A1232.3), "Extraordinary behavior of sun" (F961.1), and "Transformation: man to stone" (D231).

6. Don Cameron Allen, *The Legend of Noah: Renaissance Rationalism in Art, Science and Letters* (Urbana, Illinois: University of Illinois Press, 1963), pp. 128–29. Other discussions of the Jewish theory appear in the bibliographical note, Appendix A, in Lewis Hanke, *The First Social Experiments in America* (Cambridge, Massachusetts: Harvard University Press, 1935); "Tribes, Lost Ten" in Cecil Roth (ed.), *The Standard Jewish Encyclopedia* (London: W.H. Allen, 1959), p. 1837; Allen Howard Godbey, *The Lost Tribes a Myth: Suggestions Towards Rewriting Hebrew History* (Durham, North Carolina: Duke University Press, 1930); a brief article ("Lost Ten Tribes of Israel") by A.F. Chamberlain in Frederick Webb Hodge (ed.), *The Handbook of American Indians North of Mexico,* I (Grosse Pointe, Michigan: Scholarly Press, 1968; reprint of a work originally published in 1912), p. 775. The theory's strongest European backer in the nineteenth century was Edward King, Viscount Kingsborough, who devoted almost a lifetime to the attempt to demonstrate it. This it the thesis advanced in his nine-volume *Antiquities of Mexico* (1830–1848). For a discussion of other nineteenth-century titles see Roy Harvey Pearce, *The Savages of America: A Study of the Indian and the Idea of Civilization* (Baltimore: Johns Hopkins Press, 1953), p. 62, note.

7. Roger Williams, Thomas Mayhew, John Eliot, Cotton Mather, Samuel Sewell, and William Penn, to name a few.

8. William J. Ghent, "James Adair," in *Dictionary of American Biography,* I (New York: Charles Scribner's Sons, 1928), pp. 33–34.

9. James Adair, *The History of the American Indians* (New York and London: Johnson Reprint Corporation, 1968), p. 10.

10. Ibid., p. 377, for instance.

11. See, for example, the section titled "General Observations on the North American Indians," pp. 375–448.

12. Ibid., dedication, p. 2. Also see p. 2 of the preface.

13. Ibid., pp. 191–220.

14. Henry Rowe Schoolcraft, *Algic Researches* (New York: Harper and Brothers, 1839), p. 5.

15. Henry Rowe Colcraft, *Alhalla, or The Lord of Talladega: A Tale of the Creek War* (New

York and London: Wiley and Putnam, 1843). Colcraft is a pseudonym for Schoolcraft, who explains that the name "is in strict conformity with family tradition, supported by recent observations in England. In the latter country, however, the name is uniformly written Cal, however it may be pronounced" (p. 3). Although in his introductory remarks Schoolcraft says the poem was written in 1826, the published version is dated Sault Ste. Marie, 1832. The book also contains four poems evidently written by Schoolcraft: "There Is A Time To Die" dated New York, 1843, "Lines" on the death of Captain M.M. Dox, signed Michilimackinac, "The Chippewa Girl," and "Shingabawossin," both of which are undated (pp. 114–16).

16. This epithet was given to Brinton by W J McGee and refers to Brinton's well-known critical nature and dogged refusal to go along with otherwise accepted views without some proof of their validity.

17. The first forty-eight volumes contain the informative essays, some of which are quite lengthy. Beginning with Volume 49 (1931–32), the *Annual Reports* became merely a formal statement of what the director of the bureau and his staff accomplished during the year. These volumes were rarely more than twelve pages long.

18. By this time Mooney had published ten articles dealing with Indian topics and with Irish folklore as well as an undated monograph on linguistics. For a complete listing of his publications see the bibliography in L.G. Moses, *The Indian Man: A Biography of James Mooney* (Urbana and Chicago: University of Illinois Press, 1984), pp. 277–80.

19. James Mooney, "Sacred Formulas of the Cherokees," *Annual Report* 7 of the Bureau of American Ethnology, 1885–86 (Washington: Government Printing Office, 1891), p. 311.

20. The two works were *Sacred Formulas of the Cherokees,* which appeared in the seventh *Annual Report* of the Bureau of American Ethnology, and *Myths of the Cherokee,* which appeared in the nineteenth *Annual Report.* In the 1920s Fran M. Olbrechts went back to the same area and did additional work there, the results of which appeared as "The Swimmer Manuscripts," *Bulletin* 99 of the Bureau of American Ethnology (Washington: Government Printing Office, 1932).

21. Joel Chandler Harris, *Nights With Uncle Remus* (Boston and New York: Houghton Mifflin and Co., 1883), xxviii.

22. James Mooney, "Myths of the Cherokee," *Journal of American Folklore* 1 (1888): 97–108. See especially page 106, where Mooney says that he plans to prove that the Uncle Remus stories are of American Indian origin.

23. James Mooney, *Myths of the Cherokee* (New York: Johnson Reprint Corporation, 1970; reprint of a work originally published in 1900), p. 232. Gerber's article is "Uncle Remus Traced to the Old World," *Journal of American Folklore* 6 (1893), 145–57. The essay was a version of a talk Gerber gave at the 1892 meeting of the American Folklore Society.

24. Ibid.

25. Ibid., pp. 232–33. Arguments such as this are generally associated with a school of folklore and myth theory called solar mythology, for obvious reasons.

26. Mooney, *Myths of the Cherokee,* pp. 233–34.

27. The tar-baby story is Type 175 in the Aarne-Thompson tale type index and is also listed under K741 in Stith Thompson's *Motif-Index of Folk Literature* (Bloomington and London: Indiana University Press, 1966), IV, p. 335.

28. A motif is usually defined as the smallest single narrative element that has the power to persist in tradition, while a type is a larger unit made up of several motifs or, in other words, an entire tale.

29. Mooney did, however, do some work with non-American Indian folklore, most notably with Irish materials.

30. Letter to H.W. Henshaw, January 28, 1892, Bureau of American Ethnology Archives.

31. Letter to John Wesley Powell, February 9, 1893, Bureau of American Ethnology Archives.

32. The article is "Biloxi Tales" and appears in Volume 6 of the *Journal of American Folklore* (1893): 48–50.

33. David I. Bushnell, Jr., "Myths of the Louisiana Choctaw," *American Anthropologist* 12 (1910), 526–36.

34. See Frank G. Speck, "A Comparative Study of the Native Mythology of the South-Eastern United States," M.A. thesis (Columbia University, 1905), and his later articles, "The Negroes and the Creek Nation," *Southern Workman* 38 (1908), 106–10, and "Notes on Creek Mythology," *Southern Workman* 38 (1909), 9–11.

35. John Witthoft and Wendell S. Hadlock, "Cherokee-Iroquois Little People," *Journal of American Folklore* 59 (1946), 413–22.2

■ ■ ■

SETTING THE STAGE

■ ■ ■

CHAPTER ONE

Preliminary Reflections

In most parts of North America, open conflict between the Native Americans and the European-Americans has ended. The clash of cultures began soon after Europeans set foot ashore. It has continued for four centuries in forms as diverse as frontier atrocities and congressional debate. Over the conflict between invaders and beleaguered, there hangs a pall of tragic inevitability. On every frontier in the New World, in South America, Mexico, Florida, Virginia, New England, and Canada, friendly coexistence turned into violence. With very few exceptions, the outcome was the same—subjugation of the Native Americans. In the encounter the Native Americans lost high percentages of their population to virulent plagues, lost almost all control over their occupied lands, lost the ability to determine their ecological niche, lost the cultural momentum that was theirs in 1500, and in many cases, lost their heritage. An appalling number of Native American societies simply ceased to exist. So many societies of the Eastern Woodlands became extinct so early that even the historical and ethnographic records are virtually blank. For their part, the Europeans gained continents, all the wealth contained therein, an extraordinary number of new agricultural plants, a few new diseases, and a new sense of destiny.

The tragic story of this exchange is a matter of history in most places, and that fact has permitted the Euro-Americans a new interest in the cultural heritage they displaced. In the last decade many volumes of information about Native Americans, living and dead, have rolled off the presses. Anyone who offers a contribution to that flood owes the public some explanation of why another book should appear, what purpose it might serve.

This volume is about the Native Americans of the Southeast, from the Carolinas to the Plains. Except for a few pockets here and there, Native Americans are no longer on that land. They were finally "Removed," as the rhetoric of the day put it, in the 1840s. Their struggle with the Europeans and

Euro-Americans had been going on since the early sixteenth century, and it ended in Oklahoma and Texas after three centuries of diplomacy, warfare, trading, and disease. To be sure, the survivors have emerged with a vigorous new social adaptation to their circumstances, and the conflict continues in the courts, but the old Native American world of the Southeast is gone.

The societies of the Southeast are inherently interesting, because they had formed some of the most complicated social systems on the continent, and anthropologists and historians are still arguing over how they worked. In the four centuries before the Europeans appeared, the Southeast was the scene of population expansion accompanied by movement of peoples and ideas over a large area. They developed individual cultural characteristics while exchanging goods and ideas with neighbors. Architectural arrangements of pyramidal mounds and an explosion of iconographic art forms in shell, wood, and copper are material clues to the complexity of the cultures in the Southeast. Powerful chiefdoms created cultural spheres centered on river basins. They were participants in an exchange network which included the Caribbean, Mexico, the Southwest, the Upper Mississippi Valley, and the Northeast. For anyone interested in the development of cultures and the processes of cultural dynamics, the Southeastern peoples are of permanent interest.

From the grimmer side, any study of the processes of acculturation and frontier patterns cannot ignore the tragedy of the Southeast. The multitude of difficulties involved in studying the Native American Southeast—inadequate historical documentation, late gathering of ethnographic data, rapid acculturation by the inhabitants, the complexity caused by the long-term presence of competing European powers, the obscurity of the location of materials—only increases the rewards in understanding. This book, I hope, will help more people to surmount those difficulties and attain some understanding of those past societies.

There is also a sense in which the old Southeast is part of a larger picture. Most of the tribes we now associate with the Plains moved to that region only in recent centuries. From earlier, more eastern locations they participated in some of the same supercultural phenomena which linked otherwise culturally divided societies in the Southeast. In some cases the Southeastern tradition can shed light on a Plains practice, and vice versa. Most people do not much care for comparative examination of their cultural traditions, because that approach seems to deny the uniqueness of the local culture. Many Cherokee may feel uncomfortable with discussion of the antecedents of one of their sacred myths, in the same way that many Christians resent being told that Biblical narratives had ancestors in Mesopotamia. The discovery of such relationships, however, only serves to highlight the achievements of each society participating in a larger network of ideas, for basic concepts seem always to be altered, adapted, when fitted to an existing body of knowledge and social system. The diffused idea becomes a localized idea, and comparative study of the process can reveal much about how societies work together.

From the 1880s to the 1920s, various ethnographers sponsored by the government and philanthropic institutions collected what data could be found. It was the "golden age" of Southeastern ethnography, and a burst of publishing produced a collection of books that is still the basis of what is known about Southeastern cultures. Even so, a small number of scholars have continued the collection and study of information about the old Southeast. The best general Southeastern ethnography, in fact, was published as late as 1976,[1] and archaeologists continue to unearth and publish major new insights into the cultural patterns of the Southeastern Native American world. That means that the general ethnological understanding of that world is continually being revised and refined by succeeding generations of new scholars.

Although far too many of the Southeastern peoples are extinct, the larger groups are alive and well, albeit on more western land. The Southeast is now largely occupied by Euro- and Afro-Americans, but for the peoples who trace their Native American ancestry back to the region, the "Removal" is simply a complication in an unbroken chain of culture. The old Southeast is their heritage, and it is a rich one. It is presumptuous for any Euro-American, particularly one descended from settlers in Georgia, to think that he can offer insight to a Native American, but this book is offered with the hope that the descendants of the peoples who are the focus of it may find it helpful in seeing their heritage in a slightly different light. It may be enough to hope that this book does not offend.

A final reason for continuing to study the old Southeast lies in a personal article of belief, no less strongly held for being unscientific. I believe that when a people totally replaces another on the land, the new population owes it to their predecessors to preserve the memory of their saga. It is the path of wisdom to learn from one's predecessors, of course, but we also owe them the metaphysical courtesy of remembering them. As archaeologists know, the land itself remembers those who have dwelt upon it. Can the present inhabitants do less?

The Southeast in this volume is seen through the filter of folklore. The classic collection of Cherokee tales and legends was published in 1900, and its Muskhogean companion volume came out in 1929 and is still available in reprint.[2] A few later collections have been published in the intervening decades, but not many. What is the purpose of another publication, then?

Collection.

First, this volume is intended to be a collection of texts. All of them have been previously published, but many of them are in journals and out-of-print volumes which are unknown and not readily available to the general public.

Until now, anyone who wished to learn the legends of the old Southeast had to embark on an exploration of holdings in large libraries. This volume offers a sampling, but not by any means an exhaustive collection, of the traditional narratives of Native America. The reader who simply wants to read the stories as an introduction to this rich body of lore can do so by following the listing of the texts given at the beginning of the book.

Other collections of Native American materials are now available in bookstores, but they do not focus on the Southeast. This collection includes texts from outside the region, but only when they shed light on the lore of the Southeast. Here are materials for anyone who wishes to encounter a world of thought which exists now only on the printed page.

Southeastern Ethnographic Studies.

This volume is intended to be more than just a collection, however. New insights have been offered to students of the Southeast in the last few years by archaeologists, ethnohistorians, and ethnologists, and they form the backdrop for these examinations of traditional narratives. It is not so much that study of legends can clarify ethnographic reality, although that is the hope of every folklorist, but that deeper understandings of the social systems of the Southeastern peoples can give us new ways of reading the texts. Serious students of Southeastern cultures will begin with Hudson's major work, *The Southeastern Indians*.[3] While that volume does not replace the encyclopedic works of Swanton, Speck, and other early scholars, it is the reigning classic of Southeastern ethnology. The reader may find it helpful as a constant reference companion for the reading of this volume, just as it did for the writing of it. Ethnographic details will frequently be noted as the texts are examined, but they form the background for the study, not the purpose. This series of studies is not intended to be an ethnography, but a book of folklore.

Folklore Studies.

In North America the study of folklore has been the companion discipline of the study of linguistics and ethnography since the inception of those social sciences in the late nineteenth century. It is a significant fact that Franz Boas, the "father" of American anthropology and the first president of the American Anthropological Society, was also a founder of the American Folklore Society. Almost all of the Southeastern ethnographers were members of both organizations and published their findings in the journals of each. This present publication is intended to find its small niche in the joint collection of both disciplines.

Folklorists are almost by nature comparativists, because much of the achievement of the discipline revolves around the organization and indexing of traditional materials in their many forms and locations. Until recent decades, the folklorist has tended to focus on the diffusion of lore, leaving the unique and local to the historian. Recent shifts of interest among professional folklorists have turned attention to stylistic questions and studies of the performance of narrators. For the Southeast, these new emphases are too late. When Haas offered a final plea for collection from Southeastern informants in 1947, she suggested that only two decades remained for the final gathering of the old data, at least in the original tongues.[4] That time has now passed, and we are left with a body of materials still not analyzed, even from the perspective of comparative study. This volume hopes to offer some insights into possibilities of understanding materials which have long been in our hands and hidden on the shelves of our libraries.

Other than Hudson's work, there are two reference works which were constantly consulted in the writing of this book, and the general reader may wish to learn about them. In 1929, the same year that John R. Swanton published his collection of Muskhogean texts, Stith Thompson issued his classic *Tales of the North American Indians*.[5] While it is a collection of texts representative of all areas of the continent, the footnotes are a compendium of references to locations of texts up to that date. As an index to the early collections, therefore, it is unsurpassed, and it stands today as the beginning point of all studies of Native American folklore. Earlier than that, however, Thompson had brought the work of Finnish folklorist Anti Aarne to completion as an exhaustive index of the types of tales (each one numbered!) found in the oral literature of Europe.[6] While that classic work would seem to be irrelevant for a study of Native American lore, it is invaluable for comparative purposes and will be mentioned in this study from time to time.

In the 1950s Thompson crowned his achievements of a lifetime as one of the leading folklorists of the world, by publishing his six-volume *Motif Index of the Folk Literature of the World*.[7] Based on the recognition that the only way to trace the diffusion of folk narrative is to break down larger texts ("tales") into smaller units of action and detail called "motifs," the work indexes Thompson's lifelong categorizing of motifs. His system of motif recognition and recording takes some time to learn, but it is repaid by one's being able quickly to list the locations of related textual material. Without this work, the present collection of studies would have required years to assemble; with it, it was a matter of months. For the benefit of those who have no interest in this process, most of the references to motifs have been removed to endnotes so as not to impede the encounter with the texts.

Educational Use.

I am a teacher, and the classroom is never far from my mind. As a teacher of anthropology and folklore, I am convinced that the general public benefits from these academic disciplines primarily in terms of exposure to alien cultures. Learning about alternate ways of seeing the world and living in it is difficult but rewarding, for it is the only weapon against our unconscious assumption that we are always right. Our "ethnocentrism," as that attitude is known, gets in our way whenever we deal with people of other cultures, whether for trade or cultural exchange. To the extent to which we gain humility by learning to appreciate differences, we are better inhabitants of this shrinking planet.

Thus I confess that as I wrote, I frequently envisioned myself speaking to my undergraduate student friends, and I suspect that this book would have gotten itself organized into classroom chapters even if I had not wished it. If it serves any students of folklore or Native American thought as a textbook or enrichment source, I will be pleased. As a teacher, I place high value on the transmission of knowledge, and I hope this volume may contribute to that process.

CHAPTER TWO

The Native American Southeast

When the Spaniards under Hernando DeSoto toured the Southeast from 1539 to 1542, their late medieval European eyes saw "provinces," monarchs, and nobility. What they were really confronting was an extraordinarily complicated international system of chiefdoms, each with its own characteristic peculiarities and sets of relationships to each other. The various chiefdoms apparently agreed on basic concepts, but each adaptation of the superculture was unique; the result was strong cultural individuality within an apparent regional sameness.

Studies by ethnographers, archaeologists, and ethnohistorians since DeSoto's time have only deepened our awareness of the complexity of Southeastern societies. If that awareness were more general, the "Hollywood Indian"—a simple universal savage given to grunts and mindless violence—could never have gotten a foothold, particularly as regards the Eastern Woodlands. As it is, few seem today to be aware that the diversity among the two-hundred-plus Native American societies was much greater than that which separated the nations of Europe, and recent demographic study has suggested that the North American population may have been larger than Europe's when the two worlds collided. When the Europeans entered the Southeast, they were invading a region that was already thoroughly international.

For one thing, the Southeast was the home of speakers of every one of the five major language families of Eastern North America, in addition to a few more of unknown affiliation, called "isolates." The Cherokee and their neighbors spoke a version of Iroquoian, while the vast majority of people in the mid-South spoke various dialects of Muskhogean, some not even mutually intelligible despite the family relationship. The Catawba and their neighbors of the Carolinas spoke Siouan, as did the Biloxi of the Gulf Coast, although their linguistic kinspeople were mostly on the far side of the Mississippi River. The Quapaw and Osage north of the Arkansas River marked the beginning of the

Siouan cluster of the Upper Mississippi Valley and the Plains. On the western edge of the Southeast were the Caddo, whose fellow Caddoan speakers were stretched out to the north—Wichita, Pawnee, and Arikara. Even Algonkian was spoken, not only by the peoples of the Virginia area but also by wandering groups of Shawnee. The Timucua of north Florida, doomed to extinction under the Spanish, spoke an isolated tongue which has been identified as related to the Arawak family. And there were linguistic isolates whose ancestry is mysterious; among these are the Yuchi, the Tunica, and the Tonkawa. Some peoples became extinct so early that it is not possible even to study their language or other characteristics.

Such linguistic diversity immediately tells us that the Southeast was some sort of international zone created by prehistoric migrations and political events, and we should expect more complexity rather than less.

One of the major factors promoting complexity was the "town" system. The English translation does not really communicate the idea. Called *talwa* by the Creeks, *okla* by the Choctaw, and other names by the other peoples, the town as the basic political unit seems to have been universal in the Southeast. One was born into a talwa and owed it lifelong fidelity. The talwa had a location, but the location did not define the talwa. Coosa, for example, the "mother" talwa of the Upper Creeks, could and did change locations several times through the historic period, but it was always Coosa. When a talwa split, it "gave birth" to an offspring town, but members of the new group always maintained the "oldtown" as chief identity. This was referred to as "being of one fire" with each other, a reference to the sacred fire which burned in the council lodges or "temple" area and was the source for all fires at the annual "new fire" ceremony.

Through the centuries talwas changed physical locations. During the historic period some are known to have made radical changes to surprising new places. The primacy of the talwa as the social unit made it possible for a talwa to ally itself with otherwise unrelated talwas without undergoing major cultural change. The result was the phenomenon of the confederacy. The most well known is the Creek Confederacy, but all the other nations seem to have been confederacies of a similar type. "Creek," by the way, is a European name, and "confederacy" is the European description of what they saw, an aggregation of talwas frequently acting as if they were a coherent single society. Despite common activities, such as war or negotiations with Europeans, the talwas were free agents.

Take the Creek talwas, for example. We now know that the mother town Coosa occupied the headwaters of the Coosa River in northwest Georgia at the time of "Contact"—the initial encounter with Europeans. Kasihta and Coweta, leading towns of the Chattahoochee Creeks, told Europeans that they were latecomers, having migrated in recent centuries from farther west; it is a fair speculation, however, that their ancestors were related to the Okmulgee site at

Macon, Georgia, around 1000 B.C. Tukabahchee, another mother town, may have been Shawnee and a fairly recent immigrant to the Tallapoosa River, but the evidence is inconclusive. The Koasati moved from the Tennessee Valley to the lower Coosa after DeSoto's journey, and the Alabama moved eastward from the Tombigbee, probably more familiar with the Choctaw and Chickasaw than Coosa and Tukabahchee. They were known for keeping their customs separate from the Coosa talwas, even though they became thought of as "Creeks." One observer in the eighteenth century noted that six separate languages were spoken in the vicinity of Fort Toulouse at the Coosa-Tallapoosa junction—by "Creeks."

All of the Southeastern peoples were agricultural peoples, but they varied in the intensity of their agrarian pursuits (number of species and crops per season) and the method of adapting to local conditions. They tended to settle in, and eventually to control, river valleys, using the uplands for hunting. Some peoples placed the talwa center on the floodplain for the agricultural part of the year, but others had to find high land overlooking the water to avoid the floods. In the Mobile Delta, they utilized the idea of permanent towns on the bluffs and temporary villages in the low delta, a pattern the French later adopted.

Those peoples who lived near the coast, of course, developed their own diverse ways of relating to their environment, and the ubiquitous heaps of ancient shell testify to their use of the saltwater world. Like beads on a string, the societies ran from the Rio Grande to Tampa Bay: Karankawa, Tonkawa, Atakapa, Chitimacha, Bayagoula, Mugoulasha, Pascagoula, Biloxi, Maubila, Pensacola, Chatot, Apalachee, Timucua, Calusa. The Chitimacha's use of the *atlatl* (spear-thrower), known to persist into historic times, may be a coastal characteristic; by the arrival of the French, the atlatl for the interior peoples was an obsolete or symbolic weapon.

Political systems also varied among the Southeastern groups. They seem to have agreed on the basic notion that politics was mostly a male activity and that a council of elders should make decisions by consensus. They met around the sacred fire within specialized architecture. Usually, males advanced in status and attained participation in the council by building up achievements as warriors.

One of the cultural characteristics that seems to have been generally held across the Southeast was first deduced from the Cherokee records, but seems applicable across the board. The political organization reflected the recognition of two different modes for the people: war and peace. The peace council, considered preeminent, was presided over by the primary chief, but when war was declared, an entirely different set of men took charge. The war organization was probably a development of permanent warrior societies, and it was set up along military lines, rather than by council. The peace status and its structure were symbolized by the color white, and the alternate war system was indicated by red. The two colors thus took on many levels of metaphor, and this basic color symbolism was recognized across the Southeast.

Success as a warrior was understood to be very similar to success as a hunter. Both required personal courage and skill, but they also required additional power from spirit or animal powers. Visions and dreams were ways in which supernatural assistance was granted to men, frequently after the man was tested severely. As a man's gifts from the animals increased, so did his success in war and the hunt, and so did his status in the warrior system. Just as hunting involved the notion of a personal relation between the hunter and the hunted, or with the "Master of Animals" who gave permission for the kill, so war was a matter of relationship between the warriors. The demonstration of power over the enemy seems to have been at least as important as actually killing him. This produced painful executions of prisoners that Europeans saw as torture, but the Southeasterners apparently saw them as tests of the prisoners' power. Southeasterners, like Native Americans elsewhere, were trained to die well. Young men were expected to follow the red path. It was the way to renown and status. It has been argued that the rebellion of the young men which led to the Creek War of 1814 was inevitable, because the long peace had deprived a generation of war and the opportunity to grow in the talwa.

Killing within the people, whether talwa or confederacy, was another matter. Not only did one not achieve status by killing a townsman, one incurred a cosmic debt. A death required a death, not in a sense of revenge, but because of a balance that had to be maintained. There are indications that the family of the victim had the right to decide when the balance was achieved, and in some cases it is known that payment of goods was sufficient to satisfy everyone. Nonetheless, the death of the killer, regardless of circumstances, could be demanded, and was.

Beyond a man's younger life as a warrior, however, there was the possibility of exchanging red for white and becoming a white elder or chief. Probably the most distinguishing characteristic of a white chief was concern for the people, and this was normally demonstrated as a set of actions from youth. Just as the successes of a hunter/warrior showed his power, the chief-to-be gave meat from a successful hunt to the widows and orphans and defended the weak. Such men were destined to become "beloved men" worthy to guide the fortunes of the talwa.

In addition, one could also follow the path of the doctor. Just as the Southeasterners believed that illnesses were caused mostly by animals (and were therefore relationship problems), they understood that healing came from the same sources. In visions and dreams the animal powers would bestow upon a seeker special knowledge—a cure for a specific disease, or a song to give immunity from a disease. Those who had gathered many such cures had great power, and the doctors were one of the few specialized groups in Southeastern life. They were the healers, the repositories of religious and historical lore, and the powerful seers who could choose to wield their knowledge against people as well as for them.

All of these ideas were common across the Southeast. Beyond these similarities in viewpoint, however, there was considerable diversity. In some societies there seem to have been some political roles achieved by heredity. The Natchez, although destroyed as a people by the French in 1729, were observed to have an extremely complex system of classes with fixed rules of marriage into the classes below. Apparently not all the elements of the system were recorded, leaving anthropologists arguing to this day about how it worked. The Natchez had a ruling family called "Suns," and the French were impressed at what they saw as similarity to the monarchies of Europe. Two centuries earlier, DeSoto had encountered indications of this class distinction across the Southeast, but by French times most talwas—Cherokee, Creek, Choctaw—exhibited much more egalitarian behavior before they began to evolve new adaptations to the European presence. The Natchez and Timucua were the major reminders of the earlier political complexities of the Southeast.

While these ideas surrounding politics and war were generally accepted across the Southeast, if not eastern North America, ways of burying the dead differed greatly. Almost every mode of disposal of the dead was practiced in the Southeast, from extended burial under the house to cremation to exposure on a scaffold away from the town, with burial of the bundled bones at a later time. Some, particularly the Atlantic Coast peoples and the Biloxi, even practiced mummification, a rare technique.

While women were generally excluded from both warfare and the political structures that revolved around it, a few women are known to have breached the barriers by sheer strength of ability. For the most part, the women's world was the important world of the family. The Southeastern tribes, as distinguished from the majority of the others in North America, were matrilineal, in that the children "belonged" to the mother, not the father. Each person took the mother's clan and talwa, and the mother's lineage was one's family. One important consequence of this basic cultural fact was that the paternal role, the duties and privileges that patrilineal groups assign to "father," was filled by the mother's brother. Kinship terms for the Southeasterners, as for most people, served as a means of establishing the nature of relationships between people, and between people and animals. To call someone "uncle" or "mother," therefore, was to make a statement about the kind of relationship that existed. In the Southeast, "mother" was a much stronger term than "father," and "uncle" shared with "mother" the respect due to those who discipline and train. Grandparents, on the other hand, were expected to lavish affection and indulge whims. One could joke with grandparents, but not with parents, and to call anyone "grandfather" was to insist on a close, affectionate relationship.

Another consequence of matrilineality, which both outraged and delighted Europeans, was that unmarried women were free to seek pleasure or children from anyone they chose. Since a child couldn't be illegitimate, the women were free to bear at will, and many Europeans found themselves besieged by young women eager to secure the foreigner's exotic "power" for their soon-to-be-conceived child. As might be expected, Europeans had ambivalent attitudes regarding this practice. Priests thundered against it, but soldiers indulged themselves. It is little wonder that there were frequent defections of Europeans into Native American life from the time of the early explorations on.

The Europeans were also unprepared for the discovery that laws of fidelity were as strong after marriage as freedom was before it. Adultery was severely rejected, with different punishments across the Southeast. Among the Creeks, first offenders lost their noses, while death followed the second occurrence.

Several difficulties hinder us from understanding Native American life in the Southeast. One is the very adaptability of the Southeasterners. From French times on, they demonstrated an ability to evolve their institutions rapidly so as to deal with the rapidly changing world of the Europeans. It was a survival skill for them, but it also resulted in a great deal of change before ethnographic information was gathered. There had already been massive changes in the interim beween DeSoto's sixteenth-century journey and the arrival of the French. Population loss due to disease brought by the Spanish is thought to have been the major factor, because it is difficult to maintain complex social structures, particularly ranking and hereditary preferential treatment, when catastrophic reduction in population occurs. Thanks to DeSoto and other early explorers, we know that the world they saw at the time of Contact was much more complex than existed two centuries later. Even in later times, very little serious collecting of ethnographic data was done, and we are left to piece together clues found in various journals and fill in gaps with archaeology.

The reason why this is important is that in the centuries of Europe's medieval period an extraordinary set of societies developed in the American Southeast. They are known to have been involved in some sort of "superculture" that used elaborate ritual regalia, shared symbols and art forms, and created complicated architectural centers of earth. The remains of the "Southeastern Ceremonial Complex," as it is called, have provided the pieces of a gigantic jigsaw puzzle. All students of the Contact period in the Southeast sense that there are important messages contained in the engravings on shell, copper, and stone, could they but be read properly. Several major studies of the iconography of the SCC have been written, the latest being a massive study of the shell engravings that were dispersed throughout the world after the plundering of the Spiro mound on the Arkansas River in the 1930s. The interpretation focuses on the use of the shells as status indicators in the ranking system of warriors, but the actual iconographic meaning of much of the material remains a matter for debate.[1]

Certainly the Southeastern Ceremonial Complex forms an enigmatic backdrop for any study of traditional narrative, because it is likely that some of the art forms are illustrations of the legends, or at least of beliefs which lie behind the legends. This consideration adds a visual dimension to the study of Southeastern verbal art, but it is doubtful that there will ever be a definitive interpretation of these materials. In this book, a text will sometimes by accompanied by a drawing of one of these designs as a suggestion that it may be an illustration of the myth. Such linkages cannot be proven, of course, but they are fun to ponder.

Collecting the Narratives.

Unfortunately, the collection of the narratives was even later than the ethnography, and several informants made it clear that there was much more which could no longer be recalled. Nonetheless, it was done, and it has provided for posterity what was available by the late nineteenth century, four centuries after Contact and four decades after Removal.

During the nineteenth century local historians in the Southeast recorded some materials, but it was mostly ethnographic and had the drawback of usually being retellings of oral history from veterans of the latter years of the pre-Removal Southeast. A better approach was taken by W.O. Tuggle in Oklahoma in 1881 and 1882. While working there he interviewed many Creeks and compiled the texts, doubtless somewhat rewritten from notes. His material was used by Swanton and others, but the full collection has only recently been published.[2]

Albert S. Gatschet was the first professional ethnographer who collected materials from Native Americans in the Southeast. In 1881 he collected Catawba linguistic materials from Billy George in North Carolina.[3] From there he went to Louisiana, where in 1881 and 1882 he "collected an abundance of linguistic material from the Chitimacha."[4] His classic work, still worth reading despite the great expansion in our knowledge since that time, appeared in 1884.[5] In 1885 the tireless Gatschet collected a text "in the Yuchi language from a young man of that tribe at Wialaka (Oklahoma)." The informant was "a pupil of the mission school at Wialaka, Creek nation, on the Arkansas river near the present settlements of the Yuchi."[6]

The next year he was in Lecompte, Louisiana, where he collected materials from the last Biloxi. His informants were Bankston Johnson, Betsey Joe, and her daughter Maria.[7] Six years later, in 1892, James O. Dorsey, the great collector of the Siouan peoples who was eager to attack the problem of the isolated Siouans in the Southeast, followed Gatschet's lead and visited Lecompte. For two months he also collected texts from Bankston Johnson, Betsey Joe, and Maria. "In order to record any of the texts in the original Biloxi, it was necessary to have present not only the aged woman who told the myths to the others, but also her daughter and son-in-law, as only the last could be induced to dictate the myths sentence by sentence and in an audible voice, the others prompting him from time to time."[8] That proved to be the last of the information about the Biloxi. Dorsey and John R. Swanton, Southeastern ethnographer for the Bureau of American Ethnology, wrote the final word on the Biloxi.[9]

Swanton, meanwhile, was busy collecting Muskhogean material, primarily in Oklahoma. While that work was going on, beginning in the summer of 1887, James Mooney collected for the bureau from the Eastern Cherokee in North Carolina. His major informant was Swimmer, an aging doctor who knew a great deal about the Cherokee heritage. The majority of the narrative texts came from him and from John Ax. Mooney did not reveal his method of collecting, but his attention to linguistic detail in the published texts suggests that he took down the information verbatim in Cherokee, then translated it later. In 1900 Mooney published *Myths of the Cherokee*.[10] Despite the additional collections of Cherokee material through the years since, it remains an irreplaceable classic.

On the other side of the Southeast, between 1903 and 1905, George A. Dorsey, under auspices of the Carnegie Institution, collected materials from the Caddo in western Oklahoma.[11] He was specializing in the Caddoan language family, and he ultimately produced volumes of traditional narratives for each of these peoples: Caddo, Wichita, Pawnee, Skidi Pawnee, and Arikara.[12]

In 1904 and 1905 Frank G. Speck was in Oklahoma collecting material from the remaining Yuchi in Oklahoma. While he was there, he "incidentally obtained" material from neighboring Taskigi.[13] His Yuchi informants were Jim Brown, Louis Long, John Wolf, George Clinton, John Big Pond, Jim Tiger, Henry Long, and Fagoeonwi', "all of whom held civil or religious offices in the tribe."[14]

In 1907 Swanton assessed the situation in the Southeast:

The Tonkawa are represented by forty-seven persons in Oklahoma, the Attacapa by less than a dozen mixed bloods near Lake Charles, La., and possibly as many more in Oklahoma. Of the Chitimacha there cannot be seventy-five all told, and probably are not many over fifty. Close to Marksville, La., are thirty-three Tunica, and a few live in the Choctaw nation and elsewhere, making a total of perhaps fifty.[15]

Several of these remnant groups were visited by ethnographers in the next few decades.

David I. Bushnell, Jr., of the bureau collected from a band of Choctaw living at Bayou Lacomb in St. Tammany Parish, Louisiana. In 1908 and 1909 materials were "related to the writer by two women, Pisatuntema (Emma) and Heleema (Louisa), and a man Ahojeobe (Emil John)."[16] In 1910 he went back to collect more texts from Pisatuntema; he published them immediately.[17]

Swanton's major period of field collecting was from 1908 to 1914. His focus was Muskhogean, and he produced the definitive ethnographic volumes for the Choctaw, Chickasaw, Creeks, and Lower Mississippi Valley groups, making him the premier ethnographer of the Southeast.[18] He produced a single volume of folk narrative texts in 1929, still the classic Muskhogean collection.[19] The Creek materials were collected in Oklahoma. "The Alabama stories are from the Alabama Indians living in Polk County, Tex., and the Koasati stories from some of the same informants and from the Koasati near Kinder, La." When he was on the Alabama-Coushatta reservation in 1911 and 1912, Charles Thompson served as translator for him.[20]

> The Hitchiti stories were obtained from a few speakers of the Hitchiti language in the northern part of Seminole County, Okla., part of them having been recorded directly, while part were written down in the original by an Indian. The Natchez collection, so called, was secured from one of the few remaining speakers of the ancient Natchez tongue residing near Braggs, Okla., a man named Watt Sam.[21]

In 1914 Swanton collected materials from the Chitimacha of Bayou Teche, Louisiana. "Unfortunately but four individuals have a speaking knowledge of the old tongue; and, still more unfortunately, only a very few texts may be obtained from these, the greater part of the features of the language being accessible only by a painful system of cross-questioning, which must be in large measure blind."[22]

Speck collected in 1913 from the Siouan-speaking Catawba in North Carolina. His major informant was "Mrs. Samson Owl, who left the Catawba reservation upon her marriage with a Cherokee and moved to the home of the latter in the mountains of western North Carolina."[23] Four years later Swanton made an additional Catawba collection at the reservation in North Carolina.[24] From 1921 to 1931, Speck made occasional return visits to the Catawba. He described his informants:

> Mrs. Samson Owl (nee Susan Harris) living at Cherokee, North Carolina, aged 83 in 1930, narrator of 21 tales. She was born at the mouth of Sugar (Sugeree) Creek on Catawba River above the Catawba reservation, York County, South Carolina. Mrs. Margaret Wiley Brown of the Catawba Nation who spent her life on the reservation, and died in 1922 at the age of 85, narrator of 33 texts. Mrs. Brown said that...her father was a very old man when he died, as she thought, in about 1845. He bore the marks of smallpox, evidence of his being a victim of the epidemic of 1800...Mrs. Sally Gordon (nee Sally Brown), daughter of Margaret Brown of the Catawba reservation, born 1865, narrator of 62 texts.[25]

Because a significant number of Cherokee had remained in the East, they continued to attract ethnographers after Mooney. For two months in 1927 Frans M. Olbrechts collected Cherokee materials from Will West Long and his half-brother Morgan Calhoun in Big Cove, North Carolina.[26]

Linguists as well as ethnographers were trying to collect samples of the languages, particularly those in danger of vanishing. In 1928 and 1929 Gunter Wagner collected materials from Yuchi of central Oklahoma under the auspices of the Council of Learned Societies.

> By far the greatest part of the tales was told by Maxey Simms of Sapulpa, Oklahoma...The other tales were obtained from George Clinton, Sally Clinton, and their daughter Ida Clinton of Bristow, Oklahoma, and by Andy Johnson of Sapulpa. They were translated partly by Maxey Simms and partly by Mrs. Ella Townsend of Bristow, Oklahoma...[27]

From 1931 to 1941 Howard N. Martin, a Euro-American who had grown up with Native Americans in Livingston, collected narratives from Alabama and Koasati in Polk County, Texas. His nineteen informants included C.M. Thompson, chief from 1928, McConico Battise, Bronston Cooper Sylestine (who died in 1969 at age 89), Charles Boatman (Koasati), Billy Harrison Battise, Frank Sylestine, and Gustin Battise. He published texts in several articles; a book-length collection was issued in 1977.[28] Other collectors of Alabama-Koasati materials included Frances Densmore in 1932.[29]

In 1940 linguist Mary R. Haas collected materials from Creeks in Oklahoma.[30] In 1947 she published a summary of the collecting possibilities for linguists. She pleaded for fast action: "Some good story-tellers are still left among these tribes and additional material is therefore obtainable, whereas in another fifteen or twenty years this will not be the case."[31] If her plea was heeded, little published material has resulted. Recent collections are few, but there are some. In 1954-56, James H. Howard collected Cherokee materials from Stewart R. Shaffer in Albion, Michigan. "The bulk of the material, however, was collected by James Shaffer, the grandson of Stewart, who mailed it on to me after talks with his grandfather."[32] In Oklahoma Betty Lombardi, teacher of folklore and English in Tallequah, has recently demonstrated that there are still significant opportunities for collecting, especially by Native Americans themselves. Her students collected Cherokee materials which indicate that the ever-adaptable Cherokee culture is alive and well, albeit in contemporary form.[33]

While this is not an exhaustive list, it includes the major collections of Southeastern material which have been made. The significant thing to note, of course, is the lateness of the collecting effort, discouragingly long after Removal, at least from the viewpoint of understanding Southeastern cultures before Contact. As we shall see, there were significant accretions from Europeans and Africans in the intervening years.

Oral Narrative in the Southeast.

In Euro-American society, literacy provides a way of preserving the essential lore of the culture, and the oral narratives can safely be left to evolve in the uncontrolled processes of oral transmission. In non-literate societies more structure must be established to maintain stability in traditions considered essential. An early Natchez informant, a priest, expressed his awareness of the difference. When the French visitor explained Christian beliefs, the priest "hearkened to me with great attention, and promised to repeat all that I had told him to the old men of his nation, who certainly would not forget knowledge of such fine things by means of the speaking cloth, so they name books and manuscripts."[34]

Providing security for oral transmission called for some sort of formal system. Among Plains people, for example, legends were literally owned by individuals. The narrative belonged to the ritual associated with a sacred bundle, and the owner and protector of the bundle was expected to preserve the myth along with the contents of the bundle. When the time seemed right, the owner carefully selected the new owner, who bought the bundle from him and received careful schooling in the meaning of it. The Plains peoples had thus provided an institutionalized way of reducing change in myth and assigning responsibility for the preservation of oral narrative to specific individuals.

In the Southeast there are a few indications of that sort of system, but not enough for a detailed reconstruction. The evidence is from only a few peoples, which leaves open the question of how widespread any of the mentioned practices were. In the early eighteenth century DuPratz found a priestly class of specialists among the Natchez. He reported on his discussions with these guardians of the sacred fire, and he indicated that they were the official repositories of the myths. Apparently there were some rigid transmission rules: "The old men who keep the ancient word (it must be remembered that this is the tradition) never speak before the women. Even among the men they choose to teach it to those whom they recognize as having the most intelligence."[35]

There are hints of the same sort of system in other Southeastern peoples, but the doctors seem to have been the repository rather than priests, perhaps reflecting only the cessation of the fire guardianship.

> The first class [the healers, one of whom officiated at every busk] communicated their knowledge to novices for a certain consideration. They would take from one to four pupils at a time, have them go through a preparation of fasting and sweat bathing somewhere away from the village and then inculcate their mysteries...I have been told that there were also graduates in the telling of myths...These graduates, of whom there were several in each town, were evidently the repositories of learning, the keepers of the sacred myths, the historians, and the guardians of the supernatural mysteries.[36]

The impression given here is that there was an institutionalized transmission system, but the doctors were apparently more plentiful than were the fire guardians of the Natchez.

These "graduates in the telling of myths" were undoubtedly well known by everyone, and they may have been the people who used the mnemonic devices known throughout the Eastern Woodlands and Plains. Europeans had early commented on the *wampum* (bead) belts used by speakers at formal councils to remind themselves of the historical or mythical episodes they were to tell; in the Plains the same devices were used, but they seem to have been more usually painted on skin. Both practices seem to have existed in the Southeast. The Creek migration legend recorded in 1735 was accompanied by a painted skin used as a mnemonic device by the narrator. Milfort noted half a century later that they used wampum belts.

> Since my arrival among the Creeks the old chiefs had often spoken to me of their ancestors, and they had shown me the belts, or species of chaplets, which contained their histories. These chaplets were their archives; they are of little seeds like those which are called Cayenne pearls; they are of different colors and strung in rows; and it is on their arrangement and their pattern that their meaning depends. As only the principal events are preserved on these belts and without any details, it sometimes happens that a single chaplet contains the history of twenty to twenty-five years.[37]

It is not clear what relationship existed between the official preservers of lore and medicine-men and doctors, who seem to have comprised several different groups. The Cherokee had what appears to be a similar system.

> The sacred myths were not for everyone, but only those might hear who observed the proper form and ceremony. When John Ax and other old men were boys, now some eighty years ago, the myth-keepers and priests were accustomed to meet together at night in the *asi*, or low-built log sleeping house, to recite the traditions and discuss their secret knowledge. At times those who desired instruction from an adept in the sacred lore of the tribe met him by appointment in the asi, where they sat up all night talking, with only the light of a small fire burning in the middle of the floor. At daybreak the whole party went down to the running stream, where the pupils or hearers of the myths stripped themselves, and were scratched upon their naked skin with a bone-tooth comb in the hands of the priest, after which they waded out, facing the rising sun, and dipped seven times under the water, while the priest recited prayers upon the bank...Before beginning one of the stories of the sacred class the informant would sometimes suggest jokingly that the author first submit to being scratched and 'go to water.'[38]

To use such a selective system of oral transmission does not, of course, mean that only those chosen ones knew the lore. On the contrary, most adults had probably heard the legends enough times that they could themselves tell them, but they did not bear the responsibility of preserving them. It may be that collectors were in the presence of much more lore than they could record, because their informants did not have the right to communicate it. Radin has given an indication of reluctance to have such information recorded among the Winnebago, and the same phenomenon may have occurred in the Southeast.[39] Dorsey complained of that among the Quapaw:

I met with considerable difficulty on account of the reluctance of the people to communicate to me the information which they regarded as the peculiar right of a class of men whom they called the *Wapinan.* A wapinan they defined as a *nika quwe* or mysterious man, answering to the *wakan* man of the Dakota tribes.[40]

The consequence was that he published no collection of Quapaw narratives. For the Choctaw there is a hint of a more democratic treatment of oral transmission. Adam Hodgson, who toured the Southeast before Removal, wrote:

After parting with the Rev. Mr. Kingsbury on the banks of the Yaloo Busha, we proceeded through the woods, along an Indian path, till evening, when we reached the dwelling of a half-breed Choctaw, whose wife was a Chickasaw, and whose hut was on the frontier of the two nations...He told me, that great changes had taken place among Indians, even in his time—that in many tribes, when he was young, the children, as soon as they rose, were made to plunge in the water, and swim, in the coldest weather; and were then collected on the bank of the river, to learn the manners and customs of their ancestors, and hear the old men recite the traditions of their forefathers. They were assembled again, at sunset, for the same purpose; and were taught to regard as a sacred duty, the transmission to their posterity of the lessons thus acquired.[41]

A century later Bushnell found the same general knowledge among the Mississippi Choctaw:

From her father Pisatuntema learned many of the ancient tribal myths and legends...Often, however, while telling the legends, she would be interrupted by others who would suggest or add certain details, but all were familiar with the subjects and at no time did they differ on any essential points.[42]

The Creeks also may have had an institutionalized educational training program for everyone. Swanton noted, "Among the Creeks I was told that when a story-teller finished his narrative he would spit, and then another would have to contribute a story in return, and in this way the cue was taken up by one after another 'until the children went to bed.'"[43]

There were taboos which surrounded the telling of sacred narratives. In some cases the sense of taboo was retained without a clear idea of the consequences. A Creek informant who told Swanton a migration legend also told him "that such traditions must be repeated in a certain manner word for word, for a mistake would cost blood."[44] His Natchez informant, Watt Sam, said that certain stories, including those about the tie-snake, "must be told only during cold weather. Otherwise bad luck would follow."[45]

This "bad luck" was more concretely understood elsewhere. The taboo on telling certain kinds of narratives was observed over much of the Woodlands and Plains; the danger lay in snakes. Here is a brief sample:

Omaha: "Myths must not be told during the day, nor in summer, as violation of this rule will cause snakes to come."[46]

Omaha: Among the Omaha Indians, where "story-telling is an important part of home-life," the favorite season is winter, and there is "a superstition which prevents the telling of stories in the summer season, as the snakes may hear and do mischief." But as Miss Fletcher further informs us, this taboo is lifted for the children, who "carry the songs out among the summer blossoms, and the snakes do them no harm."[47]

Ojibwa: The Ojibwa and certain other Algonkian tribes of the Great Lakes give as a reason for not telling the "tales of the fathers" in summer, that "frogs and other disagreeable things would enter into the camp"; moreover, during the winter, the great Nanibozhu is at leisure, and can listen to the tales of his own mighty deeds.[48]

Winnebago: The old people do not like to tell their stories after the spring opens. The children are told that they will see snakes if they should listen to tales during warm weather.[49]

Creek: According to both the early writers and present-day Indians, in ancient times the Indians would not willingly kill a wolf or a rattlesnake. I was told that not many stories were related about the former because it was considered the friend of the red men and they were afraid it might injure them.[50]

This taboo against telling myths in the summer and during the day was early noticed as a widespread one, but apparently no rationale was given to the collectors. I think it is possible to suggest a reason why this taboo was so widely observed, however. The Skidi Pawnee of the Plains preserved a body of astronomical lore which stands out as different from all other North American lore. While their folklore is related to the other Caddoan collections, they emphasize astronomical meanings of legends more than any other people. One of their connections was the identification of a "Coyote Star" (Antares?) in the summer sky. What they designated "Coyote tales" were not to be told

... during the summer months, or rather during those months when the snakes are visible; for it is supposed that the tutelary god or star of the snakes is in direct communication with the star of Coyote, for during these months the Coyote-Star is early visible in the eastern horizon, and, not liking to be talked about, directs the Snake-Star to tell the snakes of those who talk about him that they may bite them.[51]

It may be that here we have the full explanation of the taboo on summer telling of legends; other peoples may have accepted the taboo along with the diffusion of legends, but only a people as knowledgeable about astronomy as the Skidi would have retained the rationale.

Curiously, the Cherokee seem not to have been involved in this wide distribution of the taboo. "With some tribes the winter season and the night are the time for telling stories, but to the Cherokee all times are alike."[52] Why the Cherokee should be different is not known.

As the taboo indicates, Native Americans made distinctions among the kinds of stories they told. Folklorists have long since become aware of the ethnocentrism of simply applying European categories, or "genres," to non-European lore. Many attempts have been made to determine the Native American categories, but no scheme has been found to apply across the board. Unfortunately, we have little information about the Southeastern way of organizing material, and every collector has offered his collection with a different set of categories. One note on genres was taken from the Yuchi:

> The following two classes may be distinguished in the myths: the sacred, relating to the culture hero and the deeds of the animal creators, and the commonplace, relating to the Rabbit trickster, various animals and their exploits, etc. The latter class, subject to much variation and change at the hands of different individuals, is extremely characteristic of the whole Southeast... The culture hero concept is closely connected with religion and ritual, while the trickster concept is not.[53]

We are left with a problem of what to call the various narratives. It is clear that the European distinction between tales and legends does not work very well in North America. The notion of "tale"—a sequence of motifs that has achieved permanent form, with formulas indicating the fictional nature of the narrative—seems inapplicable to almost all North American narratives, except possibly the trickster tales, for they weren't considered fictional entertainments. As Swanton noted, "My informant affirms that these are true stories."[54] Even with the trickster stories, the fiction/nonfiction distinction is forced, because the trickster is also frequently confounded with the culture hero of myth.

The separation of myth from legend on the basis of the cosmic activities of divinities, which seems clear in European studies, is made difficult in Native American folklore because it is often difficult to tell whether a given character is "divine" (even that word seems ethnocentric) and whether the action done is cosmogonic or just a yarn. As many of the narratives in this volume show, animals are people and can change form, and they sometimes do powerful acts befitting European gods, but then so can some humans. Setting up genres by form and content seems impossible, and we don't have enough information from the Southeast to argue from function or performance style.

Students of Native American folklore quickly recognize that the basic element of narrative is the motif or episode, for they float from one string of motifs to another with apparent ease, even within the repertoire of a single teller. Sometimes several motifs seem to have established a more permanent relationship to each other, in that they are usually found together in the same narrative, and these could fairly be termed "tales" to distinguish them from floating motifs. Hultkrantz, dean of the history of Native American religions, has suggested that all narratives other than purely historical legends (none of which is included in this collection) should simply be termed "myths."[55] All these difficulties, made worse by the lack of information from the Southeast, have led me to use tale, legend, and myth as almost interchangeable terms, if only to emphasize our lack of knowledge about native genres.

The one primary fact which hangs over all Southeastern folklore studies is the lateness of the collecting. Comparative study serves, above all else, to suggest how much of the richness of the ancient Southeastern heritage is forever lost. Treasures of symbolic interpretation such as *Lakota Myth* can only cause envy in the student of the Southeast, because such esoteric understanding is no longer available. All too frequently heard is the comment, which is also a sad folkloric epitaph, that "there was once a long myth of this kind, most of which has been lost."[55]

THE WAYS
OF THE WORLD

CHAPTER THREE

The Above World

For human beings, survival demands an awareness of the way the world works. No matter how we look at the world around us, it is endlessly complex. In order to reduce that complexity, every human society posits a relatively small number of principles that seem to explain and predict the dynamic forces of the non-human natural order. This lore is crystallized into patterns called belief systems, and those patterns find expression in all areas of social life, from the verbal, aural, and visual arts to organization, customs, and economics. All together, the belief systems and their expressions comprise our "culture," the thought and behavior that make us part of one society and not another.

Native Americans of the Southeast, like all human societies, created a set of similar cultures that are both admirable and frustrating. "Admirable" because they survived and even thrived in a single region over many centuries, at least until the arrival of the Europeans. "Admirable" also because their cultural expressions are considered aesthetically excellent by many people from other cultures. "Frustrating" because the pre-Columbian Southeastern ways of looking at the world are not completely recoverable, thanks to the length of time the Native Americans have been adapting to the presence of Euro-Americans and Afro-Americans, the tragedies inherent in the expansion of Euro-America, and the lateness of the gathering of so much of the ethnographic information.

One of the clearest and most widespread beliefs of Native Americans is that the sun is a major power in human lives. The sun appears in many practices and art forms in the Southeast. There is evidence that there was a general belief in a higher spirit, but, as is true of so many animistic peoples, that "high god" did not appear in rituals and legendry. The sun, however, both as the celestial body and as its earthly representative, fire, did take a direct role in the cultural life of the people. The people were understood to be in direct contact with the sun by means of fire, especially the "sacred fire" that was the ritual center of each major town. All fires were extinguished at the annual first-fruits festival, generally called by the Creek name *poskita,* anglicized into *busk.* In a major ceremony a "new fire" was made at the town's center. From the new fire all other fires were begun for the new year. As might be expected, care was taken that the sacred fire was not polluted, and everyone seems to have known the rules surrounding the use of fire.

Each sacred fire was distinct from the others, defining the individual's *talwa,* poorly translated as "town." As already noted, the town seems to have been a universal organizational principle in the Southeast. Each person owed first allegiance to his or her town, which was defined by the sacred fire. Even as towns grew large and split, the "offspring" towns continued to regard their parent's fire as theirs also. Thus close relations between towns were expressed in terms of fire; towns that recognized a close linkage were referred to as being "of one fire." That phrase served as a useful political metaphor when ambassadors wished to stress the closeness of the two talwas or clusters of talwas, as when Kasihta, a lower Creek talwa, asserted it was "of one fire" with the Chickasaw. This sort of claim may only reflect the current politics, but it might also enshrine historical fact. Although Tukabahchee was a leading Creek talwa in the late eighteenth century, some have suggested that it was originally Shawnee. When Tecumseh visited the Creeks in 1811, he stayed at Tukabahchee, whose council asserted it was of one fire with the Shawnee.[1]

In the late prehistoric era the symbols of the sun and fire were widespread, and most Muskhogeans and Cherokee are known to have had ritual features organized around the importance of the sun.[2] Swanton and Haas surveyed the data and listed as participants in solar worship the Natchez, Yuchi, Creek, Choctaw, Chitimacha, Caddo, Cusabo, Timucua, Cherokee, Tunica, and Biloxi.[3] The addition of Mugulasha and Bayogoula of the lower Mississippi Valley (from French records) suggests that the sun/fire belief complex was virtually universal in the Southeast.

One of our earliest indications of widespread solar worship is a portrayal of sixteenth century Timucua making a first-fruits offering to the sun.[4]

From the Mississippi Valley there is tantalizing testimony from the Natchez of the early eighteenth century. So important was the sun in their complex social system that the leading family were known as the Suns, and the primary chief was called the Great Sun.[5] Unfortunately, the French observers recorded just enough information about the Natchez social system and beliefs to spark disputes among anthropologists that continue to the present day. The major problem lies in the nature of the ruling class; as given by the French, the marriage and kin system does not appear to be a stable one, but it is not clear whether it was a fault of French reporting or an actual flaw in the Natchez social structure. Even more unfortunately, the French did not record much of their legendry, possibly because it was part of a still functioning ritual and political system and was too secret to be shared with the Europeans by the Natchez who knew the materials. One French observer, however, did record from the Great

An offering to the sun

Sun an impressive legend that gives us insight into the seriousness of their concern with the sacred fire.

Polluting the Fire ■ ■ ■
NATCHEZ

You know that there are always two guardians in the temple to care for the sacred fire. But once in the past it happened that one of these two men went out for some purpose, and while he was away his companion fell asleep and let the fire go out. When he awoke, seeing the fire extinguished, fright seized him. But as his companion had not yet come back he determined to conceal his fault, because he was easily able to do it, in order to escape the death which he had merited. He called then to the first passer and begged him to bring him fire with which to light his *calumet* (pipe), a thing which this person did willingly, well knowing that it is not permitted to touch the eternal fire except to tend it, and that no other use could be made of it.

Thus this fire was relighted with profane fire. Immediately sickness took hold of the Suns. In a few days they were seen to die in rap:d succession, and it was necessary to send after them into the world of spirits many people to serve them.[6] This mortality lasted four years, without anyone being able to guess what had occasioned it. Nine great Suns who succeeded each other died in this interval, and a multitude of people with them. Finally, at the end of this time the guardian himself fell ill. This bad man, feeling that he was not able to live a long time, had word sent to the great Sun at once that he had something to communicate to him of such great importance that if he died without revealing it all the Natchez would die. The great Sun went to see him as quickly as possible. As soon as the sick man perceived him his whole body trembled and he appeared unable to speak. However, he spoke these words, although with difficulty:

"I am going to die, so it makes no difference to me whether the sickness or a man kills me. I know that I am a bad man for having for so long a time concealed, in order to preserve my life, what I am going to tell you. I am the cause of the death of my nation, therefore I merit death, but let me not be eaten by the dogs."

The great Sun understood by these words that this man was guilty of some great crime, and that it was necessary to reassure him in order to draw from him his secret, which appeared to be of the last importance. He therefore told him that whatever he had done he might be assured that he would not be put to death and that he would be buried, that what he had promised him was as true as it was true that the Sun, their father, lighted them every day, and that he should hasten to speak before death prevented him. On this promise the bad guardian confessed all that he had done, which I have related to you.

Immediately the great Sun assembled the old men and by their advice it was resolved to go that very day to wrest fire from the other temple. That was executed and the Suns ceased dying.[7]

Unfortunately for our understanding of the Natchez sun/fire complex, the Natchez uprising against the French in 1729 led to their virtual extinction as a separate nation, and only refugee bands remained as part of the Chickasaw, Creek, and Cherokee.

The Yuchi, already set apart by being a linguistic isolate, called themselves "Children of the Sun," an impressive claim in a world of solar worship. Their legend supports their claim.

The Cedar Tree ▪ ▪ ▪
YUCHI

An unknown mysterious being once came down upon the earth and met people there, who were the ancestors of the Yuchi Indians. To them this being taught many of the arts of life, and in matters of religion admonished them to call the sun their mother as a matter of worship. Every morning the sun, after rising above the horizon, makes short stops, and then goes faster until it reaches the noon point. So the Unknown inquired of them what was the matter with the sun. They denied having any knowledge about it, and said, "Somebody has to go there to see and examine." "Who would go there, and what could he do after he gets there?" The people said, "We are afraid to go up there." But the Unknown selected two men to make the ascent, gave to each a club, and instructed them that as soon as the wizard who was playing these tricks on the sun was leaving his cavern in the earth and appeared on the surface they should kill him on the spot. "It is a wizard who causes the sun to go so fast in the morning, for at sunrise he makes dashes at it, and the sun, being afraid of him, tries to flee from his presence." The two brave men went to the rising place of the sun to watch the orifice from which the sun emerges. The wizard appeared at the mouth of the cave, and at the same time the sun was to rise from another orifice beyond it. The wizard watched for the fiery disk and put himself in position to rush and jump at it at the moment of its appearance. When the wizard held up his head the two men knocked it off from his body with their clubs, took it to their tribe, and proclaimed that they had killed the sorcerer who had for so long a time urged the sun to a quicker motion. But the wizard's head was not dead yet. It was stirring and moving about, and to stop this the man of mysterious origin advised the people to tie the head on the uppermost limbs of a tree. They did so, and on the next morning the head fell to the ground, for it was not dead yet. He then ordered them to tie the head to another tree. It still lived and fell to the ground the next day. To insure success, the Unknown then made them tie it to a red cedar tree. There it remained, and its life became extinct. The blood of the head ran through the cedar. Henceforth the grain of the wood assumed a reddish color, and the cedar tree became a medicine tree. [8]

Tuggle collected another text which varies only a little from Gatschet's. The Sun incident is contained within a larger creation story from the Yuchi, but told by a Creek.

Mother Sun ■ ■ ■
YUCHI

"Who will make the light?" it was said.

Yohah, the Star, said, "I will make the light."

It was so agreed. The Star shone forth. It was light only near him.

"Who will make more light?" it was said.

Shar-pah, the Moon, said: "I will make more light." Shar-pah made more light, but it was still dark.

T-cho, the Sun, said: "You are my children, I am your mother, I will make the light. I will shine for you."

She went to the east. Suddenly light spread over all the earth. As she passed over the earth a drop of blood fell from her to the ground, and from this blood and earth sprang the first people, the children of the Sun, the Yuchis. [9]

This text reveals a fact which was obscured in the first one—the sun is female. The same is true of the Tunica, the Biloxi, and the Chitimacha.

Shaming of the Sun ■ ■ ■
TUNICA

Once a very beautiful girl married Kingfisher. When she asked him for food he caught some minnows and brought them to her. This made her ashamed. She told him that he should remain on the water and eat minnows. She herself would go up into the sky to live. She sang and danced, and, as she was going up into the sky, she radiated light all about her. She became the Sun and now illuminates the whole world. It is for this reason that the Tunica Indians dance the sun dance.[10]

It was collected from one of the few surviving Tunica, and it may be suffering from obsolescence. A text from the Biloxi may have the same problem, but it seems to be a variant of the same legend.

Shaming of the Sun ■ ■ ■
BILOXI

When the Ancient of Otters was about to go to see the ball play, his grandmother objected.[11] But he replied, "That makes no difference. I will view it from afar, and then I will return home." Off he went. On reaching the place, he was standing afar off when a woman sent some one to him, saying, "Tell that person to go home. He emits a very strong odor." Then the man went to the Ancient of Otters and delivered the message. "That woman in the distance says that you are to go home, as you emit a very strong odor." "Yes," replied the Ancient of Otters; but he still remained there. Then another person was sent to him with the same message. "Yes," replied the Ancient of Otters, "I was about to start homeward, but I am here still." Nevertheless, he did not move, so another messenger was sent to him. When he beheld him coming, he started off at once, without waiting for his arrival, as he suspected what his message would be.

On reaching home, he walked to and fro, saying nothing. Then his grandmother said, "For what reason have you come home?" And he replied, "A woman said that I smelt very strong, so I came home." His grandmother laughed at him for some time, and then said, "I said to you that it would turn out thus, but you would not heed at all, and you went anyhow." By and by, she went out to dig some medicine. Having brought the medicine home, she administered it to the Ancient of Otters and made him vomit. Then she urged him to try his luck again. "Return to the place where you were before you started home, and after remaining a while, come home. If they say anything to you, say, 'I have just come back after eating some stewed fish.' Hasten to return home." So the Ancient of Otters departed.

When he arrived there and was standing there viewing the players, the woman said to someone, "Tell that person to come back and I will play with him." So the messenger said, "Yonder distant woman says that you are to go thither and she will play with you." To this the Ancient of Otters replied, "I have just returned after eating some stewed fish," and did not move from his position. Again she sent a messenger, who said the same words, but with like want of success; but this time the Ancient of Otters never said a word. When the third messenger was seen in the distance, the Ancient of Otters started off at once, and went home.

When he got home his grandmother made for him an ordinary-sized bed and a very small one, too. She set them up in the other room of her house. She made the Ancient of Otters lie down on the larger one, and she covered him with bearskins. As he was lying there and his grandmother was sitting close to the fire the Woman was coming in the distance, her garments rattling on account of the silver that she wore. On reaching the house she asked the old woman, "Where is that person?" The old woman replied, "I have not seen anyone at all." "I refer to the person who stays here," said the visitor. "Pshaw! Is it that ugly boy whom you wish to see?" said the old woman. "That is he," said the visitor. "He was sitting around here for a while after eating some stewed fish, and I think that he is now lying down with unwashed hands," said the old woman. The visitor entered the house, making her garments rattle as she moved. Addressing the Ancient of Otters, she said, "Lie farther over!" But he did not move. She thought that she would get over him and lie down on the other side, but in attempting it she fell to the ground, and her garments rattled exceedingly as she kept falling about. She rose to her feet and said, "I am much ashamed tonight. Though you shall not be able to see me well during the day, I shall be there." Then she went up above when day came, and they say that she is still there. They say that because of the treatment of the Sun Woman by the Ancient of Otters, i.e., his making her ashamed, she went up above, and she is still there. And because of the words of the Sun Woman she is always one whom people can never see well.[12]

The Chitimacha female sun was paired with the male moon.

Sun and Moon ■ ■ ■
CHITIMACHA
The sun and moon were created for man and wife. The moon was male and intended to vivify and illuminate all things upon the earth: but having neglected to strengthen itself by baths it was condemned to remain in the state in which it came from the hands of its creator, light, pale and without vigor, continuing in ceaseless pursuit of its wife, the sun, without being able to overtake her. The sun, on the contrary, having paid more attention to taking her baths and her bitters (amers) merited the prerogative of shedding her benefits on the world and mankind. It has always been held in great veneration among them and has often stopped in its course to give them time to overcome their enemies, to secure their

prey, and to attain the other objects of their travels.[13]

None of these texts seems to explain the shame of the female Sun, but our ethnographic knowledge of the Southeast is by no means complete. If there is importance in the sex of the Sun, as seems reasonable, the only other representative of that view might be helpful. The Cherokee had this to say:

The Daughter of the Sun ■ ■ ■
CHEROKEE

The Sun lived on the other side of the sky vault, but her daughter lived in the middle of the sky, directly above the earth, and every day as the Sun was climbing along the sky arch to the west she used to stop at her daughter's house for dinner.

Now, the Sun hated the people on the earth, because they could never look straight at her without screwing up their faces. She said to her brother, the Moon, "My grandchildren are ugly; they grin all over their faces when they look at me." But the Moon said, "I like my younger brothers; I think they are very handsome"—because they always smiled pleasantly when they saw him in the sky at night, for his rays were milder.

The Sun was jealous and planned to kill all the people, so every day when she got near her daughter's house she sent down such sultry rays that there was a great fever and the people died by hundreds, until everyone had lost some friend and there was fear that no one would be left. They went for help to the Little Men, who said the only way to save themselves was to kill the Sun.

The Little Men made medicine and changed two men to snakes, the Spreading-adder and the Copperhead, and sent them to watch near the door of the daughter of the Sun to bite the old Sun when she came next day. They went together and hid near the house until the Sun came, but when the Spreading-adder was about to spring, the bright light blinded him and he could only spit out yellow slime, as he does to this day when he tries to bite. She called him a nasty thing and went by into the house, and the Copperhead crawled off without trying to do anything.

So the people still died from the heat, and they went to the Little Men a second time for help. The Little Men made medicine again and changed one man into the great Uktena [the great serpent of the Cherokee discussed in the next chapter] and another into the Rattlesnake and sent them to watch near the house and kill the old Sun when she came for dinner. They made the Uktena very large, with horns on his head, and everyone thought he would be sure to do the work, but the Rattlesnake was so quick and eager that he got ahead and coiled up just outside the house, and when the Sun's daughter opened the door to look out for her mother, he sprang up and bit her and she fell dead in the doorway...

When the Sun found her daughter dead, she went into the house and grieved, and the people did not die any more, but now the world was dark all the time, because the Sun would not come out. They went again to the Little Men, and these told them that if they wanted the Sun to come out again they must bring back her daughter from Tsusgina'gi, the Ghost-country, in Usunhi'yi, the Darkening-land in the west. They chose seven men to go, and gave each a sourwood rod a hand-breadth long. The Little Men told them they must take a box with them, and when they got to Tsusgina'i they would find all the ghosts at a dance. They must stand outside the circle, and when the young woman passed in the dance they must strike her with the rods and she would fall to the ground. Then they must put her into the box and bring her back to her mother, but they must be very sure not to open the box, even a little way, until they were home again.

They took the rods and a box and traveled seven days to the west until they came to the Darkening-land. There were a great many people there, and they were having a dance just as if they were at home in the settlements. They young woman was in the outside circle, and as she swung around to where the seven men were standing, one struck her with his rod and she turned her head and saw him. As she came around the second time another touched her with his rod, and then another and another, until at the seventh round she fell out of the ring, and they put her into the box and closed the lid fast. The other ghosts seemed never to notice what had happened.

They took up the box and started home toward the east. In a little while the girl came to life again and begged to be let out of the box, but they made no answer and went on. Soon she called again and said she was hungry, but still they made no answer and went on. After another while she spoke again and called for a drink and pleaded so that it was very hard to listen to her, but the men who carried the box said nothing and still went on. When at last they were very near home she called again and begged them to raise the lid just a little, because she was smothering. They were afraid she was really dying now, so they lifted the lid a little to give her air, but as they did so there was a fluttering sound inside and something flew past them into the thicket and they heard a redbird cry, "Kwish! kwish! kwish!" in the bushes. They shut down the lid and went on again to the settlements, but when they got there and opened the box it was empty.

So we know the Redbird is the daughter of the Sun, and if the men had kept the box closed, as the Little Men told them to do, they would have brought her back home safely, and we could bring back our other friends also from the Ghost country, but now when they die we can never bring them back.

The Sun had been glad when they started to the Ghost country, but when they came back without her daughter she grieved and cried, "My daughter, my daughter," and wept until her tears made a flood upon the earth, and the people were afraid the world would be drowned. They held another council, and sent their handsomest young men and women to amuse her so that she would stop crying. They danced before the Sun and sang their best songs, but for a long time she kept her face covered and paid no attention, until at last the drummer suddenly changed the song, when she lifted up her face, and was so pleased at the sight that she forgot her grief and smiled.[14]

Here the Sun is angry rather than ashamed. The killing of the Sun's daughter is coupled with the widespread Orpheus legend, which in other tribes stands as a separate legend without the solar motif. (See Chapter 11.) The Cherokee told another legend which does incorporate the element of shame.

Incest of the Sun and Moon ■ ■ ■
CHEROKEE

The Sun was a young woman and lived in the East, while her brother, the Moon, lived in the West. The girl had a lover who used to come every month in the dark of the moon to court her. He would come at night, and leave before daylight, and although she talked with him she could not see his face in the dark, and he would not tell her his name, until she was wondering all the time who it could be. At last she hit upon a plan to find out, so the next time he came, as they were sitting together in the dark of the asi, she slyly dipped her hand into the cinders and ashes of the fireplace and rubbed it over his face, saying, "Your face is cold; you must have suffered from the wind," and pretending to be very sorry for him, but he did not know that she had ashes on her hand. After a while he left her and went away again.

The next night when the Moon came up in the sky his face was covered with spots, and then his sister knew he was the one who had been coming to see her. He was so much ashamed to have her know it that he kept as far away as he could at the other end of the sky all the night. Ever since he tries to keep a long way behind the Sun, and when he does sometimes have to come near her in the west he makes himself as thin as a ribbon so that he can hardly be seen.[15]

This is an astounding legend to find in the Southeast, because it is found among the Eskimo and Mackinaw tribes and in South America (Witoto, Zaparo, Cuna, and Carib), with a scattering in the Plateau and Plains.[16] The Cherokee text is not alone in the Southeast, however. Texts from the Biloxi and the Caddo indicate that the incest motif can occur without involving the sun, whom the Caddo see as male.

Moon ■ ■ ■
BILOXI

When a child felt the Moon person its hand made a black spot on him. This caused the Moon person to feel ashamed, and when night came he disappeared.

Therefore, as they say, he always stays up above, and has a black spot. Sometimes he is dressed in money alone, and subsequently he disappears. Therefore [i.e., on account of the money] it is sometimes light at night.[17]

The Caddo also knew the moon incest motif, which they included as part of a longer creation myth.

The Creation ■ ■ ■
CADDO

In the beginning the sun, stars, moon, and earth did not exist as they are now. Darkness ruled. With the lapse of time came a man, the only living being. Soon after his arrival a village sprang into existence with many thousands of people, and the people noticed that the man seemed to be everywhere. For a time he disappeared, and when he came back he had all kinds of seeds. He called all the people together and told them that the seeds were for them to eat, and gave them to everyone. He told them that soon Darkness would go, and the people would see, for Darkness had promised that they should have a man by the name of Sun, and that he should be given power by the Great-Father-Above; and that whenever his time should come to give them to the Sun he should be called or taken away from his mother, from our great mother Earth below; that the direction where the Sun should come from should be called "east," and the way of its going down should be called "west." He also announced to the people that he was the first being created and that he had been given power by the same Great-Father-Above, and that he had to carry out his work. He then told the people that it was very necessary that they should have one man abler and wiser than any other man among them, to be their head man; that they should call him "chief"; that whatever the chief should command should be done by the people; that they should look upon him as a great father. The unknown man told the people to return to their homes, hold a council among themselves, and select a chief.

When they had returned and assembled there was in the council a man by the name of Coyote, who told the people that the unknown powerful man should be called Moon, because he was the first man created on earth. The people decided that the Moon should be their head man or chief...

(After a migration) when Moon came to his people, the few he had left, he told them the name of the place in the ground from which they had come. He told them that the direction to their right-hand side should be called north, or cold side, and the direction to their left-hand side should be called south, or warm side. While Moon was talking the Sun came up out of the east, passed them, and went down in the west. He went too fast to do them any good at all. Coyote announced that he was going to stop the Sun from going so fast. He started eastward early in the morning, and when he came to a good place to stop he waited for the Sun to come up. When the Sun came up he found Coyote waiting for him. Coyote told the Sun that he had come there for the purpose of seeing him; that he wanted to talk with him, for he was in trouble. The Sun said that he had not very much time to stop and talk. Coyote told the Sun that he would go with him and talk to him as they went along. They started on, walking very slowly. Coyote kept telling about things that had lately happened. When the Sun was nearing the west Coyote told him that he was going to defecate, and asked him to wait a while. He started out behind the bushes, and just as soon as he was behind them, where the Sun could not see him, he ran away from the Sun and the Sun stood there waiting for him to return. After a while the Sun grew tired of waiting and started on very slowly, looking back every little while and watching for Coyote to catch up with him, but Coyote did not appear. The Sun went down very slowly, still waiting for Coyote. This is the reason that the Sun lingers and goes down very slowly ...

Time passed on and the people noticed that their chief, Moon, paid no attention to them and seemed to have nothing to say. He did not call them together any more, but stayed at his home all the time. The people began to think there must be something wrong, and so there was, for Moon himself was doing very wrong things. He knew that he was setting his people a bad example, and he believed the people had already found out something about him. Medicine-Screech-Owl knew all about this, for he had more powers than Moon himself. Moon was living with his family near the center of the village; he was the chief, unmarried, and lived with his father and mother and one very young sister. Here was the beginning of his mistakes. Unknown to his father and mother, for a long time he kept going by night to see his own sister, not letting her know that he was her own brother. He abused her and treated her very meanly sometimes. For a long time she did not know who he could be, for she had no one to tell her. It finally occurred to her that it might be her brother. One night she made up her mind to find out who he was. She put some black paint on her fingers, and that night when the man came she passed her painted fingers across his forehead and made black marks, which the man knew nothing about until the next morning. In the morning, when he came in, she saw the marks on his forehead, and she knew that he was the man who had abused her. When he learned that the people were finding out about him he became so ashamed of himself that he wished to leave his people. He remembered that when he came into the world the Great-Father-Above had promised him that someday he should call him away from his people; that he should be placed where the people could see him at night, and that he should be with the people all the time. He knew that the time was now approaching when he should be called away from his people, and soon he was called away from them. Great-Father-Above took him away and placed him far above, where the people could see him and the shame-marks on his forehead. [18]

A very different complex of legends argues that light had to be stolen from its original owner. Here is an Alabama text.

The Rescue of the Sun ▪ ▪ ▪
ALABAMA

An old woman put the sun into an earthen pot and kept it there. Rabbit wanted it and stayed at her house dancing. Rabbit said to the people assembled, ''Sing for me so that I can dance.'' ''We don't know how to sing for you,'' they answered. ''Sing 'Rabbit, Rabbit, Rabbit,''' he said. So they sang ''Rabbit, Rabbit, Rabbit,'' and he danced. While he was dancing, he said, ''Move it [the pot] toward me,'' and they moved it toward him. Again he said, ''Move it toward me. I am dancing like a crazy person.'' After they had moved it toward him farther, he seized the sun. They chased him as he ran away but he kept on with it. On the way he struck the pot repeatedly against the bushes but it did not break, so he again took it and ran on. Then he struck it against a hornbeam tree and broke it in pieces.

Then all creatures assembled and counselled, and all the flying things tried to move it but it did not move. The Tciktcikano (a bird like a wren) tried to move it and it rose a short distance but fell back again. He said, ''If another should help me I could carry it up,'' so Buzzard and Tciktcikano helped each other. Grasping it on each side they flew up with it. They carried it up and placed it in the sky, and when they came back the people said to Buzzard, ''You shall eat animals that have died.'' They said to Tciktcikano, ''You shall wash in cold water every morning and so you will never be sick.''[19]

When we consider that in the Southeastern view the sun and fire are the same, we should not be surprised to find that there are several other texts of this story, but they all deal with the theft of fire (Motif A1415). Perhaps the most famous is the Cherokee legend.

The Theft of Fire ▪ ▪ ▪
CHEROKEE

In the beginning there was no fire, and the world was cold, until the Thunders (Ani'-Hyun'tikwala'ski), who lived up in Galun'lati, sent their lightning and put fire into the bottom of a hollow sycamore tree which grew on an island. The animals knew it was there, because they could see the smoke coming out at the top, but they could not get to it on account of the water, so they held a council to decide what to do. This was a long time ago.

Every animal that could fly or swim was anxious to go after the fire. The Raven offered, and because he was so large and strong they thought he could surely do the work, so he was sent first. He flew high and far across the water and alighted on the sycamore tree, but while he was wondering what to do next, the heat had scorched all his feathers black, and he was frightened and came back without the fire. The little Screech-owl (Wa'huhu') volunteered to go, and reached the place safely, but while he was looking down into the hollow tree a

Spider and fire gorgets

blast of hot air came up and nearly burned out his eyes. He managed to fly home as best he could, but it was a long time before he could see well, and his eyes are red to this day. Then the Hooting Owl (U'guku') and the Horned Owl (Tskili') went, but by the time they got to the hollow tree the fire was burning so fiercely that the smoke nearly blinded them, and the ashes carried up by the wind made white rings about their eyes. They had to come home again without the fire, but with all their rubbing they were never able to get rid of the white rings.

Now no more of the birds would venture, and so the little Uksu'hi snake, the black racer, said he would go through the water and bring back some fire. He swam across to the island and crawled through the grass to the tree, and went in by a small hole at the bottom. The heat and smoke were too much for him, too, and after dodging about blindly over the hot ashes until he was almost on fire himself he managed by good luck to get out again at the same hole, but his body had been scorched black, and he has ever since had the habit of darting and doubling on his track as if trying to escape from close quarters. He came back, and the great blacksnake, Gule'gi (the Climber), offered to go for fire. He swam over to the island and climbed up the tree on the outside, as the blacksnake always does, but when he put his head down into the hole the smoke choked him so that he fell into the burning stump, and before he could climb out again he was as black as the Uksu'hi.

Now they held another council, for still there was no fire, and the world was cold, but birds, snakes, and four-footed animals, all had some excuse for not going, because they were all afraid to venture near the burning sycamore, until at last Kanane'ski Amai'yehi (the Water Spider) said she would go. This is not the water spider that looks like a mosquito, but the other one, with black downy hair and red stripes on her body. She can run on top of the water or dive to the bottom, so there would be no trouble to get over to the island, but the question was, How could she bring back the fire? "I'll manage that," said the Water Spider; so she spun a thread from her body and wove it into a tusti bowl, which she fastened on her back. Then she crossed over to the island and through the grass to where the fire was still burning. She put one little coal of fire into her bowl, and came back with it, and ever since we have had fire, and the Water Spider still keeps her tusti bowl.[20]

The culture hero who steals fire for the people here is a spider, a figure who is otherwise missing in the Southeast. There is one sign that there may have been a stronger role for the Spider in Mississippian times, because an image of a spider with a fire sign is one that has been found from a variety of locales from Tennessee to Illinois.[21]

Whoever the earlier fire-bringer may have been, Rabbit is the figure now found in the Creek texts.

The Theft of Fire ▪ ▪ ▪
HITCHITI

Rabbit ran away with the fire and scattered it. At that time people were forbidden to build a fire except in the busk ground. It was customary to build a fire just to have a dance.

Rabbit knew when there was to be a dance at the busk ground and thought, "I will run away with some fire." He considered the matter and decided how he would do it. He had his head rubbed with pine tar so as to make his hair stand up. Then he set out. When he arrived at the busk ground a great number of people were gathered there. While Rabbit was sitting about and the people were dancing, they said that he must lead and he agreed. "Now, lead," they said, and he got up and danced ahead of them around the place where the fire was. As he went many people followed him and Rabbit started the song. He was dancing along, the rest following him. While they were dancing very hard Rabbit ran round near the fire and bent his head as if he were going to take hold of it. They said, "When he is leading Rabbit always acts that way." He kept on acting that way and circled about as he did so. Presently he poked his head into the fire and ran off with his head ablaze, while the people shouted, "Hulloa, catch him or throw him down."

They shouted at Rabbit as he ran away, and they chased him, but he disappeared. Then they made it rain and on the fourth day said the rain must have put the fire out. So it stopped and the sun shone and the weather was fine. But Rabbit had built a fire in a hollow tree and stayed there while it rained, and when the sun shone he came out and set out fires. Rain came on again and put the fires all out but he again built a fire inside of a hollow tree. When the sun shone he would set out fires and then rains would come and put them out, but they could not stop them entirely. People took fire and ran off with it. Rains kept on putting the fires out at intervals but when they stopped all the people distributed it again, and when the rain stopped fire was established there for good. This is the way it is told. Therefore, they say that Rabbit distributed the fire to all people.[22]

Even in a fragmentary form the legend is still recognizable.

Theft of Fire ■ ■ ■
CHITIMACHA

Fire was originally given—probably by Ku'tnahin—into the custody of an old man. This man was blind, but he was always able to feel the presence of an intruder in search of his fire and chased him away with his stick. One time, however, he beat about so much with his stick that, although he was successful in forcing the thief to drop the fire he had carried away, he at the same time knocked some of it into a log, and the man obtained fire from that.[23]

The Alabama story of the theft of the sun by Rabbit is the equivalent of the many other variants of the theft of fire. It may be that the Alabama felt a need to identify the object stolen as the sun because they had a slightly different legend of the origin of fire.

Bears and Fire ■ ■ ■
ALABAMA

Bears formerly owned the Fire and they always took it about with them. One time they set it on the ground and went on farther eating acorns. The fire nearly went out and called aloud. It was almost extinguished. "Feed me," it said. Then some human beings saw it. They got a stick toward the north and laid it down upon it. They got another stick toward the west and laid it down upon it. They got a stick at the south and laid it down there. They got another at the east and laid it down and the Fire blazed up. When the bears came to get their Fire, it said, "I don't know you any more." They did not get it back and so it belongs to human beings.[24]

These different understandings of the nature of the sun remind us that the Southeast was a place of diverse cultures. They also warn us that a general cultural phenomenon, such as solar worship, may hide a variety of approaches, details, and beliefs.

The Sun and Fire form one major organizing principle for the world view of the Southeast. Another is the tradition of investing the cardinal directions—east, west, south, north—with various meanings. This "quadripartite view" was widely known and practiced across North and Central America, although the meanings changed somewhat from nation to nation. While there is little proof now, there is reason to suspect that most of the Southeastern peoples participated in the quadripartite tradition. The Cherokee assigned colors and other attributes to the four directions, but the existing evidence makes it difficult to estimate how strong the color-direction symbolism was for them.[25] There is a single early indication that the Creeks may have had a similar system, but otherwise the assumption has to rest on the square architecture of the "square grounds" and the four-log fire.[26]

The quadripartite view was not restricted to color-direction symbolism, however. There is at least one good indication that the wind was also broken into four directional winds.

The Winds ▪ ▪ ▪
YUCHI

The Wind came out of the east and was lying somewhere, they say. He had four young men; they were his sons. One of them once said, "Let us go and look at the earth." That's why they went, and they haven't come back yet. So the young man went west and was gone a long time; he has never come back. Soon after, the second young man went and did not come back. Then the third young man went and he did not come back. None of them came back.

Now the Wind said, "I will go myself." He prepared and got everything ready. He told them to bring him a chair. They brought him a large terrapin. Then he ordered his pipe, telling them to bring him a bullfrog. Then he called for his pipe-stem. They brought a kind of snake and made a pipe-stem. He told them to get his tobacco. They brought him snake dung for tobacco. He told them to get his ammunition bag. They got him another snake for the ammunition bag. And when he told them to bring a belt for the ammunition bag, they brought him a bullsnake's hide for that. Then the Wind was ready.[27]

He got up and started toward the west, the way the young men had gone before him. He followed their trail, traveling a long while, and at last came to a creek. Across the creek on the opposite bank he saw a white rooster. A short distance back there was a house. Now when the rooster saw him it flew over and alighted on the roof of the house. Then someone came out and crossed the creek in a little boat to meet him. Then the man in the boat told Wind to get in with him and go across. But Wind said that he had his own way to get across. So he put the terrapin in the creek and got on his back and the terrapin carried him across. Then they went on and soon reached the house. When Wind got to the house, the man gave him a chair and told him to sit down. Wind said that he had his own chair. He took the terrapin and sat down on him. The man then asked Wind to smoke with him. Wind said that he was willing, but that he had his own tobacco. And taking the snake dung, he put it in the frog's mouth, filling it up.

"Now all that I need is a little fire to light my tobacco with," said Wind. But he had his own fire. Taking the joint snake he had with him he struck a fire, and

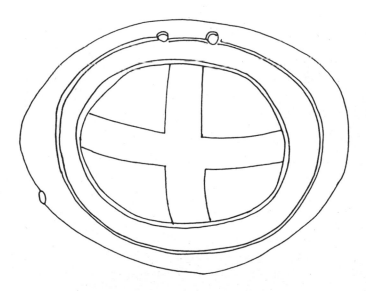

Sun and fire gorgets

soon had a light for his pipe. He lighted it in that way. Then taking the other snake which was the pipe-stem, he inserted this in the frog's anus. So the pipe was finished, and in that way Wind could smoke with his host.[28]

Now the owner of the house was a bad man; a man who could not be killed. He was made of iron. So he was Iron Man.[29] Wind knew all about that, and he even knew that Iron Man had killed his four young men. Then Wind decided to kill him. When he smoked, he drew in a great deal of smoke and blew it on Iron Man. And that is the way he killed him.[30] When Iron Man was dead, his wife came up and said to Wind,

"You killed my man. Let's marry."

But Wind said that he would not. He asked her where his four young men were and what had become of them. Then she told him all about them. She told him to go where he would find a certain dead tree near the water. She told him that if he would go and cut this tree down and throw it in the water, the four young men would come up from it. Then she guided Wind to the tree and said to him, "Cut it down." She got an axe and Wind cut the tree down. Then he threw it in the water as Iron Man's wife had told him. And the four young men came out of the water. When they stood on the ground they all looked black. They recognized Wind, but they told him that they were not under his control any longer. "Well, I'll make something different out of you, then," he said to them. Then one of the young men said, "What shall I be?" But Wind did not answer him, for that.

"I'll be a wolf," said the second. So the Wind told him to go into the woods, and he went.

Wind asked the third what he would be. "I'll be a crow," said he. Then Wind asked the fourth what he would be. "I'll be a raven," said the fourth young man. Wind told him to go into the forest. Now the first young man who had spoken too soon was the only one left. And Wind said to him, "What will you be?" "I'll be a dog," said he. "Well, you go and stay with the wolf," said Wind to him. And he went.[31]

Now Wind was through with the young men. He said, "Someday I will go back where I came from. As I go I'll leave nothing in my way."

Wind has never come back; he is there yet. But someday he will come. That is what the old Yuchi say.[32]

The four winds are probably attested to in Mississippian times by a few designs on gorgets, but the interpretation is speculative.[33]

The Chitimacha also told a tale which suggests the four winds. It is "The bird whose wings made the wind" (A1127), a motif whose distribution is otherwise restricted to the Northeastern Algonkin.[34] Why the Chitimacha knew this alien motif is a question for which I have no answer.

Wind gorgets

The Broken Wind ■ ■ ■
CHITIMACHA

A little boy named U'stapu was lying in a bunk close to the shore of a lake. His people had come there from the prairies in order to cross, but the wind was too high. As he lay there U'stapu discovered a boy fanning with a fan of turkey feathers. This was the boy that makes the west wind. Then U'stapu said to his people: "I can break the arm of the boy that makes the west wind." All laughed at him, but he took up a shell, threw it at the boy who was making the wind, and broke his left arm. Therefore, when the west wind was high, the Indians used to say this boy was using his good arm, and if it was gentle, they said he was using his broken arm. Before that time the west wind used to be very bad, because the west-wind maker could change hands, but since then it has been much gentler. It is possible that this boy made the other winds also.[35]

Another important structural principle of the Southeastern world view was the dualism of the upper world and underworld. In the mythology the sky is represented by birds and other inhabitants, while the underworld, which is water, is represented by water creatures. Many legends tell of the doings of these various creatures, but the primary expression of the dualism is the legends of the battles between the Great Bird and the Underwater Serpent/Panther. The Cherokee call the bird *Tlanuwa* and the serpent *Uktena,* while terms from the other peoples are not known. The Alabama, Hitchiti, and Koasati share a simple version.

The Eagle's Nest ■ ■ ■
ALABAMA

A man traveling about became frightened at a big eagle which he saw moving along and got into a hollow tree. Then the eagle took him, tree and all, carried him to his little eaglets, and laid him down there. The eaglets sat on the top of a high hill. When day came the mother bird went away and in the evening came back.

Then the man watched the eaglets. When they grew bigger and could fly some, and just after their mother had started away, the man came out of his log, mounted upon the back of one of them, and came down. He tried to come toward the ground, and if the bird flew up a little, he struck it on the head and it came on down again. If it turned round and flew up again, he again hit it and it descended farther. It came on, and, when it had almost reached the ground, he heard its mother screaming behind. But the eaglet came on down and when it reached the earth he got off and ran away.[36]

This is called the "Roc" motif (B31.1) from its occurrence in the Old World, but it is widely found in North America. Texts of it have been recorded from the Plateau, the Plains, the Southwest, the Northeastern Algonkin, and the Seneca. Here is the way it appears in Cherokee lore, with the addition of the serpent.

The Nest of the Tlanuwa ▪ ▪ ▪
CHEROKEE

The Tlanuwa were about the size of a man. These birds lived at the same time the other powerful birds and insects lived. These powerful birds could carry off a baby for their food.

A grandmother was taking care of a baby. A Tlanuwa came and carried it off. The grandmother thought: "What can we do?"

She decided that she would make a rope of linden withes [thin branches]. She gathered some of them, stripped them, boiled them, and made a rope.

She went to the top of the cliff in which the Tlanuwa lived. She tied pine limbs into the rope every now and again to rest her feet upon as she climbed down.

In the Tlanuwa's nest were two young birds. The grandmother had with her a hatchet of stone, and with it she killed the fledglings. Then she threw the rope into the water and said, "This rope must become an Uktena." (This was near Vdhi:guhi, "pot in it liquid-place" [on the Tennessee River eight miles south of Chattanooga].)

She saw the two big parent birds come back. When they found the nest empty, they hovered about it in order to find out who had killed their young ones. Then they saw the Uktena, and one bird seized it in its claws and flew up into the air with it while the other bird kept striking pieces off the Uktena. As these pieces fell to the ground, all of them became standing pillars of rock. [Note by Obrechts: "Morgan's grandmother, who told him this story, saw them (the pillars) when she came back from the west."][37]

A version from the Natchez, but probably derived from the Cherokee during the Natchez habitation with them, has the Tlanuwas killed as well as the Uktena.

The Tlanuwa ▪ ▪ ▪
NATCHEZ-CHEROKEE

One time a young man said, "If I had children and those birds took one of them I would kill them." People told him not to say such a thing, but he persisted. This youth grew up and married in the course of time and had a child. One day, when the child was large enough to run about, it was playing around while its mother swept the yard, the father being off hunting.[38] Then a tlanuwa flew down and carried the child away. When the father came home and his wife told him what had happened he did not seem to be angry but said, "I am going to kill him." He lay down and fasted for seven days.[39] Hitherto people had always failed to shoot this bird, because when they sent an arrow at it it caught the arrow in mid-air. After the seven days' fast was completed the man went to a creek or river nearby, dived into it, and brought up a turtle. Taking this, he went to the top of the precipitous cliff on which the bird's nest was built, and, tying one end of a grapevine at the top, swung down to the nest. He tied the turtle to the end of the grapevine and hung it in front of the nest. Inside of the nest he found some young hawks *(tlanuwas),* which he killed and threw into the water. Then he hid himself at the top of the cliff and waited for the return of the old birds. By and by they came back carrying an infant with them, and finding that something was wrong they flew round and round without alighting. Then they flew high up into the air, let the child they were carrying fall, and beat it to pieces before it reached the earth. After that they dived into the water and pulled out a snake which they also carried high up in the air and treated as they had the child, letting the pieces fall into the water. After that one tlanuwa flew up against the turtle, broke a wing upon it and fell into the water, and after a while the second bird did the same thing. Then the young man went down to the nest again, untied the turtle and carried it back to the place from which he had obtained it. He went to the other side of the river where the bank was low, made a canoe and pulled both tlanuwas out of the water. He pulled off their feathers, which were a fathom long, and made a box for them.[40] Afterwards some more tlanuwas came, but they were red in color. They lighted on a tree near by, and he shot one and put its feathers into the box where he kept the others. After that a great many people in his town began dying of a bloody flux. He thought to himself, "Those red feathers must be the cause of it." So he took the red feathers out and threw them into the water, and the disease was stopped. The person that saw these feathers was Watt Sam's father's great-great-grandmother. It was somewhere in the east.[41]

This collection of Roc texts is part of a very widespread tradition, as mentioned above. Many of the same tribes that tell variants of the Roc legend, however, go a step farther and identify the bird as the Thunderbird (A284.2). Thompson observed that "it is impossible to separate with any degree of precision this motif [Thunderbird] from that of Roc, for stories of the adventure with the Roc are told of the thunderbird, but many other forms of the visit to the thunderbird appear."[42] The range of the Thunderbird is from the Northwest through the Plains and the Central Algonkin to the Iroquois. Two notes from the Central Algonkin are of interest in understanding the Southeastern legends.

The Thunderbirds ■ ■ ■
MENOMINI
Far, far away in the West where the sun sets, there floats a great mountain in

the sky. Above the earth the rocks lie tier on tier. These cliffs are too lofty to be reached by any earthly bird. Even the great war eagle cannot soar so high. But on the summit of this mountain dwell the Thunderbirds. They have control over the rain and the hail. They are messengers of the Great Sun himself, and their influence induced the Sun and the Morning Star to give the great war-bundle to our race. They delight in fighting and great deeds. They are the mighty enemies of the horned snakes, the Misikinubik. Were it not for the Thunderers these monsters would overwhelm the earth and devour mankind. When the weather is fair, then watch when you travel abroad, for the snakes come out to bask in the sun, but when the weather is cloudy you need fear nothing, for the Thunderers come searching from behind the clouds for their enemies, the Misikinubik.[43]

In northern Minnesota in 1958 collectors of Ojibwa legends were told various things about the Thunderbirds. While they are notes rather than texts, they add to the picture.

The Thunderbird ■ ■ ■
OJIBWA
On the reservations at Fond du Lac and White Earth, we were told the story of the young thunderbird who struck the side of a hill and broke his wing. He was then caught between the precipices. When he tried to free himself, he kept on striking against the rocks, and he repeatedly broke his wing as he did so. This explains the continuous flash of heat lightning... [T]he *animikig* (thunderbirds) were associated with the four cardinal directions, and they were said to control the four winds.[44]

Taken together, these many aspects of the Thunderbird belief, which are held by so many tribes over such vast distances and across all known cultural boundaries, suggest that this is a body of mythology which is ancient in North America. The tension between the Thunderbirds and the Underwater Serpents is a dualism of ancient origin, and it is still present in the lore of the Southeast. It may be that the much-debated "forked-eye design" of the Southeastern Ceremonial Complex should be seen as a convention denoting lightning, and all who wear it as Thunderbirds, or related to that function.[45]

It is important to note, however, that the "thunderbird legends" in the Southeast do not all refer to thunderbirds, and that fact suggests that there has been some local alteration in the continental pattern, possibly because thunder is conceived differently in the region. With the Cherokee that is certainly true, for the major explanation for thunder is that it is caused by Kanati and his two sons, whose story will be presented in another chapter. Nonetheless, the Tlanuwa is an important part of their lore. The Biloxi have identified as thunder the marooned hero of a legend not otherwise connected with thunder; that text will

Thunderbirds

also be presented when we consider the legendary adventures. Among the Chitimacha, "a thunder-bird belief appears to have been non-existent, thunder having originated from Ku'tnahin (the creator)."[46]

Thunder Helper ■ ■ ■
CREEK

A boy went along on a hunting party with three of his uncles. While they were away from camp he took charge of it, prepared *sofki* (a maize dish) for them and did any other work that was necessary. The camp was on a small stream and one day he heard a kind of roaring in this stream. He went in the direction of the sound and saw something standing up over the water, partway up which another creature had wrapped itself. The latter was white about the neck. The thing it was wrapped about was quivering and making a thundering noise. This was Thunder and the creature coiled about it was a Tie-snake or Strong-snake *(Stahwanaia).* Each of the contestants asked the boy to help him, saying, "My friend, help me."

The boy did not know at first which being to assist, but finally he aimed an arrow at the white neck and pierced it, whereupon the snake loosened its coils and fell into the water dead. Then Thunder said, "You are just a boy, but you shall always be my friend."

Then the boy went back to camp, and presently his uncles returned from hunting. Thunder had told him that when they all went home from their camp he must walk behind his uncles, and he did so. He added, "When you get home, ask your oldest uncle to give you a medical course (a fast for four days), and if he refuses ask the others in turn." So the boy asked the oldest uncle, but he said, "You are too young." He asked the next younger and he refused. The youngest, however, said he supposed he had better do so, and he did. In those days the Indians were always going on war expeditions and when the fast was over the boy said to his uncle, "Let us travel," meaning "Let us go to war." When they got close to the enemy's town the boy told his uncle to remain where he was for a while. Then he went off into the woods a short distance and made a circle and came back in the form of a rainbow. His uncle followed him and the boy went along making it thunder and lighten until by his powers his uncle saw him destroy the entire town. After that they returned home.[47]

The Cherokee variant of this legend is less clearly oriented toward prowess in war conferred by Thunder.

Thunder Helper ■ ■ ■
CHEROKEE

Once Thunder was fighting an Uktena. A man saw the fight. The Uktena asked the man for help. Thunder asked the man to help him.

At first the man wondered whom to help; then he decided to help Thunder. When the man arrived upon the scene, the fight was over: Thunder had killed the Uktena.

Thunder said, "You will be my *vghiwi:na;* you call me *edu:tsi.* '[48]

Thunder commanded his two sisters to bring "horses," which were two huge snakes.

"Get on!" Thunder said. All got on.

They whooped, and at every whoop, lightning flashed and thunder sounded.

When we think it thunders, it is but the Thunder People whooping in the air.[49]

An interesting text from the Caddo expresses very well the dualism of the bird and serpent, without ever specifying either.

Lightning and the People ■ ■ ■
CADDO

In the beginning Lightning lived upon the earth with the people, but he became so powerful and killed so many of the people that they feared and hated him. One time after he had become angry and killed a number of the people, the chiefs of the tribe called a council to determine what to do with him. They decided that he could no longer live with the people, but would have to go away. Lightning pleaded to stay, but the chiefs would not change their decision and told him that he would have to go.

Not long after Lightning had gone a great monster that lived underground among the rocks began to carry away the people. They tried in every way to kill him, but could not, for he always disappeared under the ground where they could not reach him. Lightning appeared to them and told them that he would kill the monster if they would let him come back and live with them. He said that he wanted to come back to earth, and that he would kill all monsters and make the earth a safe place for the people to live on, and would not do any more harm himself if they would let him come back. The people decided to let Lightning come, because there was no one else powerful enough to kill the great monster.[50]

It appears from these various texts that the nations of the Southeast shared more than one tradition of Thunder. The ancient tradition of the Eastern Woodlands, as we have mentioned already, is that of the Thunderbirds versus the Underwater Serpent. The Thunderbird may or may not be the same as the eagle, and some people see them as quadripartite, while others think of them as a species or family. Hudson suggests the peregrine falcon as the natural inspiration of the Tlanuwa, which he equates with the winged figure of the

Southeastern Ceremonial Complex.[51] That same figure is one which we have suggested could be identified as the Thunderbird, primarily on the basis of the lightning sign at the eyes known as the "forked-eye design."

Here the reference seems to be to the ongoing battle between the thunder-bird and the Uktena, but Lightning is never identified, and his foe is simply a "great monster." Nonetheless, it seems to belong to the thunderbird tradition. In the Caddo collection the text is immediately followed by "The Brothers Who Became Lightning and Thunder," a non-thunderbird legend which parallels the Cherokee tradition of Kanati and his two sons, the thunders. The presence of the Thunderbird in the Southeastern legends must therefore be seen as an alternative to the tradition of Thunder as a human sort of person. We may speculate that this is the sort of situation that may develop in folklore when a new body of lore is adopted from new influences, whether refugees or trading of goods and ideas.

Sparse as the materials are, they at least do give us a picture of a sky world dominated by the Sun and its representative Fire, but also the home of the Thunders and other birds who form one side of a major dualism—the war between the Above and Under Worlds.

CHAPTER FOUR

The Under World

In opposition to the Above World is the Under World, which consists of water. Like the Western mythological tradition, but unlike the Western philosophical tradition, which wants to know the source of the water, the Southeastern view simply assumes its existence. Some western North American traditions affirm creation in a different way, but the Eastern Woodlands people were in agreement on the water. We begin our examination of the Under World with an apparently simple story.

Of all the Southeastern texts collected by Swanton, the best represented is the legend of a man who was transformed into a snake. There are eight texts from the Creeks alone, two from the Cherokee, and single texts from the Yuchi, Hitchiti, and Alabama. Texts from the Seneca and Menomini complete the Eastern Woodland occurrences. Here is a Creek text about the "Snake-man."

The Snake-Man ■ ■ ■
CREEK

Two old men once went hunting and camped at a certain spot. One of them was very fond of fish and said, "I want some fish." Just then they noticed water dripping from the top of a tree nearby, and the man who was fond of fish said he would go up to see what caused it. Arrived there, he found water in the top of the tree and some fish swimming in it, splashing the water over by dashing around. He said, "That is what I have been wanting," and threw them down. Then he climbed down and ate them. The other said, "There may be something wrong about fish found up in a tree that way," but his companion cooked and ate them nevertheless. The other did not like fish, so he did not touch them.

But after the first man had eaten he stretched out and said that his bones ached and that something was the matter. The other said, "I told you they might not be good, but you would eat of them." Then the body of the fish eater began to assume a curious shape, more and more like that of a snake, until he had altogether turned into one. He could still talk, however, and he said, "I have many kindred. Tell them I will be at the square ground *(tcuko thlako)* and ask them to come there." Then he went into a little stream near by, whereupon the water bubbled up into a great boiling spring. The man that turned into a snake belonged to the Deer Clan.

At the time appointed the kindred of this man assembled at the square ground to see him, and when he came it was with a powerful current of water as if a dam had broken and they were all swept away; perhaps they were turned into snakes. Thus the water-snake was a kind of person. These water-snakes had horns of different colors, yellow, blue, white, green, etc.[1]

On the surface this legend seems to be a fairly straightforward didactic lesson pertaining to food taboos: whatever you do, don't eat fish found swimming in a pool in the top of a tree or at its roots. This is a peculiar taboo, in that the circumstances seem so unlikely as to be a useless taboo. Other Creek texts put it more reasonably. Look at the food involved in this text, also from the Creeks.

The Snake-Man ■ ■ ■
CREEK

Two friends went out hunting. They came to the shore of a great lake, and on the shore found a big egg, which one of them brought back to camp. His friend told him it might not be good, but he said, "I am going to cook it anyhow." So he cooked and ate it, and then the two lay down to sleep on opposite sides of the fire. During the night the one who had eaten the egg awakened his companion. "My friend, what is the matter?" said the other. "Look and see what is the matter with me." His friend looked and saw that the legs of the other were glued together. By and by the same one called to his friend to look at him again, and he found that from his body on down was the tail of a snake. At daybreak he said again, "Look at me now," and behold he had turned completely into a snake and lay there in a big coil. Then the Snake said, "You must leave me, but first pilot me to the hole from which we got water." They got there and the Snake went in, whereupon the earth, trees, and everything else caved in, producing a big water hole. Then the Snake raised his head out of the water and said, "Tell my parents and my sisters to come and see me." So the friend went home and told them, and they asked him to guide them back to the place where the Snake had been left. When they got to the shore the Snake showed himself in the middle of the pond. He came to the bank and crawled out, and he crawled over the laps of his parents and his other friends, shedding tears. Then he returned into the water and they went home. So the Tie-snake was created from a human being.[2]

Here the food which causes the transformation is an egg instead of fish. And here is another alternative:

The Snake-Man ▪ ▪ ▪
CREEK

Two men went hunting together. They traveled all day and when they encamped for the night exchanged stories with each other. One said that if you mixed together the brains of a black snake, a black squirrel, and a wild turkey and ate them you would turn into a snake. The other replied, "If that is the case I believe I will try it…"[3]

Perhaps a comparative chart will help make sense of this diversity. Here is a listing of the Eastern Woodlands texts of the Snake man legend.

	Two Men	Food	Tree	Trans	Concl.	Source
Creek 1	*	F	*	HWS	Town	Sw. 1929:32f
Creek 2	*	F	*	HWS	Person	Sw. 1929:33f
Sumu	*	F	*	HWS	Town	Conzemius 1932:130
Creek 3	*	F	*	HWS		Sw. 123:158
Creek 4	*	F	*	WS	Town	Sw. 1928:71
Creek 5	*	F	*	WS	Town	Nelson 1954
Yuchi	*	F	*	WS	Town	Wagner 31:66f
Hitchiti	*	F	*	WS		Sw. 1929:97
Creek 6	*	B		TS	Exp	Sw. 1929:30f
Creek 7	*	B		TS	Exp	Sw. 1929:31f
Creek 8	*	E		TS	Exp	Sw. 1929: 34
Alabama		E		WS		Sw. 1929: 154
Cherokee	*	M		WS		Mooney 1900: 304f
Cherokee	*	M		Lizd		Trav. Bird
Menomini		M		Fish	Exp	Sk/S 1915: 476
Seneca	*	F		Fish	Exp	Cur. 1910: 111f

KEY: F = Fish B = Brains
E = Eggs M = Meat
HWS = Horned Water Serpent
WS = Water Serpent
TS = Tie-Snake
Exp = Expansion

Of the eight Creek texts, five feature the eating of fish as the cause of the transformation, two focus on brains, and one emphasizes eggs. If diet is the central focus of the legend, it is curious that even informants from the same tribes do not agree on what, exactly, is taboo. The detail of the food is not unimportant, because it probably reflects a taboo well understood by the hearers, even though the idea of fish in a tree seems strange. We may conclude from this what we already know to be true, that the Creeks were a confederacy of towns (talwas) with different customs, traditions, and even languages. The disagreement among texts may demonstrate the creation of local variants by different talwas.

Other Eastern tribes increase the diversity, because the Alabama have eggs, the Seneca have fish, and the Cherokee and Menomini have meat. Nonetheless, the majority focus on fish. These details of the food which caused the transformation are called "allomotifs," because they can replace each other in the legend without changing the structure. If we chart the legend sequence for all the Eastern Woodlands versions, we get this flow-chart.

				Lizard		
	Meat	⇨		Fish		
	Brains					
	Eggs	⇨		Tie-Snake	⇨	Expansion
Two men ⇨	Fish ⇨	Tree	⇨	Horned WS	⇨	Town flooded

As we can see, there are two other instances of allomotifs: the kind of creature the man becomes and the consequences of the transformation. Perhaps the Under World will be better illuminated by examining the water creatures presented in this legend.

What Kind of Snake?

Of the sixteen texts only a Cherokee variant, the Seneca and Menomini legends, has anything other than a snake, and those creatures (lizard and fish) are all water creatures. All agree on one major fact: not only is the water person a transformed human being, he is apparently an identifiable mythological figure. In three of the Creek texts it is a "tie-snake," and three others make specific reference to his multicolored horns, a characteristic feature of the Horned Water Serpent. Six do not specify the kind of water-snake. It appears that there are at least two mythological serpents involved in the variants of the legend, the Tie-snake and the Horned Water Serpent. Did the Creeks believe in two water-snakes, or one with two images? The evidence is a little ambiguous.

The Tie-Snake.

Swanton summarized the descriptions he obtained:

> The "tie snake" is an inch and a half in diameter and short, but it is very strong. It is white under the throat, but black over the rest of the body, and its head is crooked over like the beak of a hawk. It lives in deep water, usually in deep water holes from which it makes excursions into the woods, drawing its prey down into the water to its den. There are many tales told of this tie snake...[4]

Another legend of the water serpent tells of the journey of a young man to the underwater lodge of the water serpents, where he is befriended.

Journey to the Underwater Lodge ■ ■ ■
CREEK

A chief sent his son with a message to another chief, and delivered to him a vessel as the emblem of his authority.[5]

The son stopped to play with some boys who were throwing stones into the water. The chief's son threw his vessel upon the water and it sank. He was frightened. He was afraid to go to the neighboring chief without the vessel, and he did not like to return home and tell his father of the loss. He jumped into the stream and, reaching the spot where the vessel had sunk, he dove into the water. His playmates waited a long time for him, but he did not reappear. They returned and reported his death.

When the chief's son was beneath the surface of the stream the Tie-snakes seized him and bore him to a cave and said to him: "Ascend yonder platform." He looked and saw seated on the platform the king of the Tie-snakes. The platform was a mass of living Tie-snakes. He approached the platform and lifted his foot to ascend, but the platform ascended as he lifted his foot. Again he tried, with the same result. The third time he tried in vain. The Tie-snakes said, "Ascend."

He lifted his foot the fourth time and succeeded in ascending the platform and the king invited him to sit by his side.[6] Then the king said to him:

"See yonder feather; it is yours," pointing to a plume in the corner of the cave. He approached the plume and extended his hand to seize it, but it eluded his grasp. Three times he made the attempt and three times it escaped him. On the fourth attempt he obtained it.

"Yonder tomahawk is yours," said the Tie-snakes' king.

He went to the place where the tomahawk was sticking and reached out his hand to take it, but in vain. It rose of itself every time he raised his hand. He tried four times and on the fourth trial it remained still and he succeeded in taking it.

The king said: "You can return to your father after three days. When he asks where you have been, reply: 'I know what I know,' but on no account tell

87

him what you do know. When he needs my aid walk toward the east and bow three times to the rising sun and I will be there to help him."

After three days the Tie-snake carried him to the spot where he had dived into the stream, lifted him to the surface of the water, and placed his lost vessel in his hand. He swam to the bank and returned to his father, who was mourning him as dead. His father rejoiced over his son's wonderful restoration.

He informed his father of the Tie-snake king and his message of proffered aid. Not long afterwards his father was attacked by his enemies. He said to his son: "You understand what the king of the Tie-snakes said. Go and seek his aid."

The son put the plume on his head, took the tomahawk, went toward the east, and bowed three times to the rising sun.

The king of the Tie-snakes stood before him.

"What do you wish?" he said.

"My father needs your aid."

"Go and tell him not to fear. They will attack him, but they shall not harm him or his people. In the morning all will be well."

The son returned to his father and delivered the message of the king of the Tie-snakes.

The enemy came and attacked his town, but no one was harmed. Night came. In the morning they beheld their enemies each held fast in the folds of a Tie-snake, and so all were captured and the chief made peace with his foes.[7]

This legend neatly fits the pattern of the vision quest, in which medicine power is bestowed upon the seeker. Among the northern nations the vision quest is generally understood to be part of the growth of all males, but in the Southeast, as well as can be told now, it seems to have been more restricted to doctors and other specialists. In the Southeast the legend of such a quest is well known, being found among the Creeks, Hitchiti, Alabama, Cherokee, and Biloxi.[8]

Those who were befriended by the Tie-snakes were few, however, and most people found them a source of worry and wonder. Many of the references to the Tie-snake in the literature portray it as an objective danger associated with the rivers, and as a legendary figure it may serve an etiological function—the Tie-snake is responsible for drownings and vanished animals and people. This is what Tuggle learned in Oklahoma in 1881:

Tie-Snake Drowns Two ■ ■ ■
CREEK

...The wonders of the famous tie-snake were resurrected from fairy-land, and recounted to us as we passed a pool of water in a dry creek. A man and a boy had been drowned a few days ago, and the tie-snakes did it. The boy went in and the tie-snake caught him, he screamed for his father, who went to his rescue, when the tie-snakes caught him too, and both sank to rise no more. Two fresh mounds on the bank of the stream told the fate of the emigrants...[9]

In 1885 a missionary among the Oklahoma Creeks set a time for baptisms at a pool in a creek. When no one showed up for the rite, he was told, "This is a Tie-snake hole, and those Indians will not be here." So he heard the legend of the journey to the Tie-snakes' underwater lodge instead of doing a baptism.[10] A few decades later Swanton collected this from Jackson Lewis.

Water Serpent Seizes a Man ■ ■ ■
HITCHITI
A man went hunting one summer. He killed a deer and carried it along on his back. On the way he got very hot and coming to a pond he went in swimming. While he was sitting in the water he felt something against him and looking down he saw something blue lying there. He tried to get out of the water but the creature held him tight and he could do nothing. It began to drag him in and he seized a thick bush, but in vain. It kept on dragging him. It was carrying him toward a big pond. But when he was very near it his body caught against a big drift of logs and the creature left him and went into the water, while the man ran off.[11]

Swanton collected another Oklahoma Creek legend of the Tie-snake. It is localized, the narrator knew the men involved, and it was told as a personal experience story.

Water Serpent Seizes a Mare ■ ■ ■
CREEK
A Creek Indian named Ogue hili imathla, now dead, who used to live about three miles from Eufaula (Oklahoma), told this to Lewis as a personal experience. He once owned a mare which had a colt. Having missed his mare from the range, he hunted for some time, and finally found her by means of the colt, which he saw running about but always returning to a certain spot. Finally he went to this place and saw that a large tree had been uprooted there, leaving quite a hole where its roots had been—a hole partially filled with water. There he found his mare with her hindquarters under water and her head and shoulders out. As he could not get her out alone he gathered his neighbors together and they went to the place with ropes which they tied about the mare's body and pulled on all together in order to draw her out. But their efforts were at first fruitless. Making a supreme effort, however, they were successful, whereupon the water seemed to flow in from all quarters and fill up the hole. The mare was

not much hurt, and they took her away and cared for her until she recovered. Her hindquarters were at first numbed, however, and upon them was a spot about an inch and a half across from which the hair had been rubbed. The skin there became black and finally scaled off. When the hair came out again it was black and the animal was quite a curiosity on account of the black ring. Everybody, including Lewis, felt perfectly satisfied that a tie-snake had caught this mare and dragged her into the water hole.[12]

The Tie-snake worried the Yuchi, too.

Encounter with a Tie-Snake ∎ ∎ ∎
YUCHI

Once a man went hunting, and when he came to a spring he took a bath. After he had bathed he got out, and when he was putting on his clothes again a tie-snake came out of a cave; the man hunted for it and called, "They shall call you tie-snake"; then he put one foot in the water and said, "Tie it," and then it coiled around his foot, and he went off with it. He came to a pond with it and shouted, and then people came there with a knife, struck the snake, and cut it in two. Then they took him away from it, put him on their back and ran away with him; when they got back to their camping place they made medicine for his leg; when he got almost well they killed a deer, and then they went back. When they got home they again made medicine, and his leg healed. Even now the people do not bathe in the springs, because the tie-snakes are watching the water in the springs, they used to say. A person by himself is afraid of the springs, because the tie-snake would catch him; then they are also afraid of the leeches in the spring. Only two people together used to drink water from a spring; only when the medicine-makers make the medicine they cure each other; that's all.[13]

Of the texts of the journey to the underwater lodge, the Tuggle text identifies the leading snake as a Tie-snake, as does the Hitchiti, but the Alabama legend agrees with the Cherokee in speaking of the "snake-crawfish" (a direct translation of the Alabama name for the Horned Water Serpent). This horned snake is to be equated with the Cherokee uktena, so well known as to be a standard figure in the Southeast.[14]

The Horned Water Serpent is described differently from the Tie-snake, and it appears to be a completely different character, even though the behavior is the same.

This snake lives in water and has horns like the stag. It is not a bad snake. It crawls out and suns itself near its hole...If any game animal, such as a deer, comes near the place where this snake is lying it is drawn irresistibly into the water and destroyed. It eats only the ends of the noses of the animals it has killed.

The old Creeks sometimes got hold of the horns of this snake, and they were broken up into very minute fragments and distributed among the hunters of the Creek nation. These fragments are red and look like red sealing wax.[15]

Swanton further noted that the Alabama in Texas also know of the horned snake. The piece of horn was described as red, but some accounts indicate that the horns may be of various colors. The Koasati and the Natchez tell the "water-serpent transport" episode, in which a man crossing a river on the back of the Horned Water Serpent takes advantage of the journey to saw off one of the horns, reflecting the belief in the hunting medicine power of that substance.

Water-Serpent Transport ■ ■ ■
KOASATI

The Orphan stood on the bank of the river. He called, "My grandfather," upon which the turtle, alligator, loggerhead turtle came out in succession. "Not you," he said. After they had gone away the Horned Snake came out. "You are the one," he said. Then it came close to him and lay still on the water. It was very pretty, having one blue and one red horn, and he sat upon them. Then he threw a bird far off. The Snake shot forward, picked it up, and ate it. When it was finished the orphan threw another far out. While he was doing this he was sawing upon the horn with a strong rope he had. He threw another far off and the Snake went on with him. Meanwhile he kept sawing upon the horn. Now the Horned Snake said, "What are you doing to my horn?" It gave him an itching feeling. "I am doing nothing," he answered. "I like it and so I am patting it." He went on in this manner until there were no more birds. Then he shot an arrow to a great distance and the Snake went on rapidly with him. When he got to the arrow he seized it by the ligaments used in fastening on the feathers and swallowed it. When he was about to sink the man shot another. The last one stuck into the ground close to the water. At that time the horn was about cut through. Holding it, he jumped and reached the shore with the broken horn. The bank slid back under him, but he kept on and got out...[16]

This text is part of a longer story which will be given in full later on. Curiously, the Creeks do not have this episode at all. The water-serpent transport episode is of fairly widespread distribution, however, being found among both eastern (Naskapi, Micmac, Malecite, Passamaquoddy) and western (Kickapoo, Ojibwa) Algonkians, as well as the Huron, Arikara, and Dakota.[17] This list is not exhaustive, for the Mandan/Hidatsa and the Chiti-macha ought to be added,[18] and there may well be others.[19]

This brief survey of the water serpent figure in Southeastern tales provides an interesting pattern: the episode of the "water-serpent transport" is found among the Alabama, Koasati, and Natchez, but not among the Creeks. When

Horned water serpents

both Creeks and these three tribes share a water-snake legend, the Creek informants tend to identify it as a Tie-snake, while the others tend toward the Horned Water Serpent. The Cherokee legends speak only of the horned snake. In short, the horned water person, a widespread figure in the folklore of the Eastern Woodlands, appears in the Southeast to be a pre-Creek character. In many cases the Creeks substituted their unique "Tie-snake" for the Horned Water Serpent, although they retained the latter. One Creek text of the Snake-man even serves as a transition form, for the Tie-snake is described as having horns. Still, the Tie-snake and the Horned Water Serpent may just be different ways of describing a standard family of Under World beings.

The Snake-Man's Flood

These various water creatures fill the same general function in Southeastern thought, for they control the water world, perhaps as "Master of Waters." In the Snake-man legend this is expressed as a local flood caused by the Snake-man. In five of the texts the flood is minor, consisting only of a repetitious note that the hole or pond into which the Snake-man goes suddenly expands into a lake. In four others, though, the flood is grimmer. In Creek 1, 4, and 5 the people gather at the square ground to see the Snake-man, but instead a flood

sweeps them all away, presumably to join him in his new water world. Creek 2 only has him seize his sister, a fainter trace of the flood. The Yuchi text contains an interesting twist: after the man becomes a snake by eating fish found in water in a hollow tree, he is nurtured by young girls in the town (he is fed the "soft ends of corn"). When they begin to tire of this, he teaches medicine to the tribe, and then they all follow him into the water except one straggler, who becomes a rock on the bank.

These texts appear to be a compound of the Snake-man story and a flood legend. That flood merits closer attention. It is significant that two of these texts even identify the flooded town as Coosa (Creek 4 and 5). As it happens, there are other texts of the flood and destruction of Coosa that are not attached to the legend of the man transformed into a snake.

Swanton obtained from Legus Perryman an origin myth for the Tulsa, an offspring-town of Coosa. It indicates a migration from the west, the crossing of a great river, then this:

The Flooding of Coosa ▪ ▪ ▪
CREEK

One night, a long time afterward, a dance was held at which all persons were

present except a newly married couple who were in some manner delayed. When these arrived at the square, late at night, they found nothing there but a lake. They remained on the shores of the lake watching and noticed that the birds which tried to fly across fell in and were drowned. One big crane, however, flew all the way over. It said, *"Koos, koos, koos,"* and they thought that that was its name. As time went on this couple had children and their descendants formed another big town; and because the bird did fly over the submerged village in safety they named the town after it, saying, "We shall be called Coosas."[20]

In this form, of course, the plot outlines are obscured, and the folk-etymology is questionable, but other informants clarified the general Coosa legend. One said that "Coosa was Taloksu'mgi ('Town-lost-in-the-water') by the Creeks, and that it had sunk into the water until nothing could be seen of it except the ball post." Another said it had been swallowed by an earthquake.[21]

A man from Hilibi gave Swanton a different legend of the Coosa disaster.

Water-Panther Husband ■ ■ ■
CREEK

An unmarried woman in the town of Coosa went to draw water from the spring and was afterward found to be pregnant. When her child was born it was spotted. Then her brothers and some of her relatives thought this was the

Underwater panthers

offspring of a water tiger *(wi katca),* which the Muskogee now identify with the leopard, became angry with her, and wanted to kill it. But she had some old relatives who opposed them and finally prevailed. The busk ground and "hothouse" where they counselled about this stood near the river, and the girl ran to the water tiger and said, "There is an effort being made to kill my child, but they have not killed it yet." Then the water tiger said, "Let those who are disposed to defend the child move away from the rest." The woman told these what the water tiger had said, so they moved away from the town, and that night the water tiger brought on a great inundation which covered Coosa, with its square ground and all, but for years after people could see there the main timbers that braced the old *tcokofa* (ceremonial lodge). The water tiger took the woman home to live with him. Then the few persons who were left alive came together and said, "We were once a great town but now there are very, very few of us and we are ashamed of having fallen off so in numbers *(ista'kosi).* Nevertheless let us get together and make another town for ourselves," and they did so, establishing the town we now know as Tulsa *(istalsosi).*[22] Those who were engulfed in the river did not all die, and afterward people could hear a drum beaten there when they were dancing and having their good times. There is now a whirlpool on the site of the old town and close to the river. Sometimes people used to see beams whirling round in this eddy, and occasionally men sitting upon them. No bird could fly over the whirlpool, and those which tried always fell into the center of it and were drowned. But there is a small bird with a yellow

95

breast which seems to say, *"Koskoza,"* and this could fly across with perfect ease. Some maintained that the people beneath the water favored these birds and let them fly across. We name them from the noise which they make.[23]

This text introduces yet another of the Southeastern water creatures, an underwater panther. Like the Horned Water Serpent, with whom it seems to merge, this is not an unknown person in North America. "Michibichi, the Ojibwa Underwater Panther, was second in the hierarchy of deities."[24] Belief in the underwater panther is known from the Delaware, Fox, Ojibwa, Menomini, Potawatomi, Peoria, Shawnee, Winnebago, Mandan, Hidatsa, Arikara, Dakota, Omaha, and Ponca.[25] Europeans learned about the Underwater Panther early because it was carved on a rock bluff in Illinois above the Mississippi River. It is now generally referred to as the "Piasa," from the name applied to that carving, which was seen by Europeans from the late seventeenth century on.[26] If it is the Piasa that appears in carved stone and engraved shell in the Hopewell and in the Southeastern Ceremonial Complex artifacts, then the Underwater Panther is at least two millennia old in the Midwest.[27]

The Creek text of the water panther connects the Southeast, and particularly Coosa, with this ancient tradition. The visual art forms, like the verbal forms we have been following, demonstrate the flowing of the panther into varieties of serpents and birds, so perhaps we shouldn't be too surprised at the difficulty of separating one water person from another in the mythology. Another informant gave Swanton essentially the same legend about the water-panther, but he was not sure whose story it was: "That town is thought to have been Coosa, although it is possible it may have been Fushatchee."[28] The confusion is probably due to the amalgamation of part of Coosa with Fushatchee; on the basis of the census lists Swanton judged that merger to have taken place by 1761.[29]

There is no historical record of the destruction of Coosa, by an underwater panther or any other agency. If the legend of the Coosa flood reflects any actual event, it can never be known, since it had to predate the historical era. All that can be concluded safely is that the legend of a destructive flood was early attached to Coosa, a town placed by the migration legends in the Southeast before the migration of Kasihta and Coweta. But the death by flood was also told of other towns. In one of the Creek migration texts, the end of the Yamasee is told in a legend which may reflect the memory of the Yamasee War of the early eighteenth century.

The Death of the Yamasee ■ ■ ■
CREEK

The Yamasee were good people. They did not want to fight, but, being harassed, they walked deep into the water very humbly, singing pretty songs, and so that tribe was lost. The old people said that this happened because it was in the thought of God that it should be so.[30]

It appears that the flooding of a talwa or the disappearance of a people into the Under World was a migratory legend, for it was also told of the Pascagoula and Biloxi. This is one of the few examples of the European adoption and continuation of a Native American legend. It was current early in the eighteenth century, and it is still told in the Pascagoula area in romantic form. Here is a turn-of-the-century romanticized text by a Euro-American.

Death of the Pascagoula ■ ■ ■
EURO-AMERICAN

Legend says the sound (of "The Singing River") is connected with the mysterious extinction of the Pascagoula tribe of Indians. The Pascagoula were a gentle tribe of handsome men and shapely women with large dark eyes and small, well-shaped hands and feet. The Biloxi, on the other hand, were a tribe calling themselves the "first people" and extremely jealous of their position. Miona, a princess of the Biloxi tribe, though betrothed to Otanga, a chieftain of her people, loved Olustee, a young chieftain of the Pascagoula, and fled with him to his tribe. The spurned and outraged Otanga led his Biloxi braves to war against Olustee and the neighboring Pascagoula, whereupon Olustee begged his tribe to give him up for atonement. But the Pascagoula swore they would either save their young chieftain and his bride or perish with them. However, when thrown into battle against terrible odds, they soon lost hope of victory. Faced with the choice either of subjection to Otanga or death, they chose suicide. With their women and children leading the way into the river, the braves followed with joined hands, each chanting his song of death until the last voice was hushed by the engulfing dark waters.[31]

This tradition of a local flood needs to be distinguished from the almost universal legend of the great flood. Here is the Caddo version.

The Flood ■ ■ ■
CADDO

One time a long, hot, dry season came and all the waters of the earth dried up. The people wandered from place to place, trying to find things. They went to the dried-up river beds and there found many dead fish and turtles and animals that dwelt in the water, and the people cut them to pieces and threw them about, for they thought that these animals and fish were in some way responsible for the waters disappearing. While they were acting foolishly they looked up and saw a man in the sky coming toward them from the west. A wind blew, and the man approached and lighted on the ground before them. In his hand he carried a small green leaf. He told the people that they had not acted wisely and had abused him, and that he was angry with them. He motioned the leaf in four directions and drops of water fell from it. Soon the waters grew in volume and arose all over the world, even to the tree-tops, and the highest mountains except one. To this high mountain the man led a few of the people whom he chose, and they stayed on the mountain for four days, while the water rose higher and higher. As the waters rose the man caused the mountain to rise with them. He could do this because he had greater power than the spirit of Cold or Heat. After a time the waters began to go down, and green things appeared upon the earth again. Then he led the people down from the mountain. They found that many people who had been left in the water during the flood had not drowned, but had turned into alligators and other water animals.[32]

When mythological texts are compared, the details and twists of plot allow them to be grouped by similarity. These clusters of texts are called "oicotypes." In the light of this kind of general flood known in the Plains, the Southeastern local flood can be seen to be such an oicotypal group. This flood is motivated in two different ways: (1) the vengeance of a water person for the mistreatment of his children, (2) the action of the man who became a snake. The second has crystallized in the fish-in-tree/Horned Water Serpent/local flood sequence, of which there is one more text to be examined.

A Look to the South
The Underwater Serpent did not reign only in North America, however. Buried in the chart of Snake-man texts is a reference to the Sumu. Thirty years ago Rands pointed out this close parallel to the Snake-man legend as it is found in the Southeast.[33] Since the Sumu live on the Caribbean coast of Nicaragua, it is worth close attention.

The Snake-Man ■ ■ ■
SUMU
Two brothers Suko and Kuru went out fishing to the Cualigua [Kwaliwa] Creek, a tributary of Rio Oconguas [Prinsapolca system]. They caught many excellent food fishes of a species known by the Indian names *srik* or *sirik*. Then they had a gigantic river catfish at the hook. Suko immediately wanted to eat a piece of the latter, but Kuru objected as it appeared to him to be a sort of spirit. Suko, however, did not listen to his brother, and he roasted a piece of the fish and ate it. But hardly had he finished his meal when he became very thirsty. Having eaten too much, he could scarcely move, and he asked his brother for some water. The latter did as he was told, but the more Suko drank the thirstier he became, and he kept his brother continually on the run to fetch water. Finally

Kuru became tired of this and helped his brother get to the edge of the creek, so that he might drink as much as he wanted.

Arrived at the waterside, Suko lay down on the ground, and reaching with his head down in the water, he kept on drinking without stopping. Gradually his body assumed the shape of a gigantic boa constrictor, while the head retained its normal size and shape. Kuru became scared and he went home, but did not dare tell anything about what had happened. When the people inquired about his brother, he answered that he was still engaged in fishing and would come a little later.

But the neighbors noticed that something had happened and they made off all together to look for Suko. Arrived at the fishing ground, they found the boa constrictor on the branches of a very high *ceiba* or silk-cotton tree. But hardly had they perceived him when a big flood came which inundated the whole country. Everyone was drowned with the exception of Suko and the latter's wife and children.[34]

There are several familiar elements here: two brothers, unusual food (giant catfish), taboo warning by one brother, transformation into a water-serpent (boa constrictor), movement to the water, visit of family and friends, and the flooding of the "whole country." Rands observed that "in view of these similarities, there can be no doubt that the stories are historically related," but he postponed any further consideration of the parallel.[35] He did point out that the Sumu also believe in the horned water-serpent:

A very large *waula* or boa constrictor...with two horns on the head like a deer is said to inhabit certain large lagoons in the pine ridges, far away from the nearest Indian village. It is claimed that the common waula or boa turns into such a monster when it reaches old age, and that it then retreats into deep lagoons. Man has no power to kill such a boa constrictor, as bullets have no effect on it; it can be destroyed only by a stroke of lightning.[36]

If any boa constrictor can become a horned one simply by growing old, then the young man in the legend has become a Horned Water Serpent, and the parallel of the Sumu and the Southeastern texts is thus even more pronounced. Another provocative parallel is the Sumu belief in a water-tiger which is "found chiefly in the larger rivers among the rocks, and will devour any one swimming in the neighborhood or falling into the water; domestic animals and even men are said to have occasionally fallen victim to it."[37]

It is difficult to interpret the geographical gap between the Sumu and the Southeast. Present collections of folktales from the tribes north of the Sumu have no comparable texts, but that is not necessarily significant. The Meso-american sphere was the scene of so many successive cultures, each with its priests and theologians, that what remains of the earlier mythic materials is a difficult tangle to unravel. In addition, there has been relatively little collection of aboriginal folklore in Mexico and adjacent areas.[38] As has been seen, there are a few indications that at least portions of the tale complex under discussion were present in the Maya area, but there are no direct texts of the nature of the Sumu and Southeastern Snake-man tale. There are, however, elements of this legend which can be pursued even further south, and which reveal the existence of a much larger complex of which the Sumu text is a part.

The episode is found in more ambiguous form in the Guiana region, but there are references to a transformation. In one legend two brothers go fishing; one sings loudly, despite the warnings, then departure, of his concerned brother. When the youth brings back their father, they find that the boy has become "an evil beast, which was ready to kill anybody and anything." They killed him.[39] Another version tells of the boy who broke the taboo on eating after dark; he was transformed into a tiger, and when his friend brought back the boy's mother, the tiger-man killed her.[40]

These texts are legends of transformation of men into animals, and this notion is certainly not an unusual one among New World tribes. We must accordingly be cautious in accepting these non-snake texts as related to the Snake-man legend. Despite the distance, the Sumu legend is extraordinarily close to the Creek texts, and there can be little question of a relationship. Are they part of a larger oicotype?

One key motif of the complex is an element which is present in the Sumu tale but is so obscurely represented that it could easily escape notice as a significant one. When the people came to see the Snake-man, they found him "on the branches of a very high *ceiba* or silk-cotton tree."

The ceiba fills various functions in the South American traditions, from giving birth to humans to bearing fruits and vegetables. In some texts it is also the source of the waters, which indicates its cosmological status. The Cuna, for example, tell of the cutting of the great tree by the culture heroes; when it fell, "from its top came fresh and salt water, croplands, plants, reptiles, mammals, fishes and birds."[41] Among the Carib and Arawak tribes the tree as the source of the waters takes on a grimmer note, for the cutting of the tree to distribute the fruits and vegetables also releases the waters which become a flood. Roth summarized the legends concisely, using Brett's texts:

The Felling of the Tree ■ ■ ■
CARIB/ARAWAK
The bushcow/acouri/maipuri is followed to the tree by the bush rat, who then tells the people of the tree; when they and the two culture heroes decide to cut it down (in some texts the tree resists cutting in several ways), they discover that there is:

. . . a fountain of swelling waters in the stump, or under the roots, of this wonderful tree, the overflowing of which is temporarily checked by means of a rugged rock *(Carib)* or an inverted basket *(Akawai)*. Owing to the reputed wickedness of the people in the one case, and the mischief of a howling monkey in the other, the waters are let loose, and a flood occurs which overwhelms nearly everything, most of the people being destroyed.[42]

In summarizing an Akawai version Frazer says that the culture hero felled the tree only to find that ''the stump was hollow and full of water in which the fry of every sort of fresh-water fish was swimming about... The water in the cavity, being connected with the great reservoir somewhere in the bowels of the earth, began to overflow...''[43] Thus the tree does not merely contain water; it seems in some traditions to be the connecting link between the land and the waters beneath the earth.

Another tale from the Caribs tells of a boy who was taken beneath the earth by the Earthquake People, who gave him medicine power; he proved his ability as a *piai* (shaman) by knocking at all the house-posts: ''water flowed from the base of each until it covered all the ground and rose above their ankles. His mother was indeed frightened now and thought he was going to sink the earth altogether.''[44] The land floating upon the waters is a concept of very widespread distribution, but it is an important image in the area under discussion, for it provides the conceptual framework for the legend of the flood which came from the great tree. The cutting of the tree was the equivalent of pulling the stopper, and the culture hero's act to plug it again was foiled by the trickster. The flood among these tribes, then, is envisioned as an overflowing of the waters under the earth, which sets this flood tradition apart from those that see it as the result of rain from above. It also is an indication that in ancient times this tree may have been understood more fully in the role of the Cosmic Tree which holds together the various levels of the world structure. Steward refers to traditions of a local flood found among the Catio, Patangaro, Guajiro, Yaruro, and Taino, which seem to be part of the same complex.[45]

At this point, what seems most clear is that there is a linkage between the great tree, maize and other vegetables, water, and a flood, and that this folkloric complex is found most strongly in the area of the northern coast of South America. It is likely that the tradition of the twin culture heroes is part of this same complex. (See Chapter 8.) One of the miraculous deeds was the cutting of the great tree and causing the flood. It will be remembered that the great majority of the North American texts of the Snake-man legend specify that there are two men who are hunting or fishing. Since there appears to be a relation of the Twins to the cutting of the tree and the flood, motifs which in turn seem to be related to the Snake-man complex, it appears that the North American legend may be a branch of one particular Twins tradition.

In any case, the complex is well known in the Caribbean area, with extensions into the Amazonian region and the Gran Chaco. The Sumu text provides an undeniable linkage of this complex with the Southeastern texts and their cousins in North America. In the light of the fuller complex that has been uncovered in South America, we can look at the remaining evidence about the Under World in North America.

The Wider Distribution.

Our earlier conclusion that the Creek Tie-snake is an unusual adaptation of the Horned Water Serpent receives further confirmation when we examine the wider distribution of the Snake-man and related legends. The Snake-man seems to be localized in three distinctive groups other than the Eastern Woodlands: Upper Plains, Lower Plains, and Southwest. Here is the full chart of texts.

	Two Men	Food	Tree	Trans	Concl.	Source
Creek 1	*	F	*	HWS	Town	Sw. 1929:32f
Creek 2	*	F	*	WS	Town	Sw. 1928:71
Creek 3	*	F	*	WS	Town	Nelson 1954
Yuchi	*	F	*	WS	Town	Wagner 31:66f
Creek 4	*	F	*	HWS	Person	Sw. 1929:33f
Sumu	*	F		HWS	Town	Conzemius 1932:130
Creek 5	*	F	*	HWS		Sw. 123:158
Hitchiti	*	F	*	WS		Sw. 1929:97
Creek 6	*	B		TS	Exp	Sw. 1929:30f
Creek 7	*	B		TS	Exp	Sw. 1929:31f
Creek 8	*	E		TS	Exp	Sw. 1929:34
Alabama		E		WS		Sw. 1929:154
Cherokee	*	M		WS		Mooney 1900:304f
Cherokee	*	M		Lizd		Trav. Bird
Menomini		M		Fish	Exp	Sk/S 1915:476
Seneca	*	F		Fish	Exp	Cur. 1910:111f
Mandan	*	WS		WS		Maximilian 185
Mandan	*	WS		WS		Bowers 1950:199
Hidatsa	*	WS		WS		Maximilian 230
Hidatsa	*	WS		WS		Bowers 1965:360
Arikara	*	S		WS		Dorsey 1904:78,79
Gros V.	*	S		WS		Kroeber 1908:116
Blackft	*	S		WS		Wissler/D. 1908
Assinib	*	S		WS		Lowie 1909:181f
Crow	*	S?		WS?	Person	Lowie 1918:214ff

Apache	*	M	WS		Goddard 1919:64ff
Apache	*	M	WS		Goddard 1919:135f
Arapaho	*	E	WS		Dorsey/K 1903:150
Arapaho	*	E	Allig		Voth 1912:47
Ponca		RS	S	Horses	Dorsey 1890:322
Skidi P.	*	M	RS	Person	Dorsey 1904:293
Caddo	*	S	S		Dorsey 1905:65

Upper Plains. Among the Arikara, Mandan, Hidatsa, Gros Ventre, and Blackfoot, the legend is part of a larger cycle of myths.[46] Among the Mandan, at least, the cycle can be termed a major ritual myth, being connected with corn rites and the powerful grandmother figure, Old-Woman-Who-Never-Dies. The cycle involves two young men who are taken by a whirlwind to the Old Woman's lodge, from which they return by riding the Horned Water Serpent. Finding a giant serpent (unidentified) across the path, they build a fire under it. One of them eats the flesh, despite warnings, and is transformed into a large water serpent, which thenceforward lives in the Missouri River and acts as protector and spirit of the river. While the Horned Water Serpent is incorporated in this same cycle, the Snake-man in the Mandan and Hidatsa texts is described as being red-and-blue-striped and having the power to flash lightning from his single eye. In the Arikara texts the serpent shares these characteristics, but the horns are supplied in a curious way, for the snake carries on his head dirt from which trees grow.

Among the Assiniboine there is less stability in the sequence of elements. In one version the tale is a simple one of the giant snake, the eating of its flesh, and the transformation to a large water serpent. Another follows these elements with the fight between Thunder and the water serpent and the transformation of the serpent back into a man, and the third version follows the same sequence but concludes with the death of the Snake-man by frogs.[47] Here the legend shows little standardization, but it appears to be related to the Mandan cycle. The same is true of the Crow texts, for the basic elements of the Snake-man legend are present, but they are isolated tales.[48] Despite the signs of the loss of folkloric stability (probably due to the weakening of its ritual significance, as opposed to the Mandan cycle) in these texts, the details of the legend indicate that the Assiniboine and the Crow belong to the Mandan group.

The northern Plains group features a water serpent that is clearly associated with a river, the Missouri in particular. This grouping is to be expected in view of the close relationships which have existed between these tribes. The similarity of the Arikara text to those of the Mandan/Hidatsa/Crow/Siouan group—as opposed to affiliation with the other Caddoan texts—is a significant indicator that the legend passed from the Siouan Plains Village tribes to the Arikara, and possibly from the Arikara to their linguistic kinspeople to the south. This is not surprising in view of the position of the Horned Water Serpent in Mandan/Hidatsa mythology, for "Grandfather Snake" is, in other texts, the husband of "Old-Woman-Who-Never-Dies," who is the major agricultural figure in their religious structure. He figures in ritual life as the guardian spirit of the river, and offerings are made to him, particularly by travelers.[49] The Snake-man is thus no peripheral figure in these Siouan cultures. The Arapaho, Assiniboine, and Gros Ventre traditions are most likely diffused from the Plains Village peoples.

While the other Siouan Plains tribes do not seem to know the Snake-man legend itself, they do know the Horned Water Serpent, Unktehi, or Unktexi, their Neptune or divine ruler of the waters, whose name also designated a fabled monster of the deep and the whale of the salt-water. In fact, Unktehi means any large animal, for it is used also to designate some large extinct animal, whose bones are at times found by the Indians. The Winnebago know of the Waktchexi, a miraculous beast of the watery element, which had the power of imparting wonderful qualities to people who had been fasting for ascetic purposes. [50]

Lower Plains. The Apache, Caddo, Skidi, Pawnee, and Ponca form a small group that features land snakes.[51] In this last subtype, the Pawnee and Apache texts specify that the Snake-man is a giant rattlesnake; the Pawnee text in particular is thus consistent in moving the legend from a water orientation to a terrestrial one, assuming the former is earlier. This is a significant shift, for it indicates that the legend is not originally a Caddoan one.

Southwest. The Snake-man legend in the form thus far seen is not present in the Southwest, but there are several traditions that appear to be related to it. Both the Hopi and the Zuni tell the story of the destruction of a town by flood and earthquake, even though there are changes of names and a few details. The four Hopi versions are very similar. Although the Zuni texts harbor more disagreement, the plot is generally the same and can be given as one legend.[52]

The people of a town (Hopi, *Palatkwapi;* Zuni, *Itiwana)* had forgotten the moral system (the "Hopi Way"), and a priest (chief) decided to recall them to the right path by sending his son (nephew) in divine garb on four successive nights. In some versions he planted four *pahos* (prayer sticks). He was killed by the people and buried in the plaza with his hand above ground. Each day one finger dropped, and on the fourth day the sky went black, the ground shook, rumbling was heard, the plaza collapsed into a pond as water rose everywhere (even from the firepits in one version), and the corpse arose as the One-Horned Water Serpent (Hopi: *Balolookong;* Zuni: *Kolowisi).* In some texts everyone was destroyed, but in most they fled to the mountains and the town was abandoned.

In his excellent summary of Pueblo myths, Tyler has described the Horned Water Serpent as

. . . a monster with bulging eyes and a horn, to say nothing of a fan of feathers or fur. He is also specialized as the god of waters, which among the Hopis, Zunis, and most of the Keres, is not associated with disastrous floods, but with fertility and longevity. Hence we find that the Horned Water Serpent is a kindly and often even a comic god...As the god of waters, he is the god of floods and landslides, if not of the earthquakes and volcanoes that occur to the south.[53]

Separating these texts into similar groups is referred to as identifying the "oicotypes," local distinctive text groups. On the basis of the texts we have looked at, we may construct a grouping chart of the Snake-man legend as follows:

GRANDFATHER	WATER-SERPENT	TERRESTRIAL
Blackfoot Assiniboine	Menomini Seneca	Pawnee
Gros Ventre	Creek	Ponca
Crow	Hitchiti	Caddo
Hidatsa	Alabama	Apache
Arapaho	Sumu	
Mandan	Cherokee	
Arikara	Yuchi	

It does not seem possible to go any further in drawing conclusions about how this situation came about, but the Sumu connection raises the possibility that the key to understanding this myth-complex may lie south of the United States.[54]

The Snake-man

CHAPTER FIVE

The Middle World

Humans are poised between the Above World and the Under World, but the "Middle World" they inhabit seems to have been considered a younger, and possibly weaker, realm than either of them.

When Speck was doing fieldwork among the Yuchi in 1904 and 1905, he visited the neighboring talwa of Taskigi, from whom several texts were "incidentally obtained."[1] Among them was one of the few examples of a creation legend from the Southeast, the others being from the Cherokee, Creek, Yuchi, and Chitimacha. Speck warned, however, that some of the Taskigi legends might be Yuchi in origin, because "it may be expected that there has been some interchange of ideas with the Yuchi Indians, in close proximity to whom the Taskigi have lived since their removal from the East."[2]

Earth-Diver ■ ■ ■
CREEK/YUCHI

The time was, in the beginning, when the earth overflowed with water. There was no earth, no beast of the earth, no human being. They held a council to know which would be best, to have some land or to have all water. When the council had met, some said, "Let us have land, so that we can get food," because they would starve to death. But others said, "Let us have all water," because they wanted it that way.

So they appointed Eagle as chief. He was told to decide one way or another. Then he decided. He decided for land. So they looked around for some one whom they could send out to get land. The first one to propose himself was Dove, who thought that he could do it. Accordingly they sent him. He was given four days in which to perform his task. Now, when Dove came back on the fourth day, he said that he could find no land. They concluded to try another plan. Then they obtained the services of Crawfish *(sakdju)*. He went down

106

through the water into the ground beneath, and he too was gone four days. On the fourth morning he arose and appeared on the surface of the waters. In his claws they saw that he held some dirt. He had at last secured the land. Then they took the earth from his claws and made a ball of it. When this was completed they handed it over to the chief, Eagle, who took it and went out from their presence with it. When he came back to the council, he told them that there was land, an island. So all the beasts went in the direction pointed out, and found that there was land there as Eagle had said. But what they found was very small. They lived there until the water receded from this earth. Then the land all joined into one.[3]

For comparison, let's look at one of the two Yuchi texts.

Earth-Diver ■ ■ ■
YUCHI

In the beginning not a thing existed; there was only water and some animal creatures, as the old people used to tell. The fowl of the air and the sun met together: they held council [on] what they could do to find the earth. The sun took the lead at their meeting. They asked the animals in the water to search for earth; they expected the beaver could find some earth, but he could not. And then they expected the fish-otter to dive, but he also could not do it. Thereupon they asked the crawfish, who said, "If I dive into the water, the following signs will show you: if I cannot come back to the surface of the water, blood will rise up. If, however, I come back with earth, some dirty yellow water will rise to the surface." He did not know whether he could get to where the earth was, but they sent him anyway. He went down into the water, and after they had waited for a long time, they saw some dirty yellow water coming to the surface, and then the crawfish himself appeared with a little dirt between his claws. It was only very little dirt; they took it and hit it against something that was sticking out of the water, and the earth was made. Some storytellers, however, say that they just threw the earth upon the water and then the earth was made. The crawfish had dived for earth for a long time, and when he came back to the surface of the water the dirt had almost melted, just a little was left over; after the earth was made, the other animals were also created.

At first there was no light on the earth, and so they all met under the leadership of the sun to look for someone who would light the earth. They expected the glow-worm could do it; it flew around, but it only made very faint gleams of light. Then they asked the star. He also made only a dim light, and then they asked the moon too; she gave light, but it was still too dark. Then they expected the sun could do it, and up she went. Just as soon as she came up, the earth was flooded with light; all the creatures on earth were glad and sang aloud. Right at noon the sun stopped on her way. When they saw it, they said the sun should light the earth that way. And then some were saying, it only should be day and never night. Others said, it would be good if there would be day as well as night; in this way they talked with one another. After a while the ground squirrel said, "I say, the night also should be for the people to have intercourse so that they can increase." And then they all agreed with each other that day should be and night as well. The sun should make the light during the daytime and the moon and stars during the night; they all agreed that day and night should be separate. Then the ground squirrel said, "I said it and it is done that way"; every now and then he said this, and then the wildcat got mad at him; "Oh, pshaw, even if you did say it, you should say it only once," he said; he jumped on him and scratched him all over, and so the ground squirrel became spotted.

When the earth was just made it was soft, and they thought it would be good if the ground were flat. Nobody was to go over it so that it could dry. They sent the buzzard to inspect the earth; he was not to flop with his wings but only to spread them out and fly around; while he was flying he noticed tracks where somebody must have gone; he traced them and it happened to be a bullfrog whom he overtook. "Nobody is to go on the ground and here you are!" he said; he whipped him with his wings, and the bullfrog cried, and his eyebrows swelled. The buzzard flew on, and while he was flying he saw again some tracks; he traced them and when he overtook them he saw it had been a raccoon who was fishing for crawfish; he whipped him too and the raccoon's face became spotted; the buzzard was only to spread his wings, he was to fly to the other side of the earth, but he got tired and almost fell to the ground, and then he flopped; when he ascended again, the mountains were made. They had sent him to inspect the earth; he flew around but he got tired, and so he flopped and the mountains were made.[4]

In the comparison of the Yuchi text with the Taskigi, we see an illustration of the way in which individual legends are easily built into longer stories by combination. The episode called "earth-diver" is the only plot of the Taskigi narrative, and it is known in separate form from the Cherokee,[5] while the Yuchi informant combined it with "origin of light," "origin of day and night" (A1172), "buzzard creates mountains," and the origins of chipmunks' and raccoons' spots and the bullfrog's swollen eyes. The one-motif legend of Taskigi appears as a seven-motif legend among the Yuchi. It is interesting that when Speck collected the earlier Yuchi texts, he recorded as separate legends the origin of light and day/night and the chipmunks' spots; the "earth-diver" was coupled only to the buzzard's creation of mountains. It is frustrating that Swanton was told by his Creek informants that "there was once a long myth of this kind, most of which has been lost."[6]

The details of the "earth-diver" agree fairly well. The basic assumption is that the Above World and the Under World, with the animals which belong to each, already exist. The Above World people, the birds, meet in council to discuss the creation of land. They are headed by the Sun (or Eagle for the Taskigi, which may be the same thing). Apparently they need some raw material, soil which lies beneath the water of the Under World. Beaver and Otter try to get some, but fail; the Taskigi dove flies to seek some, but fails. In both texts it is the crawfish who makes the successful dive and produces the soil which the chief of the council magically expands into the earth island which floats on the top of the water.

Simple as this creation story may appear, it is one of the most widely known of all myths, and is probably one of the oldest. In North America it is found throughout the Eastern Woodlands and the northern Plains across to the Northwest. Missing in the distribution are the Northeast, the Southwest, the Northwest Coast, the Eskimo, and the Caddoan and Siouan tribes of the Plains, which have other types of creation account.[7] The distribution is not restricted to that northern and eastern sweep, however, for it is found across northern Asia and Europe to Hungary and Germany. Count studied 230 texts and concluded that "earth-diver" is "easily among the most widespread single concepts held by man."[8] Rooth later examined all the creation texts of North America alone, about three hundred of them, and found that there are only eight types of creation legend, four of which show affinity to Asia and four of which belong to the Mesoamerican world. "Earth-diver" is the major Asian connection.[9]

There appears to be some confusion in the nature of the water in which the diving is done; most see it as the primeval water, while some cast it as the great deluge, also a worldwide motif. Notice the changes brought about in the other Southeastern text.

The Flood ■ ■ ■
CHITIMACHA

When the great deluge came the people baked a great earthen pot, in which two persons saved themselves, being borne up upon the surface of the waters. With them went two rattlesnakes. So the rattlesnake was thought to be the friend of man, and it is maintained that in ancient times each house was protected by one of these serpents, which entered it whenever its owner went away and retired when he came back. While the flood prevailed the redheaded woodpecker hooked his claws into the sky and hung there. The water rose so high that his tail was partly submerged and sediment deposited upon it by the disturbed waters marked it off sharply from the rest of the body as it is to-day. After the sea had subsided considerably this bird was sent to find land, but after a long search he came back empty-handed. Then the dove was sent and returned with a single grain of sand. This was placed upon the surface of the sea and made to stretch out in order to form the dry land. Therefore the dove is called Ne-he'tcmon, "Ground-watcher," because it first saw the ground come out when the great flood subsided.[10]

This text includes several items of interest. The "earth-diver" is made part of the flood story, which also includes an explanation of the relationship between humans and rattlesnakes and the origin of woodpeckers' tail stripes[11]; the latter is known primarily in the Southwest tribes. The dove sounds as if it may reflect Biblical influence, but it is difficult to say, because we have seen the same bird in the Taskigi legend, and it also appears as an explanation of the origin of corn among the Choctaw.[12] Here is a Creek version from "Big Jack, a leading repository of native lore among the Hilibi":

Earth-Diver ▪ ▪ ▪
CREEK

Anciently there was a flood of waters, upon which floated a canoe in which were some human beings and animals of all kinds. The opossum hung to the side of the canoe with its tail in the water, and that is how it happens to have a tail practically devoid of hair at the present time. The red-headed woodpecker hung to the sky and the tip of his tail was discolored permanently. Afterwards the creatures wanted to get some earth. First the earthworm started down after it, but the fishes seized him and ate him up. Next the crawfish started down, but he did not come up again. Finally the dove flew away and brought earth from beyond the horizon, and from this the dry land of to-day was formed.[13]

Some researchers have concluded that the primeval water is earlier than the deluge, and the flood/earth-diver is a later amalgamation.[14] The flood also occurs without the "earth-diver" motif.

The Flood ▪ ▪ ▪
ALABAMA

When this world was almost lost in the waters a frog predicted it. One man seized the frog and threw it into the fire, but another said, "Don't do that." He took it, cared for it, and healed it, and it said to him, "The land will almost disappear in the waters. Make a raft and put a thick layer of grass underneath so that the beavers cannot cut holes through the wood." So he cut long dry sticks of wood and tied them together and put a quantity of grass underneath.

When other people saw this they said, "Why did you make it?" He answered, "A flood is going to cover the whole country." "Nothing like that can happen," they said. Some persons stayed about laughing at him. After some time he finished his raft and the flood came. When it arrived fish came with it and some of the people killed them and said, "We are having a good time." The man and his family got upon the raft along with the frog.

When the water rose the raft went up also, and some of the people said, "We want to get on," but no one got on. When it rose higher all of the other people were drowned. Then those on the raft floated up with it. The flying things flew up to the sky and took hold of it, with their tails half in the water. The ends of their tails got wet. The red-headed woodpecker was flat against the sky and said, "My tail is half in the water."[15]

The widespread distribution of the flood legend in the Southeast, despite the variation the texts display, argues that the flood is an old tradition there. By contrast, the few appearances of the earth-diver, once linked to the flood, pose a problem: Why are the Muskhogeans lacking in this ancient motif? It could be an accident of collecting, but that doesn't seem likely. It seems more likely that there is an alternative origin tradition. In fact, there is an alternate legend complex that seems peculiar to the Mugkhogeans and has been much collected. While it is generally referred to as the "migration legend," most texts include a significant motif—"emergence." Here is an example of the legend.

Emergence ■ ■ ■
ALABAMA/CREEK

Of their Origin or coming into the Country, some old Mingoes (chiefs) relate, that they lived under the Earth in great Darkness and saw no Sun; they hunted, but got nothing, they lived upon Linowa (Mice) which they killed with their Hands; the Ground Hog had worked a Hole through the Ground, through which some of them crept out, ran about upon the Earth, and finding a dead Deer, they brought the Meat into the Earth: the good Taste of it, and the Account of how light and fine it was upon the Earth, brought them to the Resolution, to go out of their dark Place; some stayed behind, those coming forth, began to plant Corn etc. etc.[16]

One of the earliest notices of the Alabama emergence legend was collected from Se-ko-pe-chi ("Perseverance") in 1847 in Oklahoma: "The origin of the Alabama Indians as handed down by oral tradition, is that they sprang out of the ground, between the Cahawba and Alabama Rivers."[17]

Emergence ■ ■ ■
CHOCTAW

A very long time ago the first creation of men was in Nanih Waiya (a very well-known mound near Philadelphia, Mississippi) and there they were made and there they came forth. The Muscogees (Creeks) first came out of Nanih Waiya, and they then sunned themselves on Nanih Waiya's earthen rampart, and when they got dry they went to the east. On this side of the Tombigbee, there they rested and as they were smoking tobacco they dropped some fire.

The Cherokees next came out of Nanih Waiya. And they sunned themselves on the earthen rampart, and when they got dry they went and followed the trail of the elder tribe. And at the place where the Muscogees had stopped and rested, and where they had smoked tobacco, there was fire and the woods were burnt, and the Cherokees could not find the Muscogees' trail, so they got lost and turned aside and went towards the north and there toward the north they settled and made a people.

And the Chickasaws third came out of Nanih Waiya. And then they sunned themselves on the earthen rampart, and when they got dry they went and followed the Cherokees' trail. And when they got to where the Cherokees had settled and made a people, they settled and made a people close to the Cherokees.

And the Choctaws fourth and last came out of Nanih Waiya. And they then sunned themselves on the earthen rampart and when they got dry, they did not go anywhere but settled down in this very land and it is the Choctaws' home.[18]

The geographical distribution of the emergence motif in North America, already known as a strong Mesoamerican theme, has been studied. On the basis of 120 texts, it was possible to chart the fifty Native American groups which account for their origin as emergence from beneath the earth. "The emergence type has a continental distribution along a belt hugging the eastern and southern limits of the United States, extending from the Iroquois and Delaware in the East to the Mohave and the Yokuts (Tinlineh) of California. Another belt of distribution extends north-south through the middle of the continent, from the Mandan and Hidatsa on the Upper Missouri River to the Atakapa and the Tonkawa of the Gulf."[19] That distribution fits nicely against the earth-diver distribution, with a little overlap. It looks as if there are two major origin traditions in the Eastern Woodlands and Plains, a northern one (earth-diver) and a southern one (emergence). In the Southeast the fit is neat indeed. The Muskhogeans know the emergence motif, while the Yuchi and Cherokee, earth-diver groups, do not.

The Muskhogean connection with the Southwestern/Plains emergence tradition is supported by their legends of migration from the west into the Southeast. Wheeler-Voegelin and Moore noted that "linkage between the emergence myth and migration tales is a notable feature of the North American material; over half of our versions exhibit such a linkage."[20] This linkage is characteristic of the Muskhogean emergence texts. To get a sense of the similarities and differences in the range of texts, we will look at two of them, even though they are lengthy. Each of them is a composite of legends, and they are filled with ethnographic data, which will be noted.

An eighteenth-century Creek migration text, the earliest known, has a curious history. In 1735, two years after the inauguration of the Georgia settlement, a group of chiefs of the Creek met at Savannah with the English. Oglethorpe apparently had Thomas Christie make notes on the speech of the Creek leader, Chekilli, as it came from the translator. The original text is thus really secretarial notes on an oral rapid translation. Oglethorpe sent the text, along with the pictographic skin which served as mnemonic prompter for the teller, to London, where it eventually vanished. Before the English translation was lost, however, it was translated into German and published in Germany. In the 1880s Gatschet located it and had it translated back into English and Muskhogean, then published it in a lengthy study.[21] Several decades later the original English version was located in the Fulham archives in London and was published in 1931.[22] The following text is taken from Gatschet because it is more readable, but several slight changes have been made to bring it into accord with the original; the Muskhogean names have been standardized. The narrator claimed to be head chief of all the Creeks and the son of Brims of Kasihta, leading talwa of the Lower Creeks on the Chattahoochee.

Emergence and Migration ■ ■ ■
KASIHTA (CREEK)

What Chekilli, the head-chief of the upper and lower Creeks said, in a talk held at Savannah, Anno 1735, and which was handed over by the interpreter, written upon a buffalo-skin was, word for word, as follows:

At a certain time the Earth opened in the West, where its mouth is. The Earth opened and the Kasihtas came out of its mouth, and settled nearby. But the Earth became angry and ate up their children; therefore they moved farther West. A part of them, however, turned back, and came again to the same place where they had been, and settled there. The greater number remained behind, because they thought it best to do so. Their children, nevertheless, were eaten by the Earth, so that, full of dissatisfaction, they journeyed toward the sunrise.

They came to a thick, muddy, slimy river—came there, camped there, rested there, and stayed overnight there. The next day they continued their journey and came, in one day, to a red, bloody river. They lived by this river, and ate of its fishes for two years; but there were low springs there; and it did not please them to remain. They went toward the end of this bloody river, and heard a noise as of thunder. They approached to see whence the noise came. At first they perceived a red smoke, and then a mountain which thundered; and on the mountain was a sound as of singing. They sent to see what this was; and it was a great fire which blazed upward, and made this singing noise. This mountain they named the King of Mountains. It thunders to this day; and men are very much afraid of it.

They here met a people of three different Nations. They had taken and saved some of the fire from the mountain; and, at this place, they also obtained a knowledge of herbs and of other things.

From the East, a white fire came to them; which, however, they would not use. From the South came a fire which was [blue?]; neither did they use it. From the West, came a fire which was black; nor would they use it. At last, came a fire from the North, which was red and yellow. This they mingled with the fire they had taken from the mountain; and this is the fire they use today; and this, too, sometimes sings. On the mountain was a pole which was very restless and made a noise, nor could any one say how it could be quieted. At length they took a motherless child, and struck it against the pole; and thus killed the child. They then took the pole, and carry it with them when they go to war. It was like a wooden tomahawk, such as they now use, and of the same wood.[23]

Here they also found four herbs or roots, which sang and disclosed their virtues: first, Pasaw, the rattlesnake root; second Micoweanochaw, red-root; third Sowatchko, which grows like wild fennel; and fourth, Eschalapootchke, little tobacco. These herbs, especially the first and third, they use as the best medicine to purify themselves at their Busk.[24] At this Busk, which is held yearly, they fast, and make offerings of the first fruits. Since they have learned the virtues of these herbs, their women, at certain times, have a separate fire, and remain apart from the men five, six, and seven days, for the sake of purification. If they neglected this, the power of the herbs would depart; and the women would not be healthy.[25]

About this time a dispute arose, as to which was the oldest, and which should rule; and they agreed, as they were four Nations, they would set up four poles, and make them red with clay which is yellow at first, but becomes red by burning. They would go to war; and whichever Nation should first cover its pole, from top to bottom, with the scalps of their enemies, should be oldest.

They all tried, but the Kasihtas covered their pole first, and so thickly that it was hidden from sight. Therefore, they were looked upon, by the whole Nation, as the oldest. The Chickasaws covered their pole next; then the Alabamas; but the Abihkas did not cover their pole higher than to the knee.[26]

At that time there was a bird of large size, blue in color, with a long tail, and swifter than an eagle, which came every day and killed and ate their people. They made an image in the shape of a woman, and placed it in the way of this bird. The bird carried it off, and kept it a long time, and then brought it back. They left it alone, hoping it would bring something forth. After a long time, a red rat came forth from it, and they believed the bird was the father of the rat. They took council with the rat how to destroy its father. Now the bird had a bow and arrows; and the rat gnawed the bowstring, so that the bird could not defend itself, and the people killed it. They called this bird the King of Birds. They think the eagle is a great King; and they carry its feathers when they go to War or make Peace; the red mean War; the white, Peace. If an enemy approaches with white feathers and a white mouth, and cries like an eagle, they dare not kill him.[27]

After this they left that place, and came to a white footpath. The grass and everything around were white; and they plainly perceived that people had been there. They crossed the path, and slept near there. Afterward they turned back to see what sort of path that was, and who the people were who had been there, in the belief that it might be better for them to follow that path. They went along it to a creek called Coloose-hutche, that is, Coloose-creek, because it was rocky there and smoked.[28]

They crossed it, going toward the sunrise, and came to a people and a town named Coosa.[29] Here they remained four years. The Coosas complained that they were preyed upon by a wild beast, which they called man-eater or lion, which lived in a rock.

The Kasihtas said they would try to kill the beast. They dug a pit and stretched over it a net made of hickory-bark. They then laid a number of branches, crosswise, so that the lion could not follow them, and, going to the place where he lay, they threw a rattle into his den. The lion rushed forth in great anger, and pursued them through the branches. Then they thought it better that one should die rather than all; so they took a motherless child, and threw it before the lion as he came near the pit. The lion rushed at it, and fell in the pit, over which they threw the net, and killed him with blazing pine-wood. His bones, however, they keep to this day; on one side, they are red, on the other blue.

The lion used to come every seventh day to kill the people; therefore, they remained there seven days after they had killed him. In remembrance of him, when they prepare for War, they fast six days and start on the seventh. If they take his bones with them, they have good fortune.[30]

After four years they left the Coosas, and came to a river which they called Nowphawpe, now Callasi-hutche. There they tarried two years; and, as they had no corn, they lived on roots and fishes, and made bows, pointing the arrows with beaver teeth and flint-stones, and for knives they used split canes.

They left this place, and came to a creek, called Wattoola-hawka-hutche, Whooping-creek, so called from the whooping of cranes, a great many being there; they slept there one night. They next came to a river, in which there was a waterfall; this they named the Owatunka-river. The next day they reached another river, which they called the Aphoosa pheeskaw.

The following day they crossed it, and came to a high mountain, where were people who, they believed, were the same who made the white path. They, therefore, made white arrows and shot at them, to see if they were good people. But the people took their white arrows, painted them red, and shot them back. When they showed these to their chief, he said that it was not a good sign; if the arrows returned had been white, they could have gone there and brought food for their children, but as they were red they must not go. Nevertheless, some of them went to see what sort of people they were; and found their houses deserted. They also saw a trail which led into the river; and, as they could not see the trail on the opposite bank, they believed that the people had gone into the river, and would not again come forth.[31]

At that place is a mountain, called Moterelo, which makes a noise like beating on a drum; and they think this people live there. They hear this noise on all sides when they go to war.

They went along the river, till they came to a waterfall, where they saw great rocks, and on the rocks were bows lying; and they believed the people who made the white path had been there.

They always have, on their journeys, two scouts who go before the main body. These scouts ascended a high mountain and saw a town. They shot white arrows into the town; but the people of the town shot back red arrows. Then the Kasihtas became angry, and determined to attack the town, and each one have a house when it was captured.

They threw stones into the river until they could cross it, and took the town (the people had flattened heads)[32] and killed all but two persons. In pursuing these they found a white dog, which they slew. They followed the two who escaped, until they came again to the white path, and saw the smoke of a town, and thought that this must be the people they had so long been seeking. This is the place where now the tribe of Apalachicolas live, from whom Tomochichi is descended.[33]

The Kasihtas continued bloody-minded; but the Apalachicolas gave them black drink, as a sign of friendship,[34] and said to them: "Our hearts are white, and yours must be white, and you must lay down the bloody tomahawk, and show your bodies as a proof that they shall be white." Nevertheless, they were for the tomahawk; but the Apalachicolas got it by persuasion, and buried it under their beds.[35] The Apalachicolas likewise gave them white feathers, and asked to have a chief in common. Since then they have always lived together.

Some settled on one side of the river, some on the other. Those on one side are called Kasihtas, those on the other, Cowetas; yet they are one people, and the principal towns of the Upper and Lower Creeks. Nevertheless, as the Kasihtas first saw the red smoke and the red fire, and make bloody towns, they cannot yet leave their red hearts, which, though white on one side, are red on the other. They now know that the white path was the best for them: for, although Tomochichi was a stranger, they see he has done them good; because he went to see the great King with Esquire Oglethorpe, and hear his talk, and had related it to them, and they had listened to it, and believed it.[36]

This is a Creek text; what follows is a Choctaw equivalent. The differences in detail and organization make it appear quite different from the Kasihta text, but some similarities emerge nonetheless. The major similarity, of course, is the simple fact of the sharing of the emergence/migration tradition.

Emergence and Migration ■ ■ ■
CHOCTAW

In ancient days the ancestors of the Choctaws and the Chickasaws lived in a far western country, under the rule of two brothers, named Chahta and Chikasa. In process of time, their population becoming very numerous, they found it difficult to procure subsistence in that land. Their prophets thereupon announced that far to the east was a country of fertile soil and full of game, where they could live in ease and plenty. The entire population resolved to make a journey eastward in search of that happy land. In order more easily to procure subsistence on their route, the people marched in several divisions of a day's journey apart. A great prophet marched at their head, bearing a pole, which, on camping at the close of each day, he planted erect in earth, in front of the camp. Every morning the pole was always seen leaning in the direction they were to travel that day. After the lapse of many moons, they arrived one day at Nanih Waiya. The prophet planted his pole at the base of the mound. The next morning the pole was seen standing erect and stationary. This was interpreted as an omen from the Great Spirit that the long sought-for land was at last found. It so happened, the very day that the party camped at Nanih Waiya, that a party under Chikasa crossed the creek and camped on its east side. That night a great rain fell, and it rained several days. In consequence of this all the low lands were inundated, and Nanih Waiya Creek and other tributaries of Pearl River were rendered impassable.

After the subsidence of the waters, messengers were sent across the creek to bid Chikasa's party return, as the oracular pole had proclaimed that the long sought-for land was found and the mound was the center of the land. Chikasa's party, however, regardless of the weather, had proceeded on their journey, and the rain having washed traces of their march from off the grass, the messengers were unable to follow them up and so returned to camp. Meanwhile, the other divisions in the rear arrived at Nanih Waiya, and learned that here was the center of their new home and that their long pilgrimage was at last finished. Chikasa's party, after their separation from their brethren under Chahta, moved on to the Tombigbee, and eventually became a separate nationality. In this way the Choctaws and the Chickasaws became two separate though kindred nations.[37]

Philosophically the two origin traditions differ in that the earth-diver assumes the pre-existence of water, while the emergence/migration assumes the earth itself. Some emergence myths, as found in the Southwest and Caddoans, elaborate the earth into levels, but the Southeastern version merely starts with a hole in the ground. In either case the Middle World becomes the abode of humans and other people, caught in the tension between the Above and Under Worlds.

CHAPTER SIX

The Tribes of People

One of the cultural differences that strikes the European mind when it confronts Native American legends is the attitude toward other species. Whereas Europeans tend to consider other animals and plants as subordinate creatures, Native Americans see them as people with minds and wills, who must be dealt with in the same ways as humans. Other species are structured in social and political organizations much like the human tribes. Councils of animals make weighty decisions that have impact on human life, and peaceful relations need to be maintained across species as much as within the two-legged group. We have already seen that in the Southeasterners' view the telling of myths is itself a human activity that must be done correctly if the humans are to avoid war with various other animals.

Humans made this attitude toward other animals part of their social organization. In the Southeast, every human was by birth a member of a clan; because descent was counted through the mother, her clan was automatically given to the newborn child. Each clan was understood to be in a special relationship with a particular animal, the clan *totem,* so each clan member lived in the awareness of certain taboos that must not be violated. Such taboos dealt with foods which could not be eaten and animals which could not be killed. One should never marry a person from one's own clan. As we might expect, legends surrounded each clan's totem, both explaining the characteristics of the clan and their relationships to each other. Here is a legend that deals very directly with the origins of clans.

The Origin of Animals (Clans) ▪ ▪ ▪
TASKIGI (CREEK)

The old-time beings were gathered together. They began acting in different ways and showing different qualities. Master-of-Breath observed them. Some

118

began jumping upon trees and running about. Someone asked, "What sort of beings are those?" "They are like panthers," someone answered. "Henceforth they shall go about as panthers," said Master-of-Breath. Then again, some began leaping and running. "What are they like?" someone asked. "Like deer," it was said. "Henceforth they shall go about as deer," said Master-of-Breath. Then again, some went hopping high among the leaves of trees and alighted on the branches. "What are they like?" asked somebody. "Like birds," someone answered. "They shall be birds," said Master-of-Breath. Then again, some were very fat and when they walked they made a great noise on the ground. "What are they like?" asked someone. "Like bears," was the answer. "They shall be bears, then," said Master-of-Breath. Then again, one started off to run but could not go fast. When he came back he had black stripes near his eyes. "What will that be?" (it) was asked. "It is like a raccoon," said one. "That kind shall be raccoons," said Master-of-Breath. Then one was so fat and round-bodied that when he started off he could hardly walk. "What is that kind?" (it) was asked. "It is like a beaver," someone answered. "They shall be the beavers," said Master-of-Breath. Then again, one kind was fat and could not run very fast. When this one had gone off to a distance and returned, someone asked, "What is that like?" "Like a mink." "They shall go about as minks," said Master-of-Breath. Then again, one was very swift when he started to run. He darted back and forth very quickly. "What is he like?" was the question. "Like a fox," came the answer. "That kind shall be foxes," said Master-of-Breath. Then again, one was very strong and could pull up saplings by the roots. He went off to a distance and returned. Then someone asked, "What is he like?" "Like the wind," was the answer. "That kind shall be wind," said Master-of-Breath. Then again, one started off into the mud. When he had come back out of it, someone asked, "What is he like?" "Like a mud-potato," it was answered. "Such shall be mud-potatoes," said Master-of-Breath. Then again, one of them had short legs, and his back was covered with ridges. When he started out and returned, someone asked, "What is he like?" "Like an alligator," was the answer. "That kind shall be alligators," said Master-of-Breath. Then again, one with stripes on his back went running off, and when he came back, someone asked, "What is he like?" "Like a skunk," was the answer. "That kind shall be skunks," said Master-of-Breath. Then again, one went away jumping, and when he came back to the starting place, someone asked, "What is he like?" "Like a rabbit," was the answer. "That kind shall be rabbits," said Master-of-Breath. Then again, one went off squirming along on the ground. When he returned, someone asked, "What is he like?" "Like a snake," was the answer. "That kind shall be snakes," said Master-of-Breath.

Master-of-Breath, after he had given them their forms on the earth, told them not to marry their own kind, but to marry people of other clans. All the red people know what clans they belong to and do not marry in their own clan. If they did they would not increase.[1]

Clans were a very important fact of life in the Native American world, and that fact cautions us to be sensitive to the ways in which animals appear in apparently simple animal legends. Although it is doubtful that the specific connotations of animal behavior can now be interpreted properly, it is important to remember that Native Americans in earlier days would have heard the stories on many deeper levels, for each person was intimately identified with at least one animal.

The Man Who Became a Deer ■ ■ ■
CHOCTAW

One night a hunter killed a doe and soon afterward fell asleep near the carcass. The next morning, just at sunrise, the hunter was surprised and startled to see the doe raise her head and to hear her speak, asking him to go with her to her home. At first he was so surprised that he did not know what to reply, so the doe again asked him whether he would go. Then the hunter said that he would go with her, although he had no idea where she would lead him. So they started and the doe led the hunter through forests and over high mountains, until at last they reached a large hole under a rock, which they entered. Here the hunter was led before the King of all the deer, an immense buck, with huge antlers and a large black spot on his back. Soon the hunter became drowsy and finally he fell asleep. Now all around the cave were piles of deer's feet, antlers, and skins. While the hunter was asleep the deer endeavored to fit to his hands and feet deer's feet which they selected for the purpose. After several unsuccessful attempts the fourth set proved to be just the right size and were fastened firmly on the hunter's hands and feet. Then a skin was found that covered him properly, and finally antlers were fitted to his head. And then the hunter became a deer and walked on four feet after the manner of deer.

Many days passed, and the hunter's mother and all his friends thought he had been killed. One day when they were in the forest they found his bow and arrows hanging on a branch of the tree beneath which he had slept beside the body of the doe. All gathered around the spot and began singing, when suddenly they saw a herd of deer bounding toward them through the forest. The deer then circled about the singers. One large buck approached closer than the others, and the singers, rushing forward, caught it. To the great astonishment of all it spoke, whereupon they recognized the voice of the lost hunter. Greatly distressed, the hunter's mother begged her companions to remove from her son the deer skin and antlers and feet, but they told her he would certainly die if they should do so. She insisted, however, saying she would rather bury her son than to have him remain a deer. So her friends began tearing away the skin, which already had grown to the hunter's body, and, as they continued their efforts to remove it, the

120

blood began to flow. Finally the hunter died. Then his body was taken back to the village and was buried with the ceremony of a great dance.[2]

In the Native American view, not only can humans turn into other species and vice versa, but also humans can be befriended by animals. The consequence of receiving favor from a powerful animal is to be given power in one or more areas, such as war, hunting, or medicine. The form this usually takes is probably an ancient one stemming from the hunting tradition. Among many Eastern tribes the "vision quest" as a means of seeking such animal assistance has survived to the present day. Accounts that describe it usually place it in a shamanistic context: the human takes a journey to the lodge of the species in question, passes tests, receives the gift of power, and returns to his people, with various conclusions. We have already met the man who was befriended by the tie-snakes. Here are similar legend texts.

Water People ■ ■ ■
HITCHITI

A boy carrying his bow and arrows was walking about near the water, when two women standing close to the shore said, "Follow us." Then he leaned his bow up against a tree and followed them, and presently those women said, "We are going down into the water. Go down in with us." So saying, they started on, and just as they had said, they presently went down into the water, that boy with them. When all got in, the bottom was as if there were no water there, and before they had gone far they came to where there were some old water people. Those old men said, "There is a chair. Sit down." The chair they thus indicated to him was a very big water turtle. "They spoke to me," the youth related, "and I sat down and they said, 'Do you want to lie down? There is a bed. You must lie down. The tree-tyer (tie-snake) there is the bed,' they said to me. Presently they said, 'You can go hunting if you want to.' 'I cannot go hunting because I have no gun.' But the old men said, 'Go about hunting, and when you fall down somewhere come back.' After they had said this to me I set out, and while I was walking around, there was a rumbling noise and I fell down. I lay there for a while, and then came to my senses and returned to them. When I got back the old men said, 'What did you kill?' 'I killed nothing,' I answered, 'but I fell down and was unconscious. After I had lain there for a while I came back, but I did not kill anything.' 'Let us go and look at the place where you fell,' said those old men. Immediately we started, and when we got there, a very big thing of some sort was lying there dead. 'It is just as we said,' said they, and they brought it back. Then they ate. After I had been there for a while those old men said, 'If you want to go, you may,' and I said, 'I will go.' 'You take him back,' they said to someone, and just as I thought, 'They are going to take me along,' I lost consciousness. Next I came to my senses standing close to the water, exactly where I had been when they took me off. 'My bow is standing up against a tree,' I thought, and when I got to the place, there it was just as I had thought, and I took it and started off. When I got to the place where my people lived, they were there. Then they said, 'The one who has been lost for such a long time is back.' The old men compounded medicine for me and after a while I got well,'' said the boy.

They used to tell it so.[3]

Alligator Power ■ ■ ■
CHOCTAW

One winter there were many hunters living in a village, all of whom, with one exception, had killed a great many deer. But one had met with very poor luck, and although he often succeeded in getting close to deer, just ready to draw his bow on them, they always contrived to escape unharmed. He had been away from his village three days, and during that time had seen many deer, but had not been able to kill a single one. On the third day, when the sun was overhead, the hunter saw a huge alligator resting on a dry, sandy spot.

This alligator had been without water for many days, and was dry and shriveled and so weak that he could scarcely speak. He was able, however, to ask the hunter where water could be had. The hunter replied, "In that forest, only a short journey hence, is a clear, deep pool of cold water." "But I cannot travel alone; I am too weak to go so far. Come nearer that we may talk and plan. I can not harm you; have no fear," said the alligator.

At last the hunter went nearer and listened to the alligator, who said: "I know you are a hunter, but all the deer escape from you. Now, carry me to the water and I will then make you a great hunter and tell you how to kill many, many deer." The hunter hesitated, as he feared the alligator, and then he said: "I will carry you, but not unless I may bind your legs so you cannot scratch, and your mouth so you cannot bite me." The alligator rolled over on his back and held up his legs, saying, "I am helpless; bind me and do with me as you will."

Then the hunter bound with a cord the alligator's legs and mouth. Then he lifted the animal to his shoulder and carried him to the water. When they reached the pool the hunter loosened the cords and the alligator plunged into the water. It went down, then returned to the surface three times, then went down again and remained a long time. At last he rose again to the surface and spoke to the hunter, saying: "You brought me to the water; now listen, and if you do as I counsel you will become a great hunter. Take your bow and arrows and go into the woods. You will first meet a small doe, but do not kill it. Next you will meet a large doe, but you must not shoot this one, either. Then you will see a small buck, but this likewise must be spared. Lastly you will encounter a very large, old buck. Go very close to it and kill it, and ever afterward you will be able to kill many deer."

The hunter did as the alligator told him, and never again was without venison in his camp.[4]

Bear People ■ ■ ■
ALABAMA

The people living in a certain town went about hunting. While they were doing so some of them saw a white bear, but the others could not see it. By and by one of the men hunting about killed the white bear and took it home. He returned with it shouting and happy and all divided it up, cooked it, came together and ate it. When they got through they played ball, being very joyful at their success.

Then one man said, "Are you all glad? It is wrong to be so." Later when this man was walking alone in the forest a big Bear stood in front of him and said, "They have killed my chief. I am going to kill the people. If you believe me, tell your people. If they believe you, take them to the other side of the creek." When he got home he told his people, and some of them believed him, and, when he started to move, they followed, while others did not believe him, and did not follow.

After some time a bear came to the people and they killed it. Another one came and they killed that. Still another came. Next two came. Then three came. Then four came. The number kept increasing until ten came. After that more and more came until they had destroyed all of the people.

Afterwards the man went out and the Bear met him. It said, "Kill and eat us any time you wish and we will not hurt you."[5]

These legends reveal a crucial fact about the Native American attitude toward hunting. The ability to kill game is not so much a matter of skill as it is a question of having "power" granted by the animals themselves. Any hunter is therefore by necessity involved in close relationships with a variety of species.

Because of the close identification of humans and animals in Native American thought, it is sometimes difficult to tell when stories about animals are entertainment, when they communicate clan information, and when they are mythic, in the sense that they tell of the ordering of the world in the primal time. Here are a few texts which can be read in several ways.

The Killing of the Deer ■ ■ ■
ALABAMA

When as yet there were no other deer in the world, a fawn was made and kept in a certain place, and Wildcat was set to watch it. They said to him, "Let it grow a little bigger." Then he killed it, and they restored it to life. Next they set the Wolf to watch it. After a time he killed it. They restored it to life and they set the Panther to watch it. They said to him, "Let it grow until it is almost a big buck." He killed it. Then they restored it to life again. Next Bird-that-sits-on-deer watched. While he was doing so it became big. He sat on the horn and ate ticks, and every now and then he would fly away and come back.

After that the wind blew from the north, the bird flew away to seek shelter in the moss, and while he was asleep the deer disappeared. Next morning he did not know where the deer had gone and hunted for it in vain. He said to the people, "It is gone."

The people wanted to find out where it was, so they assembled all of the prophets *(sobaile).* [6] They made a yard and kindled a fire in the center. For the same purpose they collected all sorts of medicines. One prophet sat down but could not learn anything. Another one sat down to find out but in vain. Still another sat down and could not discover anything. Last of all they asked Flying Squirrel, who began by saying repeatedly, "I do not know anything." He flew up toward the east and remained poised. He remained for a while and then came back to the ground. He flew up to the west, remained for some time, and came down. He flew up to the north, remained for some time, and came down. He flew to the south, remained for a while, and came down. Then he said, "It is standing on a palmetto *(tala)* island in a small lake far off in that direction (to the south)."

Then they wanted to summon it. For that purpose they gathered medicines and mixed them. They made a fire and their prophet stayed by it all night, and when it was almost day they heard it approaching, trumpeting. It shook the earth like a railroad train. Then the men got their bows and arrows and stood ready to shoot it, with ghosts just behind them, Panthers in the third row, Wolves in the fourth, and Wildcats last. When the Deer got close, the Wildcats became scared and did not stand. They trembled. "We want very much to defecate," they said, and ran away.

When the Deer arrived the men tried to shoot it but did not succeed; the ghosts hit it; the Panthers jumped upon it and threw it down. With the help of the Wolves they killed it. Then the Wildcats came running back and bit it in the throat, until a man told them to let it alone. "Now it is dead," he said. They stopped, and sat down licking their feet. Then the men procured sticks and tore the deer to pieces, whereupon each hair that flew out turned into a deer and ran off into the woods.

Then all of the people started off and camped in another place. They went hunting and when they came together again the people had killed a deer. The Panthers also killed one. The Wildcats, however, killed and brought back a yellow mouse. Again all went out hunting and came back, each with a deer, except that the Wildcats brought a rabbit. The next time they went out all came together again with deer except the Wildcats, who killed and brought in a turkey gobbler. The fourth time they went hunting all came together with deer but the Wildcats, who had killed and brought in a fawn. [7]

The Origin of Poison ▪ ▪ ▪
CHOCTAW

Long ago a certain vine grew along the edges of bayous, in shallow water.

This vine was very poisonous, and often when the Choctaw would bathe or swim in the bayous they would come in contact with the vine and often become so badly poisoned that they would die as a result.[8]

Now the vine was very kind and liked the Choctaw and consequently did not want to cause them so much trouble and pain. He would poison the people without being able to make known to them his presence there beneath the water. So he decided to rid himself of the poison. A few days later he called together the chiefs of the snakes, bees, wasps, and other similar creatures and told them of his desire to give them his poison, for up to that time no snake, bee or wasp had the power it now possesses, namely that of stinging a person.

The snakes and bees and wasps, after much talk, agreed to share the poison. The rattlesnake was the first to speak and he said: "I shall take the poison, but before I strike or poison a person I shall warn him by the noise of my tail *(intesha);* then if he does not heed me I shall strike."

The water moccasin was the next to speak:

"I also am willing to take some of your poison; but I shall never poison a person unless he steps on me."

The small ground rattler was the last of the snakes to speak:

"Yes, I will gladly take of your poison and I will also jump at a person whenever I have a chance." And so it has continued to do ever since.[9]

The care with which this legend discriminates between the characteristics of poisonous snakes reveals both the Native American respect for snakes (killing them was a taboo) and their intimate knowledge of them.

The Killing of Turkey ■ ■ ■
BILOXI

The Wild Turkey was killing very many human beings. He took their scalps, and wore their hair as a necklace; therefore the turkey has a tuft of hair at the present day. He took off the fingernails of the people and strung them, wrapping the strings of nails around his legs; consequently a turkey's legs are now covered with ridges just above the feet.

The people could find no way to kill the Wild Turkey because he ran so fast; therefore they set the Dog on him, and the Dog did not have to run very far before he caught the Wild Turkey and killed him. Then men made a dinner in honor of the Dog: they told him that he should be eating the very best kinds of food; but they had there all kinds of food. Then the Dog said, "I am going to eat the food which others leave." And the Dog took some mush which was there, went aside, sat down and spent some time in eating it. Therefore dogs do not eat the best kinds of food, but those which are regarded as inferior, or what is left.[10]

Red-winged Blackbird ■ ■ ■
CHITIMACHA/ATAKAPA

A person once became angry and wanted to destroy the world, so he went down into the marshes and set fire to the dry grass. A little bird perched on a tree and made fun of him. "If you don't stop talking I will kill you," said the evil-disposed man. By and by, when the bird would not stop, he picked up a shell and threw it at the bird, which it hit in the shoulder, making it bleed. That is how the red-winged blackbird came by its red wings. When the fire came along to where a giant lived, he put his sister between the valves of a shell and held her up as high as he could reach. In doing so he made the corrugations on the shells that can be seen today. "Well!" he said. "I have saved my sister." The fire started up a great quantity of deer and other game, and men went down and killed them. Then they thanked the evil-minded man for benefiting them so much.[11]

Underlying these legends about animals is an important basic principle. The general idea is that there are "owners" or guardians of the economic necessities of life. The most widespread expression of this concept is probably the motif of the "hoarded game" (A1412) in which someone pens up the game. This motif has virtually universal distribution among the hunting tribes—across the northern part of the continent, down into California, across the Plateau region and throughout the Eastern Woodlands. It appears in Creek, Caddo, Biloxi, and Cherokee collections.

Owner of the Animals ■ ■ ■
CADDO

In those times the people had little to eat. There were two people, a man and a woman, known to the people as the Buzzards, who lived at the north end of the village, and the people noticed that they always had plenty of meat and other things to eat, and they wondered how they got it. Time passed until finally Coyote came among the people and told them that he was going over to visit the two people and find out where and how they got so much meat and so many other things to eat. In those times the animals that were living with the people had some magic powers, and Coyote had power. He said: "In order to find out where and how the Buzzard people get their food, I must scheme." After studying he resolved that he would imitate a dog, and so before he came to the Buzzard home he turned himself into a very small and fine-looking dog. He stayed away from the Buzzards and watched his opportunity to place himself where they would find him. One time the Buzzards had gone out some distance from their home for some purpose and were returning, when they found the little dog by the trail. The woman liked the dog, but the man said that it was not a real dog, but someone else. The woman did not believe him. The man allowed her to take the dog home with them. When they reached home he told her that they must find out whether this was a real dog or not. He told her to pinch the dog's ear and see if it would howl like a dog. The woman pinched the dog's ear and it howled like a dog. Still the man did not believe that it was a dog. He told the woman to go and get some meat and give it to the dog, saying that if a dog it would take its time, but if it were not a dog it would eat fast; that then he would know whether or not to believe that it was a dog. Coyote stayed with them until their meat gave out, then he watched them very closely. Finally the Buzzards began to talk about going after more meat. Coyote listened. At length they started out and left their dog at home. They thought the dog would stay at home until they returned. But Coyote had a scheme, so he followed at some distance, so that they could not see him, and he watched them very closely. When they came to the place where they usually found their meat, Coyote found out all about how and where they got it, then ran back to their home and lay down, so that when the Buzzards returned to their home they found their little dog lying there fast asleep. Coyote stayed with them two days longer, and the third day he made up his mind that he must carry out his work. Early one morning he started out straight to the place where he had seen the Buzzards at work. It was a large cave or hole in the ground. The door of the place was a large rock. When he came to the place he opened it and out came thousands and thousands of buffalo. They came out so fast that before long they had spread over the western prairies before the Buzzards knew it. It was quite a time before Buzzard discovered what had happened. First he heard a strange noise like thunder. He went and looked for the little dog, but in vain, for the dog had already gone. He heard Coyote howling in the distance. Buzzard went out and found that nearly all the buffalo had escaped.

When Coyote went to his home he told the people to hurry and make some bows and arrows, for the buffalo were coming. He told them just what had happened and how he had schemed.

Buzzard was very angry at his wife and scolded her. He told her that she ought to know by this time that they were not the only ones that had powers, and that henceforth the only way that they could make a living was to go around and look for dead meat. In order to do this they turned into birds and became real buzzards. They flew around and looked for dead things to eat.[12]

Hultkrantz and other students of comparative religion have identified the concept of the "owner of the animals" as one of the basic structural elements of the world-view of hunting cultures around the globe, and Hultkrantz has argued that "such dominant complexes of ideas as the belief in the guardian spirit, totemism and the culture hero can only be understood against the background of the concept of the owner of Nature..."[13] He suggests that the owner of the animals is a springboard for the development of ideas about the ownership of other commodities important in the economic life of a tribe.

There are also, naturally, other "guardians" or "owners" in North America than the animal guardian. The plants have their guardians, have also places—and so has man, for the Supreme Being is, of course, in principle a guardian or owner of men...It is incontestable that the animal guardian as such is especially well represented here and has a far more dominant position than other types of owners, at all events in the hunting religions.[14]

One of the other "owners" controlled all the water, at least in the beginning. From the Northwest to the Northeast there is found a legend of a giant frog or other monster who owned all the water, and it was released only when the culture hero killed the frog.[15] In the Southeast the same theme is more obscure. The Alabama legend tells of a gambler who was so successful that he won all the water in the world; unfortunately, the identity of the "man" who had the right to use it as a wager is not given.

The Impounded Water ■ ■ ■
ALABAMA

There is a game called *thlakalu'nka* (the moccasin game) which is played with four square pieces of deer hide placed upon a big bearskin laid down hair side up. The players having formed two sides, a man on one side takes a bullet, moves it about in his hands and after pretending to put it under various pieces of deer hide finally deposits it under one of them when he thinks the fact will escape observation. One of the opponents then guesses under which skin it has been placed, and if he is successful his party takes the bullet; if he fails two or three times another of his party tries his skill.

One time a man who was very fond of this game and who had a very considerable family was so unfortunate as to lose all of his possessions, down to his very clothes. Finally he wagered all the water of the world and lost that, upon which all of the streams, ponds, and other reservoirs of water dried up and everyone was dying of thirst. All were seeking water but did not know how they could get it.

By and by a Bicici'hka (a small speckled woodpecker with a red head) discovered a cane as big as a tree, lighted upon it, and began pecking. But before he had made much of a hole he heard a noise inside which frightened him and he flew away. He found someone and said to him, "Something is making a noise inside of a cane." The person answered, "It is water," so he went back to the place and pecked a hole all the way through, when the water gushed out and all of the creeks were overflowed. All the creatures drank and were very happy.[16]

The Koasati text differs only in naming the woodpecker Tososohka and adding people with axes. "Some men chopped with sharp axes and some with dull ones. While they were doing so the Tososohka chopped and cut through to

128

it."[17] These texts differ from the northern tradition of the impounded water, but the reason is not far to seek. Again, the South American mythology seems parallel, for the Twins complex includes the tradition of the great tree of abundance which was cut down by the people, with the resulting flood from its trunk. The Alabama-Koasati legends appear to be an amalgam of the impounded water and the cutting of the tree.

Another legend deals with this subject of the masters of nature. The race between the crane and the hummingbird appears in all the Creek groups, and the plot seems fairly standard, with little indication of any significance to the short legend.

Crane and Hummingbird Race ■ ■ ■
HITCHITI

Heron and Hummingbird agreed to race. They said to each other, "We will race for four days, and whichever first on the fourth day reaches and sits down by a big dead tree standing on the bank of the river shall own all the fish in the water." When the time for the race came, Heron started off, while Hummingbird went along or stopped as he chose. While he was going about tasting the flowers Heron overtook him and went on past, while Hummingbird when he got ready went on and overtook Heron. He passed him and when he got a considerable distance ahead tasted the flowers again. While he was flitting about, Heron kept on, reached him, and went past, but while he was going along Hummingbird overtook and passed him once more. When night came he stopped and slept. Hummingbird sat there asleep, but Heron traveled all night. He went on past and when day came Hummingbird chased him and again overtook him. They went on and the night of the fourth day Hummingbird also slept. He sat where he was until morning and then started on, but when he got to where the dead tree stood, Heron had reached it first and was sitting on it. When Hummingbird got there Heron said to him, "We agreed that whoever got to the dead tree first should own all of the water. Now all of the water is mine." Because Heron said to Hummingbird, "You must not drink water but only taste of the flowers when you travel about," Hummingbird has since merely tasted of the flowers.

This is how it has always been told.[18]

The Cherokee variant removes the mythic element by substituting a marriage for the fish and the water, with a wry twist at the end.

Crane and Hummingbird Race ■ ■ ■
CHEROKEE

The Hummingbird and the Crane were both in love with a pretty woman.

She preferred the Hummmingbird, who was as handsome as the Crane was awkward, but the Crane was so persistent that in order to get rid of him she finally told him he must challenge the other to a race and she would marry the winner. The Hummingbird was so swift—almost like a flash of lightning—and the Crane so slow and heavy, that she felt sure the Hummingbird would win. She did not know the Crane could fly all night.

They agreed to start from her house and fly around the circle of the world to the beginning, and the one who came in first would marry the woman. At the word the Hummingbird darted off like an arrow and was out of sight in a moment, leaving his rival to follow heavily behind. He flew all day, and when evening came and he stopped to roost for the night he was far ahead. But the Crane flew steadily all night long, passing the Hummingbird soon after midnight and going on until he came to a creek and stopped to rest about daylight. The Hummingbird woke up in the morning and flew on again, thinking how easily he would win the race, until he reached the creek and there found the Crane spearing tadpoles, with his long bill, for breakfast. He was very much surprised and wondered how this could have happened, but he flew swiftly by and soon left the Crane out of sight again.

The Crane finished his breakfast and started on, and when evening came he kept on as before. This time it was hardly midnight when he passed the Hummingbird asleep on a limb, and in the morning he had finished his breakfast before the other came up. The next day he gained a little more, and on the fourth day he was spearing tadpoles for dinner when the Hummingbird passed him. On the fifth and sixth days it was late in the afternoon before the Hummingbird came up, and on the morning of the seventh day the Crane was a whole night's travel ahead. He took his time at breakfast and then fixed himself up as nicely as he could at the creek and came in at the starting place where the woman lived, early in the morning. When the Hummingbird arrived in the afternoon he found he had lost the race, but the woman declared she would never have such an ugly fellow as the Crane for a husband, so she stayed single.[19]

A comparison of the two texts demonstrates a Cherokee peculiarity. While most Native Americans recognize four as the primary organizational number (actors in stories do things four times, and so on), the Cherokee operate in sevens. In this legend the Muskhogean race lasts four days, but the Cherokee race takes seven. The Cherokee legend has become an interesting tale, but the Creek tradition is clearly in the Master of Water category. In the Guianas in South America, however, the flight of the two birds is not a race, but a team effort to steal tobacco from the island where it is kept by the fabled Amazons.[20] A Bororo variant has the hummingbird steal the shamanistic rattle from the island, and among the Surura and Toba he steals fire.[21] This latter function is also found in the Southeast, but the role of the birds is filled by the Spider for the Cherokee and the Rabbit for the Muskhogeans, as we saw in Chapter 3. The Cherokee, however, tell an interesting legend about how Hummingbird stole tobacco.[22] Among the Botocudo and Caingaing of South America, however, the hummingbird is identified as the master of waters, from whom water and fish are stolen by the other animals.[23] The Southeastern texts are linked to this complicated South American tradition of the ownership of water, as over against the northern tradition of the slaying of the hoarder.

The tribes of animals were similar to the tribes of humans in their organization and in their ability to enter into relationship with each other. The legends we have looked at thus far focus on those relationships, both in the primal time when the present order was established and in modern times when individual humans have experienced fateful encounters with animals. While many of the legends seem innocuous in their plots, they were important in Native American life because they explained the relationships between species.

Big People and Little People.

The Middle World is inhabited by more than just the animal people. There are various strange beings who also have to be dealt with, including dangerous monsters and the Little People. The belief in such creatures can be found expressed in the traditions of most societies, of course, but the elaboration of detail about them in Southeastern lore indicates the large role they played in Native American thought.

In summarizing Southeastern mythology, Speck noted that

> . . . stories of monsters clad in bone, stone, metal, or scales are very character-
> istic of the region. The monster is usually a cannibal, and is finally slain by
> persons or beings who have learned the secret of its only vulnerable spot. The
> culture hero often appears as the slayer.[24]

Here is one story of "Stonecoat."

Stonecoat ■ ■ ■
YAMASEE/CHEROKEE

Ocasta (Stonecoat) was one of God's helpers. He was sent to help the Cherokee people. He had, however, much evil in his heart as well as good. When he got to earth he was walking through the woods looking for the Indian village when he saw a man with two sticks (the bow and arrow). The man pointed one of the sticks at a deer and the deer fell down. Ocasta ran over to the deer and pulled this little stick out. On the end of it was a flint point. Ocasta decided that if a man could kill a deer with a little point of stone that he might not be safe walking around, so he went about picking up bits of flint and made a coat of them to wear.

Ocasta had only one magic power, and this was the power to disappear. He could not disappear, however, in the presence of men. Ocasta soon made many bad things for the Indian people to follow. He made witches and other bad things and went about in spirit form from one village to another, causing trouble. The people soon decided that they didn't like this fellow, and so they devised a way to get rid of him.

At that time there were seven villages or clans of the Cherokee, so each village sent a moon-sick (menstruating) woman to a place where Ocasta was often seen to pass. Soon, indeed, he came along through the woods. All seven women laid down in the woods undressed. Ocasta came and saw the first woman. "Oh!" he said. "You should be ashamed to be seen like that!" Then he went on and saw each of the others in turn. Soon he became sick from seeing so many moon-sick women. When he came to the last one he fell down and became sick from seeing so many moon-sick women. When he came to the last one he was so sick he fell down on the ground and the woman jumped up and pulled back a bit of the flint on his coat and drove a wooden stake made of basswood through his heart to hold him down.

Then all the men gathered around and Ocasta said he would leave the earth soon and to burn his body with sour wood (basswood). Then he began to teach them songs and dances that would please God and help the tribe in their hunting and winning wars and healing the sick. To some men he gave great power and these were the first medicine men. As his body burned up his spirit began to rise up and he was still singing as he ascended. He had created evil and then sacrificed himself to save the people from the evil he had made.[25]

At the other end of the spectrum in size, but by no means in power, are the Little People, a belief in whom was virtually universal in the Eastern Woodlands and is still strong today. Among the Siouans, "The Omahas and Ponkas tell of a race of 'little people,' the *Gada'zhe,* or *Ni'kashinga Man'tanaha* (Wild People), who can produce wounds under (and without breaking) the skin." "The Quapaw believe in the existence of dwarfs, whom they call *Pahi zkajika,* Small ones with white hair, and *Wakantake jika,* Small mysterious ones. They are not seen often."[26]

Each Southeastern tribe had its own way of categorizing the Little People because their attributes were perceived differently, but they agreed on their existence and importance. Speck said of the Yuchi, "Little people like dwarfs are believed to inhabit certain places in the dense woods. They are the souls of bad people who die, and they possess the power of killing those who either accidentally or deliberately intrude upon their haunts."[27]

The Little People ▪ ▪ ▪
CREEK

The Creek Indians…call them *i'sti lupu'tski,* or "little people," but distinguish two sorts, the one being longer, the others shorter, in stature. The taller ones are called, from this very peculiarity, *i'sti tsa'ptsagi;* the shorter, or dwarfish ones, subdivide themselves again into (a) *itu'-uf-asa'ki* and (b) *i'sti tsa'htsa'na.* Both are archaic terms, no longer understood by the present generation, but *itu'-uf* means "in the woods," and the whole designation of (a) probably signifies "found in the deep forest." The *i'sti tsa'htsa'na* are the cause of a crazed condition of mind, which makes Indians run away from their lodges. No others can see these last-mentioned little folks except the Indians who are seized in this manner by a sudden craze.[28]

The Choctaw elaborated a complex set of behaviors for the Little People they encountered.

The Little People ▪ ▪ ▪
CHOCTAW

Kwanoka'sha is the name of a little spirit—a man, but no larger than a child two or three years of age. His home is in a cave under large rocks, in a rough, broken part of the country.

Now, when a child is two or three or even four years old, it is often sick, and then runs away from its home and goes among the trees. When the little one is well out of sight of home Kwanoka'sha, who is on the watch, seizes it and leads it away to his dwelling place. In many instances they have to travel a considerable distance through the country. When Kwanoka'sha and the child enter the spirit's home they are met by three other spirits, all very old, with white hair. Approaching the child the first offers it a knife; the second a bunch of herbs, all poisonous; the third a bunch of herbs yielding good medicine. Now, if the child accepts the knife he is certain to become a bad man, and may even kill his friends. If he takes the bunch of poisonous herbs he will never be able to cure or otherwise help others; but if he waits and accepts the good herbs, then he is destined to become a great doctor and an important and influential man of his tribe, and to have the confidence of all his people. In this event Kwanoka'sha and the three old spirits tell him how to make use of the herbs—the secrets of making medicines of the roots and leaves and of curing and treating various fevers and pains.

The child remains with the spirits three days, after which he returns to his home, but does not tell where he has been or what he has seen and heard. Not until the child has become a man will he make use of the knowledge gained from the spirits; but never will he reveal to others how it was acquired.

The Choctaw say that few children wait to accept the offering of the good herbs from the third spirit, and hence there are comparatively few great doctors and other men of influence among them.[29]

Kashehotapolo ■ ■ ■
CHOCTAW

Koshehotapalo is neither man nor beast. His head is small and his face shriveled and evil to look upon; his body is that of a man. His legs and feet are those of a deer, the former being covered with hair and the latter having cloven hoofs. He lives in low, swampy places, away from the habitations of men. When hunters go near his abiding place, he quietly slips up behind them and calls loudly, then turns and runs swiftly away. He never attempts to harm the hunters, but delights in frightening them. The sound uttered by Kashehotapalo resembles the cry of a woman, and that is the reason for his name (*kasheho,* ''woman''; *tapalo,* ''call'').[30]

Nalusa Falaya ■ ■ ■
CHOCTAW

The Nalusa Falaya somewhat resembles man. It is of about the size of a man and walks upright, but its face is shriveled, its eyes are very small and it has quite long, pointed ears. Its nose is likewise long. It lives in the densest woods, near swamps, away from the habitations of men. In some respects it resembles Kashehotapalo.

Often when hunters are in the woods, far from their homes, late in the day when the shadows have grown long beneath the pine trees, a Nalusa Falaya will come forth. Getting quite near a hunter it will call in a voice resembling that of a man. And some hunters, when they turn and see the Nalusa Falaya, are so affected that they fall to the ground and even become unconscious.

And while the hunter is thus prostrated on the ground, it approaches and sticks a small thorn into his hand or foot, and by so doing bewitches the hunter and transmits to him the power of doing evil to others; but a person never knows when he has been so bewitched by the Nalusa Falaya until his actions make it evident.

The Nalusa Falaya have many children which, when quite young, possess a peculiar power. They possess the power of removing their viscera at night, and in this lightened condition they become rather small, luminous bodies that may often be seen, along the borders of marshes.[31]

Some tribes, like the Catawba, have preserved only a brief account of their understanding. That, however, does not necessarily indicate that there was not once a more elaborate understanding.

The Little People ■ ■ ■
CATAWBA

Many wild people live in the woods; they stay in the ground. They cry like children. They eat acorns. Tree roots, and fungi that grows around trees, the stick turtle and tadpoles they eat. Some days they carry off children. If they shoot you, you will die, you cannot know [it]. An old woman was tied to a pine tree by her hair by the wild people...They will braid a horse's tail. I rub tobacco on my head, then they cannot cause me any pain. Then, now I say, "Do not bother me again, wild people. I am alone here, I cry and I am an old woman." They are good, they don't bother me. Once [they] stole my little brother and made him sit on a big tree stump in the pond. [They] sucked the blood out of his arm completely. They taught him to be a doctor. His kin waded in the water to catch him and when they caught him he was nearly dead.[32]

The Cherokee have an equally complex tradition of the varieties of Little People, but here are only two texts of their lore.

The Little People ■ ■ ■
CHEROKEE

The Little People (yunwi' djunsti) are about two and one-half feet tall, are dressed in white, and have long hair. They live in rock slides in the cliffs where one can see "floors" that they have made—flat places that they keep swept perfectly clean. They can hear whatever you say about them. It is a bad omen to see them and death may follow.[33]

The Little People ■ ■ ■
CHEROKEE

Lincoln Trotting Bear was an old Indian who lived at Piney. Out behind his house were some big holes that went down under the ground, and he had big cages over some of these holes. There were some Little People that lived down in these holes, and every day Lincoln Trotting Bear put cornbread and other things in the cages for the Little People to eat. This old Indian died at the age of 110, when one night his house burned down with him in it. The Piney Church was not very far from where Lincoln Trotting Bear's house had been, and the Indians had their dinners and singings there behind the church. Lucinda Bear, a friend of mine, said that when they were playing out behind the church as children, they often noticed an extra child or two playing with them. At first they didn't think anything about the new children playing with them. They just figured they had come with someone else. But after a while the other children realized that no one knew who the new children were and that they had not come with anyone else in the group. They were sure that the new or strange children were the Little People from Lincoln Trotting Bear's home. At the night church services the older folks and parents forbade their children to go behind the church where the Little People were. They even had an adult stand outside the church door to make sure that no one did go behind the church.[34]

In the sixteenth century the well-ordered Middle World of the Native Americans was profoundly disturbed by the arrival of previously unknown people, the Europeans and Africans. Over the next four centuries, their unusual appearance, their technological power, their alien understandings of the world, and the devastation they caused—all these required some sort of explanation. The body of mythology expanded to accommodate explanations, as well as attitudes toward them.

Creation of the Whites ■ ■ ■
YUCHI

It was out upon the ocean. Some sea-foam formed against a big log floating there. Then a person emerged from the sea-foam and crawled out upon the log. He was seen sitting there. Another person crawled up, on the other side of the log. It was a woman. They were whites. Soon the Indians saw them, and at first thought that they were sea-gulls, and they said among themselves, "Are they not white people?" Then they made a boat and went out to look at the strangers more closely.

Later on the whites were seen in their house-boat. Then they disappeared.

In about a year they returned, and there were a great many of them. The Indians talked to them but they could not understand each other. Then the whites left.

But they came back in another year with a great many ships. They approached the Indians and asked if they could come ashore. They said, "Yes." So the whites landed, but they seemed to be afraid to walk much on the water. They went away again over the sea.

This time they were gone a shorter time; only three months passed and they came again. They had a box with them and asked the Indians for some earth to fill it. It was given to them as they desired. The first time they asked they had a square box, and when that was filled they brought a big shallow box. They filled this one too. Earth was put in them and when they were carried aboard the ship the white men planted seed in them and many things were raised. After they had taken away the shallow box, the whites came back and told the Indians that their land was very strong and fertile. So they asked the Indians to give them a portion of it that they might live on it. The Indians agreed to do it, the whites came to the shore, and they have lived there ever since.[35]

This explanation of the origin of the white men is so brief as to be missed by casual reading. The whites here are envisioned as created from the white sea foam seen on beaches. "The Creeks assert that they were made from the red earth of the old Creek nation. The whites were made from the foam of the sea. That is why they think the Indian is firm, and the white man is restless and fickle."[36] This may be a very early explanation, for it is also found in some Iroquois texts as part of their creation myth.

The Native Americans had reasons for their negative view, for through the centuries they watched the destruction of their ancient culture and the loss of the land.

A Shaman Predicts the Whites ■ ■ ■
YUCHI

A Creek chief died. When the chief was dead he appeared before Gohantone, who said to him, "This land belongs to you and your children forever. This land will be yours forever, but these whites who have just come will overwhelm you and inherit your land. They will increase and the Indian will decrease and at last die out. Then only white people will remain. But there will be terrible times."

So spoke Gohantone to the dead Creek chief. For four days he lay dead, when he came to life again. When he woke up he was well. He immediately called a great council. Shawnee, Choctaw, Creeks, and Yuchi all assembled to hear him, and he told them all that he had seen and heard. He told them that the land would belong to the Indian forever, but the white man would overrun it. So the thing is coming to pass as Gohantone said.[37]

The mechanism by which the whites were overrunning the Southeast was the cession of land by the Native Americans, who learned and adapted the ancient European legend of the fraud by cowhide.

Stealing the Land ■ ■ ■
YUCHI

A long time ago the red people may have lived somewhere under the rising sun. On this island there lived no pale-faced White people; only red men were living there. Once the water rose, covered with much water foam, right there a person came out; that person was a White man; he came to the shore, it is told; every now and then the White men left and came back again. They asked for some land, only as much as one cowhide would cover, only this much they should give them, they said. They did not want to give it, and some said, "Let us kill them." Others, however, said, "We will not kill them; as much land as one cowhide would not be much," they thought, and so they gave it to them. The

White men threw a cowhide into the water, when it was wet they cut it in little pieces. And then they stretched it; when they measured the four corners they had taken very much land. When the Indians said they had not understood it was to be done that way, they answered that they had taken just as much land as one cowhide; very much land they had taken indeed.[38]

Swanton noted that this motif of the cowhide purchase is at least as old as Virgil and was undoubtedly taken from the Europeans.

Of the various gifts of the whites to the Native Americans, the most devastating was a variety of diseases. The second was whisky, abuse of which plagues Native Americans to this day. It found its place in the legends.

Meeting the Whites ■ ■ ■
HITCHITI
(The encounter with the Europeans is placed in the context of a migration legend, which is omitted here. The Hitchiti migrated to the Atlantic shore.)

They amused themselves, using those rattles as they did so, and while they were there on the shore with them people came across the water to visit them. These were the white people, and the Indians treated them hospitably, and at that time they were on very friendly terms with each other. The white people disappeared, however, and when they did so they left a keg of something which we now know was whisky. A cup was left with this, and the Indians began pouring whisky into this cup and smelling of it, all being much pleased with the odor. Some went so far as to drink a little. They became intoxicated and began to reel and stagger around and butt each other with their heads. Then the white people came back and the Indians began trading peltries, etc., for things which the white people had.[39]

Meeting the Whites ■ ■ ■
ALABAMA
The Alabama and Koasati came out of the earth on opposite sides of the root of a certain tree and settled there in two bodies. Consequently these differed somewhat in speech, though they always kept near each other. At first they came out of the earth only during the night-time, going down again when day came. Presently a white man came to the place, saw the tracks, and wanted to find the people. He went there several times, but could discover none of them above ground. By and by he decided upon a ruse, so he left a barrel of whisky near the place where he saw the footsteps. When the Indians came out again to play they saw the barrel, and were curious about it, but at first no one would touch it. Finally, however, one man tasted of its contents, and presently he began to feel good and to sing and dance about. Then the others drank also and

became so drunk that the white man was able to catch them. Afterward the Indians remained on the surface of the earth.[40]

Another impressive thing about the whites was their literacy. The discovery of the written word struck the Native Americans with great impact, and the very possibility of such a process eventually led Sequoyah to create a similar marvel for the Cherokee. To explain the phenomenon, Native Americans borrowed a motif from the newcomers, probably Africans.

The Power of the Word ■ ■ ■
CREEK (TUKABAHCHEE)

When the Lord first made men (of all colors) they were all one people, [so] that the Lord offered them a choice, showing a piece of paper first to the red man and he could make nothing of it and let it alone, and the red man going along he found some roots and some bows and arrows and he said these are mine, and so he lived in the woods by roots and hunting.

The white man then looked at the paper and he could use it and he kept it ("and how about the black people?"). There was nothing said about them...

He said, referring to the white paper which the white man took, that if he could have had the chance he would have taken the paper and then perhaps the Indians would have had everything as the whites have.[41]

Note that the emphasis is on the ability to read, rather than just the book itself. The whites are invested with that ability already, instead of having to acquire the skill.

White Men's Book ■ ■ ■
YUCHI

The Yuchi knew the book already, it is told. It fell down from above, they took it and thought it over. It is told that the Yuchi were the first ones who found the book. They looked at the book but they did not understand it. There came a White man, he wanted to see the book, but they would not give it to him; he said he would just look at it, and then they gave it to him. As soon as he looked at the book he understood it. This White man was a "Red Coat," it is told.[42]

The origin of black Africans posed an even greater problem. The Southeastern peoples met blacks as early as 1519, and by the late eighteenth century there were many African slaves in Native American possession. The Southeastern tribes thus had both to explain the origin of blacks and to justify their servitude to whites and Native Americans. They did this by adopting a legend already worked out by the Africans.

Origin of Racial Gifts ■ ■ ■
ASHANTI

In the beginning of the world, God created three white and three black men, with the same number of women; he resolved, that they might not afterwards complain, to give them their choice of good and evil. A large box or calabash was set on the ground, with a piece of paper, sealed up, on one side of it. God gave the black men the first choice, who took the box, expecting it contained every thing, but, on opening it, there appeared only a piece of gold, a piece of iron, and several other metals, of which they did not know the use. The white men opening the paper, it told them everything. God left the blacks in the bush, but conducted the whites to the water side (for this happened in Africa), communicated with them every night, and taught them to build a small ship which carried them to another country, whence they returned after a long period, with various merchandise to barter with blacks, who might have been the superior people.[43]

Origin of Races ■ ■ ■
SEMINOLE

Listen, father, and I will tell you how the Great Spirit made man, and how he gave to men of different colours the different employments that we find them engaged in...the Master of Life sad, we will make man. Man was made, but when he stood up before his maker, he was white! The Great Spirit was sorry; he saw that the being he had made was pale and weak; he took pity on him, and therefore did not unmake him, but let him live. He tried again, for he was determined to make a perfect man, but in his endeavor to avoid making another white man, he went into the opposite extreme, and when the second being rose up, and stood before him, he was black! The Great Spirit liked the black man less than the white, and he shoved him aside to make room for another trial. Then it was that he made the red man; and the red man pleased him.

My father, listen—I have not told you all. In this way the Great Spirit made the white, the black, and the red man, when he put them upon the earth. Here they were—but they were very poor. They had no lodges nor horses, no tools to work with, no traps, nor anything with which to kill game. All at once, these three men, looking up, saw three large boxes coming down from the sky. They descended very slowly, but at last reached the ground; while these three poor men stood and looked at them, not knowing what to do. Then the Great Spirit spoke and said, "White man, you are pale and weak, but I made you first, and will give you the first choice; go to the boxes, open them and look in, and choose which you will take for your portion." The white man opened the boxes, looked in, and said, "I will take this." It was filled with pens, and ink, and paper, and compasses, and such things as your people now use. The Great Spirit spoke again and said, "Black man, I made you next, but I do not like you. You may stand aside. The Red man is my favourite, he shall come forward and take the next choice; Red man, choose your portion of the things of this world.'' The red man stepped boldly up and chose a box filled with tomahawks, knives, war clubs, traps, and such things as are useful in war and hunting. The Great Spirit laughed when he saw how well his red son knew how to choose. Then he said to the negro, ''You may have what is left, the third box is for you.'' That was filled with axes and hoes, with buckets to carry water in, and long whips for driving oxen, which meant that the negro must work for both the red and white man, and it has been so ever since.[44]

Origin of Races ■ ■ ■
CREEK (TUKABAHCHEE)
At first there were none but red men. The Lord said to three of them, ''Now I want to make some white men,'' and he told them to go to the river and wash. At first only one went and he stayed a long time in the water and when he came out he was all over white. Then another went and stayed but a short time and the water had been a little soiled, so his color was not changed. Then the third went and the water was more soiled, and when he came out he was black.[45]

This African explanation for the differences in skin color was probably easily adapted by the Native Americans, since they already explained the tail stripes of birds by staining in water. More will be said about this African source in a later chapter. The Biloxi put all this material together, including Biblical creation motifs, and produced a delightful and thought-provoking new synthesis.

The Creation ■ ■ ■
BILOXI (CHRISTIAN)
Kuti mandkce, The One Above, made people: He made one person, an Indian. While the Indian was sleeping, Kuti mankdce made a woman, whom he placed with the Indian, and the latter slept till day. Kuti mankdce departed for the purpose of making food for the Indian and the woman. After his departure, something was standing erect [it was a tree], and there was another person, who said to the Indian and the woman, ''Why have you not eaten the fruit of this tree? I think that he has made it for you two to eat.'' And then the woman stewed the fruit of the tree, and she and the Indian ate it. As they were sitting down after eating the fruit, Kuti mankdce returned. He had departed for the purpose of obtaining food for the Indian and the woman, and he returned after they had eaten the fruit of the tree and had seated themselves. ''Work for yourself and find food, because you shall be hungry,'' said Kuti mankdce in anger as he was about to depart.

When he had gone a long time, he sent back a letter to them; but the Indian did not receive it—the American took it, and because he took it, Americans know very well how to read and write.

And then the people found a very clear stream of water. The American was the first one to lie in it; next came the Frenchman. They were followed by the Indian. Therefore Indians are not usually of light complexion. The Spaniard was the next to lie in the water, and he was not white because the water had by this time become very muddy. Subsequently the negro was made, and as Kuti mankdce thought that he should continue to attend to work alone, he made the negro's nose flat, and as the water had become very muddy, the negro washed only the palms of his hands, therefore negroes are very black with the exception of the palms of their hands.[46]

In these ways the inhabitants of the Southeast explained the characteristics of the beings—winged, four-legged, or two-legged—with whom they shared the land. In the adventure stories to come, we will hear how Native Americans worked out their relations with these other creatures as they encountered them.

CHAPTER SEVEN

The Plant World

It is not enough to account for the various kinds of people in the world, for the animals and birds are not the only ones who have an impact on human life. Plants are of great importance, because many carry medicine power, and a few of them are crucial for human life.

In the Native American world one of the latter was tobacco. Although it has been used recreationally in recent years, it was for many centuries in North America a crucial resource for humans in maintaining good relations with various powerful beings in the cosmos. In the Eastern Woodlands generally, tobacco was especially prized by the Above-World and Under-World powers, and humans who made offerings of tobacco to them were almost guaranteed their good humor. Early explorers in the Mississippi Valley noted that few Native Americans would dream of embarking on a river journey without offering some tobacco to the water powers. Tobacco was therefore important in Native American life, and we would expect to find some account of its origin. In the Southeast, however, there appears to be a single legend, found among the Creeks, Hitchiti, and Yuchi.

The Origin of Tobacco ■ ■ ■
YUCHI

A man and a woman went into the woods. The man had intercourse with the woman and the semen fell upon the ground. From that time they separated, each going his own way. But after a while the woman passed near the place again, and thinking to revisit the spot, went there and beheld some strange weeds growing upon it. She watched them a long while. Soon she met the man who had been with her, and said to him, "Let us go to the place and I will show you something beautiful." They went there and saw it. She asked him what name to call the weeds, and he asked her what name she would give them. But neither of them would give a name. Now the woman had a fatherless boy, and she went and told the boy that she had something beautiful. She said, "Let us go and see it."

When they arrived at the place she said to him, "This is the thing that I was telling you about." And the boy at once began to examine it. After a little while he said, "I'm going to name this." Then he named it *i*, "tobacco." He pulled up some of the weeds and carried them home carefully and planted them in a selected place. He nursed the plants and they grew and became ripe. Now they had a good odor and the boy began to chew the leaves. He found them very good, and in order to preserve the plants he saved the seeds when they were ripe. He showed the rest of the people how to use the tobacco, and from the seeds which he preserved, all got plants and raised the tobacco for themselves.[1]

Although we have seen the arrival of special medicine plants in a migration legend, here is another version of that important event taken down in the late eighteenth century.

Gifts from Four Men ■ ■ ■
CREEK

There are in the forks of Red river (We-cha-te-hat-che Au-fus-kee), west of Mississippi (We-o-coof-ke, muddy water), two mounds of earth. At this place, the Kasihta, Coweta, and Chickasaws found themselves. They were at a loss for fire. Here they were visited by the Hi-you-yul-gee, four men who came from the four corners of the world. One of these people asked the Indians, where they would have their fire *(tote-kit-cau)*. They pointed to a place; it was made; and they sat down around it. The Hi-you-yul-gee directed, that they should pay particular attention to the fire, that it would preserve them and let E-sau-ge-tuh E-mis-see (Master of Breath) know their wants. One of these visitors took them and showed them the Pas-sau; another showed them Mic-co-ho-yon-ejau, then the *Auche-nau* (cedar) and *Too-loh* (sweet bay). (There are one or two other plants, not recollected. Each of these seven plants was to belong to a particular tribe [E-mau-li-ge-tuh].) After this the four visitors disappeared in a cloud, going from whence they came.[2]

Despite the importance of beans in the Native American diet, only one text relating to the origin of that plant has been collected.

The Origin of Beans ■ ■ ■
TUNICA

Once there were an orphan boy and his sister. Every morning they would go to the edge of the ocean to play. Under the bank there was sand. Some puppies emerged from the ocean and came to play on the sand. The girl and her brother tried to catch the puppies. One day when they came there, the puppies came out to play near the bank again. The girl chased one of them and caught it. The two of them were running toward the bank. The waves were coming toward them. When they came to the bank, the waves reached them and caught them. Then the orphan boy climbed up onto the bank alone. The girl had gone down into the water and had disappeared. The orphan boy went home.

He lived with his maternal uncle at his home. Every morning he went there and tried to find his sister. He could not find her. He went back home. One morning he forgot to go. He was just sitting at home. Once day she came back. She brought two beans. She spoke to him. She asked him a question. "Have you anything good to eat?" she said.

"No. There is nothing," he said.

"If you place the kettle on the fire, it will be a good thing," she told him. So he placed the kettle on the fire. Then she broke one of the beans and put it in the kettle. She spoke to him. "If you boil the kettle thoroughly and the bean gets done, you will eat well," she told him.

He, on his part, wanted to play, but she did not wish to play. She spoke to him. "Four days after I plant the bean I eat it," she said. He did not hear her.

Then she spoke to him once more. "Four months after I plant the bean I eat it," she said. "If I give you this bean and if you plant it, you will be able to eat it in four months," she told him. When she had finished speaking, she went back and disappeared into the ocean once more.[3]

Maize, of course, was the major plant supporting human life in the Southeast, and its importance is seen in the number of different ways its origin is described. One legend says it was brought from afar by a bird, a notion which involves two beliefs, that maize was a gift from a helpful bird-power and that there was somewhere (across the ocean?) a store of maize from which it could be procured by the bird. That is very close to the Cherokee legend of the theft of fire by spider, which we have already seen. Here is a maize text.

A Bird Brings Maize ■ ■ ■
CHOCTAW

A long time ago thus it happened. In the very beginning a crow, getting a single grain of corn from beyond the great waters, brought it to this country and gave it to an orphan child who was playing in the yard. The child named it *tanchi* (corn), and planted it in the yard. When the corn grew up high, the child's elders merely had it swept around. But the child wishing to have it a certain way, hoed it, hilled it up and laid it by. When this single grain of corn ripened it made two ears of corn. And it was really in this way, that the Choctaw discovered corn.[4]

Halbert observed that "there are several versions of the corn-finding myth, in all of which a crow and a child are the main factors." We have already seen the Chitimacha text in which a dove brings corn. In the mid–nineteenth century the "Indian Agent" in Oklahoma reported that the Chickasaw "say they got the first corn just after the flood, that a raven flew over them and dropped a part of an ear of corn, and they were told to plant it by the Great Spirit, and it grew up; that they worked in the soil around it with their fingers."[5]

On the Atlantic side of the Southeast, Speck found the episode in fuller context among the Siouan Catawba.

A Bird Brings Maize ■ ■ ■
CATAWBA

A long time ago it rained so much that the river rose and the big earth was completely under the water and the people were washed away. A few climbed up trees on an island [and remained there a] long time. The dove left [and went] far away. The first time the dove came back it brought a leaf back and the next time brought back corn. It brought back corn in its mouth. Now [the people] knew that there was dry land to go to. [This is] true, it is said.[6]

This connection with a flood and a dove betrays Christian influence, but it is difficult to separate Old and New World flood traditions in Native American mythology. These few Southeastern references to an avian source for maize do not stand alone. In 1643 Roger Williams, in his account of the New England Algonkin tribes, noted tersely:

These birds, although they doe the corne also some hurt, yet scarce one Native amongst an hundred will kil them, because they have a tradition, that the Crow brought them at first an Indian Graine of Corne in one Eare and an Indian or French Beane in another, from the Great God Kautantouwits field in the Southwest from whence they hold came all their Corne and beanes.[7]

Among the Dakota there was a memory of this episode, for Brown summarized their Earth-diver myth. "Among the seeds, brought by birds to him [the water-fowl] for planting, was corn."[8] The Arapaho sometimes account for corn in the same way. Mooney reported that the Duck brought them the sacred pipe and an ear of corn "from which comes all the corn of the world" immediately after the creation of land by Turtle.[9]

This collection of texts indicates a connection between the Earth-diver tradition and the bird-corn motif among the Dakota and Arapaho, and a flood connection among the Chickasaw and Catawba. Since the Earth-diver and the flood are also intertwined, it appears that we should understand the motif of the bird who brings maize as an adaptation of the ancient Earth-diver tradition, perhaps mingled with Biblical lore.

The Creeks have a distinctive maize legend involving a woman who is able to fill a corncrib magically.

Filling the Corncribs ■ ■ ■
CREEK

It is said that corn was obtained by one of the women of the Tamalgi clan. She had a number of neighbors and friends, and when they came to her house she would dish some *sofki* [a native dish made from corn] into an earthen bowl and they would drink it. They found it delicious, but did not know where she got the stuff of which to make it. Finally they noticed that she washed her feet in water and rubbed them, whereupon what came from her feet was corn. She said to them, "You may not like to eat from me in this way, so build a corncrib, put me inside and fasten the door. Don't disturb me, but keep me there for four days, and at the end of the fourth day you can let me out." They did so, and while she was there they heard a great rumbling like distant thunder, but they did not know what it meant. On the fourth day they opened the door as directed and she came out. Then they found that the crib was well stocked with corn. There was corn for making bread, hard flint corn for making sofki, and other kinds. She instructed them how to plant grains of corn from what she had produced. They did so, the corn grew and reproduced, and they have had corn ever since.[10]

All the texts are agreed that there is an unusual sound during the night. It is variously described: a "roaring" "like distant thunder" (Creek), "a rapping noise" (Koasati), a "noise like electricity" (Seminole). When the morning comes, the woman is gone, but the corncrib is filled with corn.

This motif of the filling of the corncrib is not found only in the Southeast. There are four examples of it from the Iroquois.[11] A woman arrives in a starving town to marry a man and aid the town. "I have come from the south to assist you and your people in obtaining food for your needs. I came because my mother sympathizes greatly with her people, and it is she who has sent me here to become the wife of your elder son." After the marriage she instructs the people to clean the corn bins. "At the dawn of day the next morning the people, awakening as if they had been frightened, heard sounds which indicated that corn was falling into their corn bins, which had been empty so long."[12]

There are Zuni and Pawnee versions, too. The filling of the corncrib is placed in yet another context, the "deserted children," but in the motif itself there is a difference between the eastern texts and these western ones. The eastern version is characterized by the gift of corn falling from above, as evidenced by the sound heard during the night. By contrast, the Southwestern motif is rooted in the phenomenon of growth, for the seeds must first be placed in the storeroom where they multiply to fill the crib.[13]

The western and eastern traditions seem related, however, even if they envision the source of the corn differently. The other major motif of the Creek legend, the shelling of corn from the woman's body, is another story.

One of the most well-known Cherokee myths, if not the most famous of all Southeastern narratives, incorporates an explanation of maize as a portion of a lengthy compound legend. Since we will be looking at the different legends which compose it in various places, we need to read the entire text, even though the maize episode is our focus. There are many texts available. This one was collected from an Eastern Cherokee medicine-man named Swimmer by James Mooney in the summer of 1887. He was told that "in the old times any one who heard it, with all the explanation, was obliged to 'go to water' after the recital; that is, to bathe in the running stream at daybreak."[14]

Kanati and Selu ▪ ▪ ▪
CHEROKEE

When I was a boy, this is what the old men told me they had heard when they were boys.

Long ages ago, soon after the world was made, a hunter and his wife lived at Looking-glass Mountain with their only child, a little boy. The father's name was Kanati, "The Lucky Hunter," and his wife was called Selu, "Corn." No matter when Kanati went into the woods, he never failed to bring back a load of game, which his wife cut up and prepared, washing the blood from the meat in the river near the house. The little boy used to play down by the river every day, and one morning the old people thought they heard laughing and talking in the bushes, as though there were two children there. When the boy came home at night, his parents asked who had been playing with him all day. "He comes out of the water," said the boy, "and he calls himself my elder brother. He says his mother was cruel to him, and threw him into the river." Then they knew that the strange boy had sprung from the blood of the game which Selu had washed off at the river's edge.

Every day, when the little boy went out to play, the other would join him; but, as he always went back into the water, the old people never had a chance to see him. At last, one evening, Kanati said to his son, "Tomorrow, when the other boy comes to play with you, get him to wrestle with you, and when you have your arms around him hold on to him and call for us." The boy promised to do as he was told; so the next day, as soon as his playmate appeared, he challenged him to a wrestling-match. The other agreed at once, but as soon as they had their arms around each other Kanati's boy began to scream for his father. The old folks at once came running down, and when the wild boy saw them he struggled to free himself, and cried out, "Let me go! You threw me

148

away!" But his brother held on until his parents reached the spot, when they seized the wild boy and took him home with them. They kept him in the house until they had tamed him, but he was always wild and artful in his disposition, and was the leader of his brother in every mischief. Before long the old people discovered that he was one of those persons endowed with magic powers *(adawehi)*, and they called him Inage Utasuhi', "He who grew up Wild."

Impounded Animals

Whenever Kanati went into the mountains he always brought back a fat buck or doe, or maybe a couple of turkeys. One day the wild boy said to his brother, "I wonder where our father gets all that game; let's follow him next time, and find out." A few days afterward, Kanati took a bow and some feathers in his hand, and started off. The boys waited a little while, and then started after him, keeping out of sight, until they saw their father go into a swamp where there were a great many of the reeds *(watike)* that hunters use to make arrow-shafts. Then the wild boy changed himself into a puff of bird's down *(atsilu)*, which the wind took up and carried until it alighted upon Kanati's shoulder just as he entered the swamp, but Kanati knew nothing about it. The hunter then cut reeds, fitted the feathers to them, and made some arrows, and the wild boy—in his other shape—thought, "I wonder what those things are for." When Kanati had his arrows finished, he came out of the swamp and went on again. The wind blew the down from his shoulder; it fell in the woods, when the wild boy took his right shape again, and went back and told his brother what he had seen. Keeping out of sight of their father, they followed him up the mountain until he stopped at a certain place and lifted up a large rock. At once a buck came running out, which Kanati shot, and then, lifting it upon his back, he started home again. "Oho!" said the boys, "he keeps all the deer shut up in that hole, and whenever he wants venison, he just lets one out, and kills it with those things he made in the swamp." They hurried and reached home before their father, who had the heavy deer to carry, so that he did not know they had followed him.

A few days after, the boys went back to the swamp, cut some reeds and made seven arrows, and then started up the mountain to where their father kept the game. When they got to the place they lifted up the rock, and a deer came running out. Just as they drew back to shoot it, another came out, and then another, and another, until the boys got confused and forgot what they were about. In those days all the deer had their tails hanging down, like other animals, but, as a buck was running past, the wild boy struck its tail with his arrow so that it stood straight out behind. This pleased the boys, and when the next one ran by, the other brother struck his tail so that it pointed upward. The boys thought this was good sport, and when the next one ran past, the wild boy struck his tail so that it stood straight up, and his brother struck the next one so hard with his arrow that the deer's tail was curled over his back. The boys thought this was very pretty, and ever since the deer has carried his tail over his back.[15]

The deer continued to pass until the last one had come out of the hole and escaped into the forest. Then followed droves of raccoons, rabbits, and all the other four-footed animals. Last came great flocks of turkeys, pigeons, and partridges that darkened the air like a cloud, and made such a noise with their wings that Kanati, sitting at home, heard the sound like distant thunder on the mountains, and said to himself, "My bad boys have got into trouble. I must go and see what they are doing."

So Kanati went up the mountain, and when he came to the place where he kept the game he found the two boys standing by the rock, and all the birds and animals were gone. He was furious, but, without saying a word, he went down into the cave and kicked the covers off four jars in one corner, when out swarmed bed-bugs, fleas, lice, and gnats (*kaluyasti, tsu'ku', tinu', dasi'-'nu*), and got all over the boys. They screamed with pain and terror, and tried to beat off the insects; but the thousands of insects crawled over them, and bit and stung them, until both dropped down nearly dead from exhaustion. Kanati stood looking on until he thought they had been punished enough, when he brushed off the vermin, and proceeded to give the boys a lecture. "Now, you rascals," said he, "you have always had plenty to eat, and never had to work for it. Whenever you were hungry, all I had to do was to come up here and get a deer or a turkey, and bring it home for your mother to cook. But now you have let out all the animals, and after this, when you want a deer to eat, you will have to hunt all over the woods for it, and then may be not find one. Go home now to your mother, while I see if I can find something to eat for supper."

Origin of Maize

When the boys reached home again they were very tired and hungry, and asked their mother for something to eat. "There is no meat," said Selu, "but wait a little while, and I will get you something." So she took a basket and started out to the provision-house (*unwata'li*). This provision-house was built upon poles high up from the ground, to keep it out of the reach of animals, and had a ladder to climb up by, and one door, but no other opening. Every day, when Selu got ready to cook the dinner, she would go out to the provision-house with a basket, and bring it back full of corn and beans. The boys had never been inside the provision-house, and wondered where all the corn and beans could come from, as the house was not a very large one; so, as soon as Selu went out of the door, the wild boy said to his brother, "Let's go and see what she does." They ran around and climbed up at the back of the provision-house, and pulled out a piece of clay from between the logs, so that they could look in. There they saw Selu standing in the middle of the room, with the basket in front of her on the floor. Leaning over the basket, she rubbed her stomach—so—and the basket was half-full of corn. Then she rubbed under her arm-pits—so—and the basket was full to the top with beans. The brothers looked at each other, and said, "This will never do; our mother is a witch. If we eat any of that it will poison us. We must kill her."

When the boys came back into the house, Selu knew their thoughts before they spoke. "So you are going to kill me!" said Selu. "Yes," said the boys; "you are a witch." "Well," said their mother, "when you have killed me, clear a large piece of ground in front of the house, and drag my body seven times around the circle. Then drag me seven times over the ground inside the circle, and stay up all night and watch, and in the morning you will have plenty of corn." Then the boys killed her with their clubs, and cut off her head, and put it up on the roof of the house, and told it to look for her husband. Then they set to work to clear the ground in front of the house, but, instead of clearing the whole piece, they cleared only seven little spots. This is the reason why corn now grows only in a few places instead of over the whole world. Then they dragged the body of Selu around the circles, and wherever her blood fell on the ground the corn sprang up. But, instead of dragging her body seven times across the ground, they did this only twice, which is the reason why the Indians still work their crop but twice. The two brothers sat up and watched their corn all night, and in the morning it was fully grown and ripe.

Adventure: Wolves

When Kanati came home at last, he looked around, but could not see Selu anywhere, so he asked the boys where their mother was. "She was a witch, and we killed her," said the boys; "there is her head up there on top of the house." When Kanati saw his wife's head on the roof he was very angry, and said, "I won't stay with you any longer. I am going to the Wa'haya (Wolf) people." So he started off, but, before he had gone far, the wild boy changed himself again to a tuft of down, which fell on Kanati's shoulder. When Kanati reached the settlement of the Wolf people, they were holding a council in the town-house (a'se egwa). He went in and sat down, with the tuft of bird's down on his shoulder. When the Wolf chief asked him his business, he said, "I have two bad boys at home, and I want you to go in seven days from now and play against them." Kanati spoke as though he wanted them to play a game of ball, but the wolves knew that he meant for them to come and kill the two boys. The wolves promised to go. Then the bird's down blew off from Kanati's shoulder, and the smoke carried it up through the hole in the roof of the town-house. When it came down on the ground outside, the wild boy took his right shape again, and went home and told his brother all that he had heard in the town-house. When Kanati left the Wolf people, he did not return home, but went on farther.

The boys then began to get ready for the wolves, and the wild boy—the magician—told his brother what to do. They ran around the house in a wide circle until they had made a trail all around it, excepting on the side from which the wolves would come, where they left a small open space. Then they made four large bundles of arrows, and placed them at four different points on the outside of the circle, after which they hid themselves in the woods and waited for the wolves. On the appointed day a whole army of wolves came and surrounded the house, to kill the boys. The wolves did not notice the trail around the house, because they came in where the boys had left the opening, but the moment they were inside the circle the trail changed to a high fence, and shut them in. Then the boys on the outside took their arrows and began shooting them down, and, as the wolves could not jump over the fence, they were all killed excepting a few, which escaped through the opening into a great swamp close by. Then the boys ran around the swamp, and a circle of fire sprang up in their tracks, and set fire to the grass and bushes, and burned up nearly all the other wolves. Only two or three got away, and these were all the wolves which were left in the whole world.

Another Maize Story

Soon afterward some strangers from a distance, who heard that the brothers had a wonderful grain from which they made bread, came to ask for some; for none but Selu and her family had ever known corn before. The boys gave them seven grains of corn, which they told them to plant the next night on their way home, sitting up all night to watch the corn, which would have seven ripe ears in the morning. These they were to plant the next night, and watch in the same way; and so on every night until they reached home, when they would have corn enough to supply the whole people. The strangers lived seven days' journey away. They took the seven grains of corn, and started home again. That night they planted the seven grains, and watched all through the darkness until morning, when they saw seven tall stalks, each stalk bearing a ripened ear. They gathered the ears with gladness, and went on their way. The next night they planted all their corn, and guarded it with wakeful care until daybreak, when they found an abundant increase. But the way was long and the sun was hot, and the people grew tired. On the last night before reaching home they fell asleep, and in the morning the corn they had planted had not even sprouted. They brought with them to their settlement what corn they had left, and planted it, and with care and attention were able to raise a crop. But ever since the corn must be watched and tended through half a year, which before would grow and ripen in a night.

Finding Kanati

As Kanati did not return, the boys at last concluded to go and see if they could find him. The wild boy got a wheel *(tikwalelu)*, and rolled it toward the direction where it is always night.[16] In a little while the wheel came rolling back, and the boys knew their father was not there. Then the wild boy rolled it to the south and to the north, and each time the wheel came back to him, and they knew their father was not there. Then he rolled it toward the Sun Land (East), and it did not return. "Our father is there," said the wild boy; "let us go and find him." So the two brothers set off toward the east, and after travelling a long time they came upon Kanati, walking along, with a little dog by his side. "You bad boys," said their father, "have you come here?" "Yes," they answered; "we always accomplish what we start out to do.—We are men!" "This dog overtook me four days ago," then said Kanati, but the boys knew that the dog was the wheel which they had sent after him to find him. "Well," said Kanati, "as you have found me, we may as well travel together, but I will take the lead."

Adventure: Panther
Soon they came to a swamp, and Kanati told them there was a dangerous thing there, and they must keep away from it. Then he went on ahead, but as soon as he was out of sight the wild boy said to his brother, "Come and let us see what is in the swamp." They went in together, and in the middle of the swamp they found a large panther, asleep. The wild boy got out an arrow, and shot the panther in the side of the head. The panther turned his head, and the other boy shot him on that side. He turned his head away again, and the two brothers shot together—*tust, tust, tust!* But the panther was not hurt by the arrows, and paid no more attention to the boys. They came out of the swamp, and soon overtook Kanati, waiting for them. "Did you find it?" asked Kanati. "Yes," said the boys, "we found it, but it never hurt us. We are men!" Kanati was surprised, but said nothing, and they went on again.

Adventure: Cannibals
After a while Kanati turned to them, and said, "Now you must be careful. We are coming to a tribe called the Undutuski, 'Cookers' [i.e., Cannibals], and if they get you they will put you in a pot and feast on you." Then he went on ahead. Soon the boys came to a tree which had been struck by lightning, and the wild boy directed his brother to gather some of the splinters from the tree, and told him what to do with them. In a little while they came to the settlement of the cannibals, who, as soon as they saw the boys, came running out, crying, "Good! Here are two nice, fat strangers. Now we'll have a grand feast!" They caught the boys and dragged them into the town-house, and sent word to all the people of the settlement to come to the feast. They made up a great fire, filled a large pot with water and set it to boiling, and then seized the wild boy and threw

him into the pot, and put the lid on it. His brother was not frightened in the least, and made no attempt to escape, but quietly knelt down and began putting the splinters into the fire, as if to make it burn better. When the cannibals through the meat was about ready, they lifted the lid from the pot, and that instant a blinding light filled the town-house, and the lightning began to dart from one side to the other, beating down the cannibals until not one of them was left alive. Then the lightning went up through the smoke hole, and the next moment there were the two boys standing outside the town-house as though nothing had happened. They went on, and soon met Kanati, who seemed much surprised to see them, and said, "What! are you here again?" "Oh yes, we never give up. We are great men!" "What did the cannibals do to you?" "We met them, and they brought us to their town-house, but they never hurt us." Kanati said nothing more, and they went on.

Thunders

Kanati soon got out of sight of the boys, but they kept on until they came to the end of the world, where the sun comes out. The sky was just coming down when they got there, but they waited until it went up again, and then they went through and climbed up on the other side. There they found Kanati and Selu sitting together. The old folks received them kindly, and were glad to see them, and told them they might stay there a while, but then they must go to live where the sun goes down. The boys stayed with their parents seven days, and then went on toward the sunset land, where they are still living.[17]

In this form this legend is peculiar to the Cherokee, except for a close Natchez text which was probably learned from the Cherokee in those years when Natchez refugees found sanctuary with the Cherokee and Creeks. This legend is part of a general complex known as "the Twins." (See Chapter 8.) Curiously, this text fails to indicate names or identification for the boys, but the display of lightning identifies them as "the Thunders," well known to all Cherokee.

Despite the boys' importance, however, the legend emphasizes their parents above them, probably because they represent a major structural principle. Kanati ("Hunter") is master of the animals and thus represents the hunting side of the tribal economics, while Selu ("Maize") represents the agricultural realm, the other half of the Cherokee subsistence base. In the story the boys are responsible for inaugurating both the universal use of maize and the necessity of hunting. The latter is signified by the boys' freeing the impounded animals, but the advent of hunting is portrayed as a loss of a state in which game animals were readily available. There is thus a reflection of the unhappy fact that successful hunting is extremely difficult, and many Southwestern stories express concern with gaining power in the hunt—heroes have it.

154

The lost "golden age" of available game is matched with loss of readily available vegetable food. The legend of Selu is the most unusual feature of the Cherokee version, for the corn element is not elsewhere found in this form of the Twins narrative. The maize legend is found in other contexts among other peoples, though; their Creek neighbors had it.

The general concept seems to be that the woman is herself corn, and when she is buried, her body becomes the source for the growth of crucial vegetable plants. The Creeks placed their tradition of the origin of maize in the context of a legend sometimes called the "Orphan" which will be given in full later on (see Chapter 9). This is the way they tell the maize portion of the legend.

The Origin of Maize (extract) ■ ■ ■
CREEK

The old woman provided corn and beans for them but did not tell him where she got them and after a while he became curious. One time when she was out of corn and beans and he was about to go hunting she told him that she would cook sofki and blue dumplings against his return. He started off but instead of going hunting slipped back to the house and peeked through a crack. Then he saw his grandmother place a riddle [basket] on the floor, stand with one foot on each side of it, and scratch the front of one of her thighs, whereupon corn poured down into the riddle. When she scratched the other thigh beans poured into the riddle. In that way the orphan learned how she obtained the corn and beans.

Afterwards the orphan went off hunting, but when he came back he would not touch the food. His grandmother asked him if he was in pain or if anything else was the matter with him, urging him to eat. When she could not persuade him, she said, "You must have been spying upon me and have learned how I get the corn and beans. If you do not want to eat the food I prepare, you must go away beyond the mountain which I forbade you to pass...Start along on this trail, but before you leave lock me up in this log cabin and set it on fire. After you have been gone for some time come back to look at this place, for here you were raised"...

Some time later the youth said to his wife, "Let us go over to the place where I grew up, for I want to see it." They went there, and when they had arrived found that all sorts of Indian corn and beans had grown up in it. That was where the corn came from. So the corn was a person, that old woman; and if it is not treated well it will become angry. If one does not "lay it by" (i.e., heap the soil about it in cultivation), it calls for its underskirt. The laying by of the corn is the underskirt of old lady corn.[18]

There are three related details in the Creek and Cherokee narratives which can give clues to relationships: the production of plants from the grave of the woman, the dragging of the old woman's body, and her body as a source of food.

The Iroquois know the detail concerning the grave. It appears in four of the twenty-five texts of their creation epic, where maize grows from the grave of the mother of the Twins. In the single Huron text the mother's grave produced pumpkins from her head, beans from her limbs, and maize from her breasts.[19] The other three are from the Seneca; in one she produced potatoes (feet), beans (fingers), squash (abdomen), tobacco (head), and maize (breasts).[20] Curtin's text has just maize from the breasts,[21] but Wright's has beans from one breast and maize from the other.[22] The Winnebago have the same tradition.[23]

The Cherokee motif of the dragging of her body over the ground is contained only in one Creek text; all the others omit it, which suggests that it is peculiar to the Cherokee version in the Southeast. It is also found in the Northeast, however. The legend stands as a separate story there, but it is found among three Algonkin tribes, the Abnaki, Malecite, and Penobscot.[24]

The Origin of Maize ■ ■ ■
ABNAKI

A long time ago, when Indians were first made, there lived one alone, far, far from any others. He knew not of fire, and subsisted on roots, barks, and nuts. This Indian became very lonesome for company. He grew tired of digging roots, lost his appetite, and for several days lay dreaming in the sunshine; when he awoke he saw something standing near, at which, at first, he was very much frightened. But when it spoke, his heart was glad, for it was a beautiful woman with long light hair, very unlike any Indian. He asked her to come to him, but she would not, and if he tried to approach her she seemed to go farther away; he sang to her of his loneliness and besought her not to leave him; at last she told him, if he would do just as she should say, he would always have her with him. He promised that he would.

She led him to where there was some very dry grass, told him to get two very dry sticks, rub them together quickly, holding them in the grass. Soon a spark flew out; the grass caught it, and quick as an arrow the ground was burned over. Then she said, "When the sun sets, take me by the hair and drag me over the burned ground." He did not like to do this, but she told him that wherever he dragged her something like grass would spring up, and he would see her hair coming from between the leaves; then the seeds would be ready for his use. He did as she said, and to this day, when they see the silk (hair) on the cornstalk, the Indians know she has not forgotten them.[25]

Other parts of the Native American world have different traditions of the origin of maize, which leaves the Southeastern and Northeastern legend of the dragging and killing of the maize-woman as a special group. The production of food from the woman's body seems restricted to the Southeast. It seems impossible to identify a source for this unusual detail, but there is a suggestive parallel from the Caribbean. One of the major figures in the South American twins legend is a Frog-woman, protector of the tree of abundance. She is associated with both fire and water and is seen as mother of the jaguars and foster mother of the twins. In some texts she is spied upon by the twins, who see her produce food or fire from her skin. The food is manioc, or cassava, a root which is a South American food staple equivalent to maize for the North Americans.

The Manioc-Woman (extract) ■ ■ ■
CARIB

The two lads now proceeded on their way and arrived at last at a clump of cotton-trees *(ceiba)* in the center of which was a house occupied by a very old woman, really a frog, and with her they took up their quarters. They went out hunting each day, and on their return invariably found some cassava that their hostess had baked. "That's very strange," remarked Pia to his brother, "there is no field anywhere about, and yet look at the quantity of cassava which the old woman gives us. We must watch her." So next morning, instead of going into the forest to hunt, they went only a little distance away, and hid themselves behind a tree whence they could see everything that took place at the house. They noticed that the old frog had a white spot on her shoulders: they saw her bend down and pick at this spot, and observed the cassava-starch fall. On their return home they refused to eat the usual cake, having now discovered its source. Next morning they picked a quantity of cotton from the neighboring trees and teased it out on the floor. When the old woman asked what they were doing, they told her that they were making something nice and soft for her to lie upon. Much pleased at this, she promptly sat upon it, but no sooner had she done so than the two lads set fire to it; thereupon her skin was scorched so dreadfully as to give it the wrinkled and rough appearance which it now bears.[26]

Apparently the Frog-woman's death does not create manioc, but the parallel with the spying, the discovery of her unusual source of food, and the burning is too close to ignore, even though the distance between the Southeast and South America is great. It seems that the Carib episode has been combined with the legend of the birth of vegetables from the grave of a woman to produce the distinctive legend of Selu in its dual form, Cherokee and Muskhogean. One researcher has traced the various New World corn myths, and particularly the group he labeled the "corn mother," to Southeast Asia.[27] He concluded that the Southeastern versions, the most complex, were probably closest to the ancient forms. That may be true, but it seems difficult to support that conclusion.

Perhaps it is enough to say that an ancient Circum-Caribbean legend merged with an ancient Eastern Woodlands story to create the complexity of the origin of maize in the Southeast. As we shall see in later chapters, the Cherokee placed the maize legend in the context of the mother of twins, while the Creeks showed their affinity with the Siouans and Algonkin by merging it with the Grandmother-Orphan legend.

■ ■ ■

ADVENTURES

■ ■ ■

CHAPTER EIGHT

The Twins

As we have seen, while the Creeks and the Cherokee possessed the same legend of the origin of maize, they placed those accounts in quite different contexts. The Creeks have made it part of the "Orphan" legend, which will be discussed in the next chapter. The Cherokee, however, have it as part of a "Twins" story. We have already looked at that text in the last chapter, and its complexity gives us a good opportunity for comparative study. In addition to the Orphan narrative which contains the maize legend, the Creeks also have a form of the Twins legend known as "Lodge-Boy and Thrown-Away" (LBTA) because it was first catalogued from the Plains versions in which the boys are called by those names. Here is the Creek text.

Lodge-Boy and Thrown-Away ▪ ▪ ▪
CREEK

(The Bead-spitter opening is omitted.)...Some time later Bead-spitter's wife was with child. Her husband was a great hunter and was off continually. One time he crossed the river in a canoe and went off hunting. When he came back, however, he found his canoe had been taken back to the side on which stood his dwelling. He shouted to his wife to come over and fetch him but she did not reply and he was obliged to swim across. In a window of his house he saw what appeared to be his wife painted and dressed in fine clothes and he said to her, "I shouted to you for a long time but it seems that you were too busily engaged in combing your hair to hear me." Then he punched at her with the butt of his gun and she fell back out of sight. He went in and then found that what he had taken for his wife was only an image of her. During his absence she had been eaten by a Kolowa (Gorilla) who had afterwards set up the image. The Kolowa had, however, left the woman's abdomen, and on opening it the hunter found a baby inside, still alive. He saved it and took care of it, throwing

the afterbirth into a thicket back of the house.

He fed his child, which was a boy, on gruel and soup. After some years had passed the child wanted a bow and arrows, and his father made some small ones for him. He was much surprised, however, when his son insisted that he make two bows with a blunt arrow and a sharp one for each. The man's suspicions were aroused at this and so, when he started out hunting one day in accordance with his custom, he stole back and watched the house. Presently he saw another boy come from the afterbirth, join his son, and play about with him. It was the first boy's twin.

Then the father crept away and began to plan how he should capture the second boy. First he thought he would turn himself into an arrow stuck in the ground at the edge of the yard and he did so, but when the wild boy came up he said, "That is your father," and he slunk away so that the man could not get at him. Next the man turned himself into a ball of white grass such as is blown along the road by the wind, and the first boy said, "Let us see which can get it," but the wild boy answered, "That is your father." The third time the man assumed the form of a flying feather with the same result. But finally the man got hold of him, he became tame, and both stayed there until they were grown up.

Adventure: Burr-Woman

One day the man said to his two sons, "If the canoe is on your side of the stream and someone shouts to you to ferry them across, it will not be I. Do not do it. A wicked old woman ate your mother, and that is the one who will shout. So do not go for her."

After their father had left them the old woman came down to the other bank and called to be ferried across. Then the wild boy said, "Did not father say that if someone called out we were to take the canoe over and fetch her?" But the other answered, "No, he said, 'If anyone shouts, do not take it over because that will be the one who devoured your mother.'" But the wild boy, whose name was Fatcasigo (Not-doing-right), insisted on going, and after they had disputed for a while he said, "If you do not agree to go I will chop you with father's ax." The other was frightened at this and went with him.

When they got to the place where the old woman was standing she said, "People always carry me on their backs and put me into the canoe," so Fatcasigo brought her down on his back. When she got into the canoe she said, "They always keep me on their backs while I am in the canoe." And when they landed on the other side she said, "They always take me out on their backs." But when Fatcasigo stood on land with her she began to shout, *"Kolowai'*, *Kolowai,'"* and stuck fast to him.

At that Fatcasigo became angry and punched her, but his fist stuck fast. He hit her with his other fist and that also stuck. He kicked her with one of his feet and that stuck. He fell down on the ground and kicked her with the other foot but that stuck. Then he butted her with his head and that stuck. His brother got sticks and beat her with them but they merely stuck to her, so that he finally became angry and struck her with his fists, whereupon he too became stuck to her like his brother.[1]

Presently the boy's father came home and shouted from the other side of the stream to be taken across. When he found that he was unable to arouse anyone he swam over. Seeing the fix into which his two sons had gotten, he said, "Did not I tell you not to take the canoe across? Now I expect you will get some sense into your heads." He went into the house, prepared his dinner, and then heated a quantity of water, which he poured over the old woman. The boys were melted loose and the old woman flew away shouting, *"Kolowai' Kolowai.'"*

Adventure: Thunderbird Eggs

Before the man started out again he said to them, "You do not seem to have much sense, but I will tell you that up in that tree yonder are some eggs. Do not climb up there and play with them." After he had started off, however, Fatcasigo said, "Did not he tell us to climb up into that tree and play with the eggs?" "No," said his brother, "he told us we must not." They disputed over it for a while until finally Fatcasigo said, "If you do not agree I will chop you with father's ax." "Go ahead, then," said his brother, so they climbed up into the tree, brought down the eggs, and began playing with them. While they were doing so a storm overtook their father out in the woods, and he came back and ordered them to replace the eggs in the nest. As they were engaged in doing this the lightning struck all about and they shouted, *"Sindadik, sindadik,"* and came down.

Impounded Animals

Next time the hunter started off he said nothing to his sons and Fatcasigo said, "Father is very angry with us. Let us follow him and see what he does." Then they discovered that he had bear, deer, and all other sorts of game animals shut up in a corral, and after he left it, they went to the place, opened the gate, and let them all out. Then they came back to the house so quickly that they reached it before them.

The next time their father went to his corral he found his animals had been let out and his anger was very great.

Adventure: Long-Finger-Nails

He said to his sons, when he got home, "On the other side of the stream lives a man named Long-finger-nails *(Kococup-tcapko)* who has some tobacco. Go to him and get me some in exchange for this lead." So they set out with the lead but on the way Fatcasigo said to his companion, "He is sending us there because he is so angry with us that he wants us to die." After they had gone on for a while they came to a deep lake which they could not cross. An Alligator, floating close to the shore, called out, "What are you doing?" They replied, "Our father told us to go to Long-finger-nails for some tobacco and we are on the way to get it." "He sent you to something very bad," said the Alligator. "He wants him to devour you. I will put you across," he added, and he did so. Then he said to them, "Let the elder boy remain behind while the younger slips up and places lead in Long-finger-nails's basket, taking out the tobacco and saying, 'I am exchanging lead for your tobacco.' Then he must run back as fast as he can."

The boys did as they had been directed and when the younger uttered the words which had been given to him Long-finger-nails made a grab for him with one hand. But in doing so he ran his fingernails so deep into a post that it took him a long time to get them out. Meanwhile the boys got back to the Alligator, mounted on his back and were nearly across the lake before Long-finger-nails reached the opposite bank. The Alligator let them land and disappeared under the water before their pursuer caught sight of him. Then the monster said to the boys, "You had a very narrow escape. Who set you over?"[2]

When the boys brought in their tobacco to their father, who had thought they were killed and eaten by that time, he said to them, "Well, did you make the trade?" "Yes, here is the tobacco," they said, and upon this their father got up and started off.

War with Father

Then Fatcasigo said to his brother again, "Our father is very angry with us. He is going to get someone to help him kill us. We will also be prepared." So they collected quantities of bees and stinging insects of all sorts and filled the house with them. "When it is time for him to come back we will set watches for him," they said, and they did so. The outermost picket was the Blue Crane *(watula)*. The next was the Wild Goose *(ahakwa)*. The next was the Pelican *(sasa'kwa ha'gi)*. The last and nearest were Quails *(kowaigi)*. The Crane was stationed farthest out because it has the loudest voice. The Wild Goose was next because it has the next loudest voice. The Pelican was next because its voice is third in strength. Quails were placed last because they make a noise with their wings when they fly up. After making these arrangements the boys lay down and listened.

By and by the boys heard the voice of the Crane and they said, "He is coming." A little later they heard the voice of the Goose, and they said, "He has gotten that far." Then the Pelican shouted and they said, "He is getting closer." And finally the Quails flew up with a whirr and they said, "He is right here; let us make ready." So they climbed up on a beam inside of the house and began throwing down bees, wasps, and other stinging things, and they kept this up until the house and yard were full of them. These settled all over their father and his warriors until they had stung them to death.

Then the boys stood up on the beam and said, "Our father must be lying somewhere about; let us go down and hunt for him." By and by they found him and said, "Our father is lying here." The boys had their bows and arrows with them, and when they found their father they took off his breechclout and rubbed an arrow over his buttocks. At once he flew up in the form of a crow, shouting "Ga ga ga ga." Thus the crow was once a human being. It eats watermelons and corn and is very destructive. It is very much afraid of a bow and arrow because its buttocks were once rubbed with an arrow. For this reason people used to keep a bow and arrows about to scare it away.

After that the boys said, "We must be bad boys. We had better separate." "Do you want to go to the east or west?" said Fatcasigo to his elder brother, and the latter answered, "I will go toward the east." The younger said, "I will go to the west, and whenever you see a red cloud in the west you will know that I am there." The elder brother replied, "And whenever you see a red cloud in the east you will know that I am there." That is the end.[3]

The opening of the story is a legend about "Bead-spitter," a text nowhere else associated with LBTA; we will look at it separately in Chapter 10. When we try to compare composite texts, it is helpful to be able to reduce lengthy texts to a shorthand. Here is a summary of "Kanati and Selu," on the left, and the Creek LBTA text on the right. The maize and Bead-spitter episodes are omitted.

Cherokee	Creek
Birth from blood +	LBTA +
	Burr-woman
	Adventure: Thunderbird-eggs +
Impounded animals +	Impounded animals +
Adventure: Wolves +	
	Adventure: Long-nails +
Father flees +	War with Father +
Adventure: Panther +	
Adventure: Cannibals.	

The opening sequences, "Birth from blood" and LBTA, serve as "allo-motifs," motifs that are interchangeable because they fill the same function in the larger story. Nonetheless, the deviation suggests two separate traditions, and that is supported by the fact that shared episodes are "Impounded animals" and "War," although they are placed differently in the sequence. The remainder of the two texts is not shared. It will be helpful to examine one more text to get the range in the Southeast; this one is from the western end—the Caddo.

The Twins ■ ■ ■
CADDO

When the world was new there lived among the people a man and his wife and one child, a boy of about twelve years. The people called the man "Medicine-Man." Now and then he went out on the hunt, and never was known to come home without killing a deer, and almost every time he came home with a big buck. One time when he was out hunting he killed a deer and then started for home, and when he reached home he found his little boy there alone and not as usual, for he looked weary and frightened. When his father asked him where his mother was he began to cry and said he did not know; that all he knew was that she took a water bucket and went down toward the creek. He said that he had run over there two or three times calling his mother, but no answer came. Then both the little boy and Medicine-Man went down to the place where the woman usually went to get water, but they could not find her. They found footprints at the edge of the water, and then the Medicine-Man knew that his wife and the mother of his only child was dead and gone; that something had taken her life; so they came back to their home and mourned for her six days. They built a fire and watched it and stayed by it for six days and nights.

The seventh day Medicine-Man told his son that he was going hunting, for their meat was about out. He went out to hunt and the little boy stayed at home alone. While his father was gone the boy would play around the house, shooting with his bow and arrows. When Medicine-Man came home he found his little son there waiting for him. Medicine-Man went out to hunt the second and the third time and found the boy safe on his return. The fourth time he went out. While he was gone the little boy went out to play. While he was shooting with his bow and arrows he saw someone coming toward him. He was not a man, but a boy of his own size, and had with him a bow and arrows. Medicine-Man's boy was afraid of him, and was about to run and cry when the unknown boy spoke to him, saying: "Don't be afraid of me, brother; I know you don't know me. I am your elder brother." The unknown boy looked queer to him. He had a rather long nose and very long hair, but Medicine-Man's boy was not afraid of him since he had spoken. He continued: "I know you are lonely; that is why I thought of coming down here to see you. Every time our father goes out for a hunt I will come to see you, but you must not tell him that I came to see you while he is gone. Say nothing to him about me. Now, brother, let us see who is the best shot with the bow and arrows." They began to play. Finally he said to his brother, "Father is coming and I must go," and he ran back to the woods. Medicine-Man was far from home when the boy saw him coming, and when he came the boy was gone, and his son did not say anything about his having been there.

Again Medicine-Man went to hunt, the second time and the third time and the fourth time. When he came home in the evening after he had been out the fourth time the boy seemed troubled. They ate and then went to bed. About midnight the boy woke up and thought of his secret brother, and he thought at once that he must tell his father about his brother. He woke his father and said: "Father, I have something to tell you, although I was told not to say anything about it to you." Medicine-Man gave very close attention. "Father, somebody comes here every time you go out to hunt, and he is not very big; he is about my size. When he first came he frightened me and I started to run, but did not know where to go, and I began to cry and the boy told me not to be afraid of him, for he was my brother. He has a long nose and wears long hair and has a bow and arrows, and we always play around here every time you go out to hunt and he treats me kindly. He seems to see you, no matter where you are, and when you start home he knows when you are coming, and then runs for the woods, and when you get here he is gone." "Well, my boy," said Medicine-Man, "we must capture the boy some way. You must go out there and play just as if I had gone away again, and whenever he asks you where I am, tell him I am out hunting. I will turn into a very small insect and stay behind the door."

The little boy ran out next morning with the bow and arrows and began to play at the usual place. Finally the other boy came, but before he came near he spoke and asked Medicine-Man's boy where their father was, and the boy said that he had gone out hunting again. The boy began to look around, and finally he said: "Who is that man behind the door?" at the same time running back to the woods.

Again the next day the boy went out to play; this time Medicine-Man placed himself at the edge of the roof of the grass house. When the boy came he asked his brother where their father was. He answered that he had gone out hunting, but the boy would not come near. He began to look around, and finally he said: "Who is that man under the roof?" and he ran back into the woods again. Then Medicine-Man said: "We must catch him some way. When he sits down near to you, tell him that something is crawling in his hair, and then he will let you look in his hair. Then catch hold of a small bunch of his hair and tie it up four times; then call me and I will be there just as soon as I can. You must not let him go until I get there." The little boy understood.

The other boy had already run away twice and this was the third attempt.

This time Medicine-Man placed himself in the middle of the fire. The boy went out and began to play. Soon the other boy came. He asked the boy where their father was and he told him he went out to hunt. The unknown boy began to look around, and finally he said: "Who is that man in the fire?" and then he ran back to the woods. The next day the boy went out and began to play and the unknown boy came again, and asked the boy the same question. The boy answered that their father had gone out to hunt. This time Medicine-Man had placed himself behind another door, and the unknown boy found him again and went back to the woods. And so the fifth time came, and this time Medicine-Man placed himself in the air, and when the unknown boy came he found him again and went back to the woods.

Medicine-Man tried once more. If he failed the sixth time he could do nothing more, for he would have used all his powers. He told his boy to go out again to play as usual, and this time his own boy did not see which way he had gone. Finally the other boy came and asked where their father was, and he told him that he was out hunting. This time the unknown boy believed him, and so he came near and sat down by him and the little boy got hold of his hair and said: "There is something crawling up in your hair, brother," and then the boy told him to get the bug out of his hair; and the boy began to do as he had been told, and when he got through he called out, "All ready, father." Medicine-Man jumped out from the grass house, and then they captured the boy and took him into the grass house and held him there for six days. At the end of the sixth day the little boy boiled some water and they washed the other boy, and Medicine-Man cut his nose off and made it look like a human nose. Medicine-Man said: "You have been coming here when I am absent and have been playing with my son and you call him brother. Now you may be his brother and stay with him and go out and play with him." The boys went out to play, and before Medicine-Man went to hunt again he went over to see the boys and told them he was going to hunt, and told them to stay at home and not to go to a certain place in the timber, where some very large squirrels lived, for they often killed little children. After their father was gone the unknown boy told his young brother they would go there and see the squirrels, and so they started. They could not find the place for a while, but finally they did, and they stood there for a good while watching the big hole in the tree.

After a while one of the big squirrels came out, and sticking his tongue out like a snake, took the younger brother into the tree. The other boy stood there watching the squirrel take his brother into the hole. He did not try to help his brother, for he knew he could get him out of the hole whenever he wanted to. After the boy had disappeared he went back to their home, and when he got there he found their father already returned from the hunt. The father asked him where his son was, and the boy told him that his brother and he were making lots of arrows, and that he came home after fire to dry the arrows with it. He took the fire and carried it to the timber, where he placed it near the tree where the large squirrel was. Then he brought some hard, red stones and put them in the fire, and when the stones were very hot he took one of them and threw it into the hole, and then another one. While he was standing there watching the hole he saw the large squirrel come out from the hole and drop down on the ground dead. Then he went over and cut the squirrel's stomach open and found his brother in there, still alive. He took him down to the river and washed him and then they both went home.

Sometimes these two boys would go out to make arrows. One time when they went out the unknown boy made two arrows for his young brother; one he painted black and the other he painted blue. They made a small wheel out of bark of the elm tree. One of the boys would stand about fifty yards away from the other, and then would roll this little wheel to each other and would shoot the wheel with the arrows. They played with the wheel every day until finally Medicine-Man's boy failed to hit the wheel, and the wheel kept rolling and did not stop until it went a long way from them, and they never found it again. The boy felt very bad, and he wanted to get the wheel back, and so the unknown boy said: "Don't worry, brother, for we can get the wheel back again." And so they started out, and they did not let their father know where they were going, nor how long they would be away from home. They went a long way and they could see the trace of the wheel all the way. Finally the unknown boy said: "Well, brother, we are about halfway now, and we must stop for a rest." They began praying to the spirits to help them. The unknown boy had two pecans, and he told his brother to watch, that he was going to put one of the nuts in the ground. Then they began to pray again, and while they were praying the pecan began to sprout, and it grew taller and larger. Finally the tree grew so tall that it went clear up into the sky and then the unknown boy told his brother that he was going up on this tree, and that he must sit near to the tree, but must never look up to the sky, but down on the earth, and that he was going to be gone for a good while, until he dropped all the bones that he had in his body; that at the last he would drop his head, and then the boy must gather all the bones up, put them on a pile, cover them with buffalo calf's hide, take the black arrow and shoot it up just as hard as he could, and when he heard the arrow coming down to tell him to get out of the way, that the arrow was coming right on him, and that the pile of bones would get out of the way. Then he started climbing up the tree and the little boy sat on the ground looking down. After a while he saw one of the bones drop, and then another and another, and so on until all the bones had dropped, and then he gathered them up and piled them together and covered them with the buffalo calf's hide. Then he shot the black arrow just as he was told, and when he heard the arrow coming down he cried out: "Look out, brother, the arrow is coming down right on you. Get out of the way." His brother jumped out from the buffalo calf's hide, and the arrow stuck right where the hide was. He said, "My father gave me very dangerous power, and so, brother, you must climb up the tree and he will give you power, too." The little boy climbed the tree, and he went clear up as far as the other boy had gone. He did not know where he was, and it seemed like a dream to him, and when the bones began to fall from his body he did not know it. All he remembered was that there was someone talking to him, but he did not see who it was, and the next thing he heard was, "Look out, brother, the arrow is coming right down on you. Get out of the way." He jumped out of the way and saw his brother standing there. His brother asked him what kind of a power he had received, and he told him that it was a great power. The boy told his brother to show him what kind of a power he had, and then the little boy began making a loud noise that sounded like thunder when it rains, and then the unknown boy let his tongue out and it looked like a flash of lightning.

They went on until they came to a large lake, and when they looked near the edge of the water they saw the trace where the wheel had passed into the water, but they could not find any place to cross. They sat down on the bank of the lake and began to pray again, and the boy planted another pecan, and soon a large tree sprang up; but this time the tree did not grow upward, but bent over across the lake to the opposite bank, and so made a bridge for them to cross upon. They went across the lake, and when they got across they saw the trace of the wheel, and a little way from the landing place they saw a narrow road leading toward the east, and a little way from the end of the road they saw that the trace of the wheel was gone. A little way from there they saw an old man going toward the lake, and then the boy who had the power of lightning said: "We must kill this man, because we know he is a bad man; he is a cannibal." When they met this old man Lightning boy said to Thunder boy: "This is the old man who took our wheel, and he has it with him now, and it is in his right side." They killed the old man and found the wheel and took it, and then they went on and they saw, a long distance from them, a smoke, and they went there and found many people. The people did not know who they were at first; they thought they were the old man, for this old man whom they had killed was their head man; and so these two brothers killed all the rest of the people. They began to look all around and finally they came to a pile of human bones. They found the bones of the wife of Medicine-Man. Only one little finger was missing. They piled the bones together and covered them with the buffalo calf's hide, and Lightning boy shot the black arrow up, and when they heard the arrow coming down they said: "Look out, Mother, the black arrow is coming right on you. Get out of the way," and the woman jumped out of the way. The boys greeted their mother, and then they all started back for their home, and when they came near to their home Lightning boy said that he was going on ahead. The other boy and his mother came on behind. Lightning boy got there first and found their father a very old man, and still weeping for his children. The yard around the grass house was overgrown with tall trees and weeds and grass, for the old man was not able to work any more. Lightning boy told him that his son and his lost wife were coming. The old man was glad, and went out to meet them. They all lived happily for a number of years; then the father and mother died. The boys were lonely then, and so they decided to leave this world. They went up in the sky, and now when the clouds gather together for a storm Lightning and Thunder, which are these two boys who once lived on the earth and killed the monsters that lived here, are seen in their midst.[4]

This text has a fragmentary form of the Thrown-Away motif, coupled with the death of the mother by a monster. The capture and domestication of the wild boy is generally the same as the Cherokee and Creek versions. Otherwise, however, it is divergent. The adventures do not match the other two sequences, and the story moves to revenge and resuscitation of the slain woman. The Caddo are in agreement with the Cherokee that the two boys become the Thunders, while that status is only weakly hinted at by the Creek text, which has them go to the east and west, identifiable by red clouds.

Careful examination of these three major Southeastern texts reveals that we seem to have three different versions of the twin heroes in the region. Despite the fact that the opening episode is a variant of LBTA, the Caddo text fits the larger Caddoan tradition of twin divinities, which has affinities to the Twins *(Ahaiyute)* of the Puebloan peoples of the Southwest, while the Cherokee and Creek versions are closer to each other. Even so, the Cherokee identification of the Twins as Thunders groups them with the Caddo, Pawnee, and Pueblo.

The number of texts of the Twins tales which have been collected in North and South America is truly staggering, leading Radin to consider the Twins corpus "the basic myth of the North American Indians."[5] On comparison it seems that there are some Southeastern distinctive traits. As we have already seen, the maize legend is peculiar to the Cherokee, and two episodes are peculiar to the Creek texts, the use of stinging insects and the transformation of· their father to a crow by the brothers. There are fairly close cognates to the Cherokee text from the Micmac, Seneca, Ojibwa, and Menomini.[6] This affinity is shown by the cannibal and wolf-ballgame episodes. The affinities of the Creek text—on the basis of the episodes of Burr-woman and Thunderbird-eggs—are with the Iowa, Omaha, and Sauk and Fox.[7]

As we might expect of so important a legend, the Twins tradition has been studied by several scholars. Reichard examined the available texts and concluded that all the LBTA legends were disseminated from the Plains area, but that was a very early conclusion based primarily on the opening sequence.[8] Sumner followed with a careful study of just the birth of the brothers; she concluded that there were three different oicotypes, or subgroups of similar texts:

Roughly, the Northeastern is an elder brother–younger brother story, in which the mother is devoured, her death avenged, the unknown child shy but not strongly animal, the elder brother lacking in supernatural power... The baby-afterbirth Southeastern tale is modified by the "twins" variety in the Southern Plains (Red River) region (i.e., Caddo). It may be characterized by devouring of the mother; instability of origin of the stronger boy, with contamination (!) by the bloodclot idea; and his wildness and badness...The "twins" tales, influenced by both these types in the Central area of overlap, are distinctive in that they contain the following episodes: mother slain by a hungry stranger who eats from her stomach; caesarian section; one or both twins deliberately thrown away; marked animal traits of the wild boy; and resurrection of the mother.[9]

This problem of subtyping is a complicated one, for it depends to a great extent on which elements are chosen for comparison. Reichard and Sumner followed the path of comparing just the opening sequence, but it appears that comparing the motif-sequences as a whole leads to some different conclusions. While Sumner's analysis made great use of the different types of origin—twins, elder brother–younger brother, baby-afterbirth—the common characteristic of the LBTA complex is the fact that they are brothers (or the functional equivalent) who have marvelous adventures.[10] Sumner did examine the adventures, and she concluded that the episodes of "Thunderbird-eggs" and "Father flees" were probably part of the original form. The almost exact correlation of distribution of the former and "Burr-woman" indicates that that motif should be added to the list; if "Thunderbird-eggs" belongs, so does "Burr-woman."

The suggested oicotype is this: the ogre kills a woman, brothers are born from the remains, wild boy tamed, boys have adventures with Thunderbirds and Burr-woman, frightening their father so much that he flees. If this hypothetical sequence is compared to the texts, only Creek, Iowa, and Sauk/Fox seem to fit it. If the Pawnee LBTA text had the Burr-woman (which does exist in another legend text), it would be in the group also. This at least identifies the Creek source group, even if it seems a bit surprising. We may theorize that all of these tribes developed a characteristic LBTA legend sequence while in close relationship, which give a good clue as to the direction of former locations of the Creeks, or part of them.

Since it seems clear that the Creek LBTA tradition is linked to non-Southeastern groups, then we need to look more closely at the Cherokee Twins. "Kanati and Selu" is unique in that it embodies the maize legend and the birth of the wild boy from blood washed from deer, a variant of the "bloodclot" motif in which a clot of blood is found in strange circumstances (frequently from the body of the slain mother). Since the maize legend forces the brothers to kill their mother, the death of the mother by a monster, as seen in the Caddo text, could not be the birth story, and the bloodclot idea works well as a replacement. One scholar has suggested that the Cherokee opening has to do with Selu's breaking a taboo, but this comparative examination

171

indicates instead that the afterbirth/bloodclot is the norm for this legend, with no trace of a broken taboo.[11] A better way of viewing this is to look at it as a structural opposition of the Under World (water) and animals (blood) against the human world.

It is an accepted axiom in the study of folklore that a motif or tale has "meaning" only within the context of each particular ethnic group which uses it, but this does not preclude the possibility of general structural meaning of figures and motifs. One of the themes of the LBTA story used by Sumner as a variable in evaluating subtypes, is the "wildness" of the Thrown-Away figure, but this aspect of the legend seems more than an incidental characteristic. In the LBTA texts this "wildness" is reflected in several ways. (1) The boy is raised in the animal world and has little knowledge of the human world. (2) He must be tricked and trapped by his father and brother, almost as if he were an animal. (3) Once caught, he must be taught—"domesticated" and "tamed" are words frequently used—and some texts even portray this physically as the breaking out of his dangerous non-human front teeth. (4) He is extremely resistant to authority; in the "dreadnaughts" episodes he is the one who forces his brother to join him in disobeying their father. (5) He also has no normal fear of dangerous animals and monsters, which produces in the surrounding humans a great fear of him. (6) He wields magical power equal to that of his adversaries, such as the Thunderbird, and he has various kinds of transformation ability. In tribal life this sort of person was a shaman, a man who had access to spiritual powers which are derived from the animal world. We have already seen some illustrations of the transformation of a normal human into this intermediate category of the human who nonetheless wields awesome power granted to him by the non-human world. (7) There is a certain overtone of Trickster-like heedlessness in his actions—i.e., he rarely is portrayed as being very concerned about the results of his actions, which places his father in the parental role of maintaining order (he must return the eggs to the nest, restore the dead animals, and so on). (8) The response of his father to him is the appropriate one for dealing with a person of such power: he is terrified and wishes to get as far away as possible from the dangerous youth. Throughout the LBTA complex there is little question that the focus is on this strange "wild" brother, the one with power, rather than the normally conceived boy.

The Cherokee Thrown-Away figure fits this general imagery fairly well. He is not human, because Selu only caused the animal blood to enter the water, but he is nonetheless human, for he accepts Kanati and Selu as his parents. His "father," Kanati, is "Master of the Animals" who controls them all until the boys set them free, so even if Kanati is seen as the boy's father, the animal heritage is indicated.

The closest similarities to the Cherokee text are from the Eastern Woodlands. The Micmac, Ojibwa, and Menomini texts follow the "ogre kills mother" opening. The Seneca text is deviant in that the mother dies in giving birth to the Twins, and the Cherokee maize legend provides her death. This is a "secularized" version of the famous Iroquois creation epic in which a woman who went to the sky fell through a hole onto the earth-island provided by the Earth-diver. Her newborn daughter became magically pregnant and gave birth to the Twins, one of whose exit from her body killed her; from her body corn and beans sprouted. The Twins then participated in competitive creation, one beneficial, one Trickster-like, until the former killed the latter. It thus seems that there is an Iroquoian tradition of the death of the mother (and the origin of corn) and an Algonkin tradition of murder. Both of those versions of the Twins can be seen to be separate from the Siouan tradition in which the Creek texts participate. The Iroquoian Twins seem more closely related to the Caddoan-Puebloan Twins. However, there is yet another affinity from a surprising source—South America.

The Twins ■ ■ ■
CARIB

A long time ago, there was a woman who had become pregnant by the Sun, with twin children, Pia and Makunaima. One day the as-yet-unborn Pia said to his mother: "Let us go and see our father. We will show you the way, and as you travel along pick for us any pretty flowers that you may come across." She accordingly went westward to meet her husband, and plucking flowers here and there on the pathway, accidentally stumbled, fell down, and hurt herself; she blamed her two unborn children as the cause. They became vexed at this, and when she next asked them which road she was to follow, they refused to tell her, and thus it was that she took the wrong direction, and finally arrived, footsore and weary, at a curious house. This belonged to Tiger's mother, Kono(bo)-aru, the Rain-frog, and when the exhausted traveler discovered where she was, she told the old woman she was very sorry she had come, because she had often heard how cruel her son was. But the house-mistress took pity on her, and telling her not to be afraid, hid her in the big cassiri jar, and popped on the cover. When Tiger got home that night, he sniffed up and down, and said, "Mother, I can smell somebody! Whom have you here?" And though she denied having anybody on the premises, Tiger was not satisfied, but had a good look round on his own account, and peeping into the cassiri jar, discovered the frightened creature.

On killing the poor woman, Tiger found the two as-yet-unborn children, and showed them to his mother, who said that he must now mind and cherish them. So he put them in a bundle of cotton (from the ceiba tree) to keep them warm, and noticed next morning that they had already begun to creep. The next day, they had grown much bigger, and with this daily increase in about a month's time they had reached man's size. Tiger's mother told them that they were now fit to use the bow and arrow, with which they must go and shoot the

173

Powis (Crax) because it was this bird which had killed their own mother. Pia and Makunaima therefore went next day and shot Powis, and these birds they continued shooting day after day. When they were about to let fly the arrow at the last bird, the Powis told them that it was none of his tribe who had killed their mother, but Tiger himself, giving them both full particulars as to how he had encompassed her death. The two boys were very angry on hearing this, spared the bird, and coming home empty-handed, informed the old woman that the Powis had taken their arrows away from them. Of course this was not true, but only an excuse; they had themselves hidden their arrows in the bush, and wanted the chance of making new and stronger weapons. These completed, they built a staging up against a tree, and when Tiger passed below, they shot and killed him. And when they reached home, they slaughtered his mother also.

The two lads now proceeded on their way and arrived at last at a clump of cotton-trees in the center of which was a house occupied by a very old woman, really a frog, and with her they took up their quarters. They went out hunting each day, and on their return invariably found some cassava that their hostess had baked. "That's very strange," remarked Pia to his brother, "there is no field anywhere about, and yet look at the quantity of cassava which the old woman gives us. We must watch her." So next morning, instead of going into the forest to hunt, they went only a little distance away, and hid themselves behind a tree whence they could see everything that took place at the house. They noticed that the old frog had a white spot on her shoulders: they saw her bend down and pick at this spot, and observed the cassava-starch fall. On their return home they refused to eat the usual cake, having now discovered its source. Next morning they picked a quantity of cotton from the neighboring trees, and teased it out on the floor. When the old woman asked what they were doing, they told her that they were making something nice and soft for her to lie upon. Much pleased at this, she promptly sat upon it, but no sooner had she done so than the two lads set fire to it; thereupon her skin was scorched so dreadfully as to give it the wrinkled and rough appearance which it now bears.

Pia and Makunaima next continued their travels to meet their father, and soon arrived at the house of a Maipuri (tapir), where they spent three days. On the third evening Maipuri returned, looking very sleek and fat. Wanting to know what she had been feeding on, the boys followed her tracks, which they traced to a plum-tree; this they shook and shook so violently as to make all the fruit, both ripe and unripe, fall to the ground, where it remained scattered. When Maipuri next morning went to feed, she was disgusted to see all her food thus wasted, and in a very angry mood quickly returned home, beat both boys, and cleared out into the bush. The boys started in pursuit, tracked her for many a long day, and at last caught up with her. Pia now told Makunaima to wheel round in front and drive the creature back to him, and as she passed, let fly a harpoon-arrow into her; the rope, however, got in the way of Makunaima as he

The Twins

was passing in front, and cut his leg off. On a clear night you can still see them up among the clouds: there is Maipuri (Hyades), there Makunaima (Pleiades), and below is his severed leg (Orion's Belt).[12]

Here we have some surprising similarities, despite the changes in detail. The death of the mother by a monster, the rapid growth of the twins, their hunting prowess, their revenge on the killer, their killing of the cassava-woman, their apotheosis into the sky—all seem related to the Twins-LBTA complex of North America. The fact that the cassava-woman, like the Cherokee Selu, is part of the Twins narrative is provocative in that it indicates that the maize legend is connected with the Twins in South America as well as among the Cherokee and Iroquois. One scholar has examined the spread of the Twins legends in South America, and he found that northern South America seems to be the source of them. "The widespread diffusion of the myth in the Amazonian basin suggests that it forms part of the common cultural background of the Carib, Tupi-Guarani and Arawak tribes."[13] Since he was restricting himself to South America, he failed to point out that the Southeast could be considered a northern distribution of the same complex, but that appears to be the case.

The Twins, then, are known as twins in South America, the Iroquoians, the Caddoans, and the Puebloans, and a special oicotype—LBTA—was developed in the central part of North America from which an extension into the Southeast via the Creeks placed it alongside the Twins version of the Cherokee.

CHAPTER NINE

The Wonderful Garments

We have seen that the Creeks and Cherokee share a legend of the origin of maize, the myth of the woman from whose body springs the wonderful plant. In Cherokee lore it occurs in the context of a Twins myth which seems to be ancient. The Creeks, however, tell the maize legend in connection with a single hero known as "the Orphan."

The Wonderful Garments ■ ■ ■
CREEK

Bloodclot

One time some people were living in a certain place, and they noticed that the dripping from the eaves of the house (I do not know whether this was during a rainstorm or not) was red. So they picked up some old pieces of pottery which had been dripped upon (called *paski'*) and put them under the bed. During that night they heard something under the bed crying like a child, so they drew out what they had placed there and found it was a baby. The old woman who found him took care of him and nursed him until he grew up. When he got to be about four feet tall, she made a bow and arrows for him, and he wandered about shooting. A long way off from where they lived was some rising ground, and the boy was told never to go to that and look beyond it. When the boy went out hunting for the first time he came in and said to the old woman, "Some things with blue heads came running." "Those were turkeys," she said; "we can eat them. Kill them. They are game." The next time he came in he said, "I saw some things with white tails." "We eat those. They are good," said the old woman.

Maize

When he got back with these various things he would find the old woman with white dumplings and other corn foods, and he wondered how she got them. One time he came back and, instead of entering the house, peeked through a crack. Then he saw the old woman shake her body, and when she shook it the grain poured out of her.

By and by the young man went over to the rising ground which he had been warned not to cross and looked over. On the other side he saw people playing ball. When he came back the old woman offered him some food but he would not eat and she said, "You scorn me, then." He had seen men and women on the other side of the hill, and he did not care for her any more.

Garments

Then the old woman told him to find a rattlesnake and a blue jay. Out of these she made him a fife (flute). That was to be an ornament for the top of his head.

Maize

Then she told him to kill the trees all about to make a field. "When you get through," she said, "take me and drag me all around over that place and burn me up, and after three months come over and look at me."

Theft

The boy did as the old woman had told him, and afterwards he put on the headdress she had made for him and crossed the rising ground again. There he met a Rabbit who made friends with him. They went on together and presently they came to a pond where there were turtles, and Rabbit said, "Let us go in and get some turtles." So they got ready, and when Rabbit said, "Dive," they dove together under water. Rabbit, however, instead of remaining down there getting turtles, came out right away, seized the youth's headdress and ran away with it. Meanwhile the youth collected a number of turtles which he tied to a cord and brought ashore. He found that Rabbit had disappeared with his headdress, but he took the turtles he had caught and went along until he came to a house. Putting his turtles into a hole which had been dug near by he went to the door and said to the old woman who lived there, "You had better make a fire and cook those turtles, and send round to invite all of your neighbors." She did so and had a feast. After the feast all met at the square ground. When Rabbit came there wearing his red coat and headdress, the rattlesnake and jay called out, "The rumor is that Pasakola has stolen that man's cap." He struck them with his flute to make them stop, but they kept on calling just the same and trying to get to their true master, so the people took them away and gave them to him.

Calling the Fish

After that the youth took the old woman's daughter as his wife. One day he went down to the river with her and washed his head in the stream, and all of the fish floated up intoxicated. Then he said to his wife, "You had better tell your mother to come down and cook this fish." So the old woman went down to the creek and found lots of big fish there, and she told the young men to go all around the edge of the town and notify everybody to come to the feast. All did so.

Split-Wife

By and by the youth told his wife to comb her hair in the center, and when she had done it he seated her on the doorstep, took an ax, and with one blow cut her in two so cleverly that he made two women out of her.

After that Rabbit thought that he could do the same thing. So he went down to the creek and washed his head and told his wife (who was sister to the wife of the other man) to tell her mother to go down and get the big fish there. She went down, but there was nothing there. Then Rabbit had his wife comb and part her hair, seated her on the doorstep and struck her on the head, killing her instantly.

Maize

By and by the youth recalled what the first old woman had told him about going back to see where he had dragged her about, and he did so. He found the whole place covered with red silk corn (probably yellow corn). Wormseed and cornfield beans were also growing in this field. So he used the wormseed as a "cold bath" (medicine) before he ate the corn and the beans, and that is why they now take it before eating corn in busking time.[1]

The motif of the wonderful garments is here introduced by the "blood-clot" motif, but the garments legend is also told in the Southeast without that introduction. The Koasati text has a child stolen from his parents by a man from an adjacent tribe; when the boy disobeys the taboo against looking toward his former home he decides to leave; the garments episode ensues.[2] Two Alabama texts are similar, but they omit the opening episode altogether.[3] The two Natchez texts also have the stolen boy, mountain-taboo, and the garments episodes, and one adds the maize legend.[4] In the Southeast, at least, the bloodclot-birth and the stolen-boy appear to be allomotifs. The Alabama,

Koasati, and Natchez have a stolen-boy episode which is shared only partially with the Creeks; the bloodclot motif seems to be not Muskhogean, but solely Creek.

The bloodclot motif is not unknown elsewhere, however. The North American occurrences have been studied and oicotypes established. The Creek connection, as we found true of the LBTA legend, seems to be with the Plains Siouan group. The Ponca, Iowa, and Pawnee all have the bloodclot boy and the wonderful garments.[5] The Omaha have the garments episode without the bloodclot opening.[6] Another Pawnee text opens with a Thrown-Away motif instead of bloodclot. That text can give us the flavor of the Plains relatives of the Creek Orphan.

Dirty Boy ■ ■ ■
SKIDI PAWNEE

Thrown-Away
There was a village in a bottom. There were several lakes around this village. The largest of the lakes was on the west side. There was a beautiful maiden among the people, and many young men tried to marry her, but she would not marry.

At last she found out that she was pregnant, although she had had no connection with any man. She was in trouble. She left the village. She went to the lake west of the village. She sat down under a bank and stayed there for many days, until she gave birth; and when she did so, she threw the child into the water. When she became able to walk she went back home.

Child of the Animals
In her dream she saw a woodpecker sitting on a limb, which asked her to come to look every day so that she could nurse the child. It told her that the birds of all kinds had taken the child in charge, and they wanted the mother to come and nurse it; that not only the birds, but the bears, otters, muskrats, minks, and other animals that stayed in the water had taken the child, too. She woke up, and the next day she went to look, and there she found her baby lying on the bank of the lake. She nursed it, laid it back, and went home. This she did for several years, and then the child disappeared. It was never brought to the bank of the lake again.

Garments
Once in a great while they would see this child going through the village. It

wore a little robe, leggings with live birds on them, and moccasins with porcupine quills, and its cap had woodpeckers all around it. It was made out of a piece of buckskin to go around the head. The woodpeckers were placed on the inside of the band with the tails sticking up, while the necks were turned around the bottom of the band with the heads pointing upward, so that the red parts of the heads were turned outside and could be seen.

When they saw the young man the people tried to talk with him, but he generally disappeared from them; and if they saw him and followed him, he disappeared on the bank, and they would afterward see him on an island.

One day he came to the camp and met his mother, who asked the boy about the island. The boy told his mother that the island was covered with sweet-smelling grass and herbs, and that all roots were fine smelling; that all things on the island were his; that he could eat grass, or eat the water plants that grew in the pond; that if he wanted anything to eat, all he had to do was to get a bow and an arrow that he had, such that when he shot at anything (as for example a bush), he would kill a rabbit or something that he could use for meat. The boy told the mother that he was sorry she did as she did; but as it was now, it seemed to have been done for his good, that he might be the child of the animals.

The people knew that this young man's name was Raktihatsiriwis, Woodpecker. So the boy made his home on the island; he never stayed in the village.

Contest

One bright, beautiful morning, as the people arose and went out, they saw many coyotes leaving the village, and among them was a beautiful red coyote, something unusual. People talked about it. It got so it was a common thing for the people to get up early and see the coyotes leaving the village and see this red coyote amongst them.

The people took such an interest in it that finally the chief came out, too, and wanted to see the red coyote. When he saw it he entered his lodge, and sent his servants to gather the people. When they were gathered the chief told them that whosoever should capture the coyote and kill it should have his daughter to marry. So the young men and the old men all went out and set to planning how to capture the red coyote. So they found a plan: Each man was to dig a hole seven feet deep, and that hole was to be his. They spread coverings over these holes and tied weights to them, and then spread a little hay over that, so that if a coyote went over it it would fall through.

Each morning the men went out to see their holes, but they found nothing in them. So instead of looking into their holes every morning when they got up, if they saw the red coyote among the coyotes that were going out and leaving the camp, they did not bother about going to see into their holes.

Dirty Boy

On the west side of the village there lived a woman and her grandson. The woman's name was Spider-Woman, and the boy's name was Burnt-Belly—he had no shirt on, and his belly was burnt on account of sitting by the fire all the time. They were very poor. Each morning the boy would run into the village and enter a lodge, and would go direct to a mortar, and he would find many grains of corn around the mortar that had dropped out while the old women were pounding their corn; and he would get four or five handfuls, so that it made quite a pile. Then he took it home to his grandmother, and she pounded it up and made mush, and that was the way they lived. There were a number of young men that used to make a practice of getting out in the morning and standing by the tipi of the old woman and the boy, and yelling, "It is raining," at the same time urinating on the tipi and making fun of the inmates.

One day it was noised through the camp that this man who had on the woodpecker cap was coming from his island to the village, and was now to marry one of the chief's daughters. So one night he came over, and on going close to this old woman's tipi he came to one of these holes, and not knowing there was a hole there, he fell in. There he stayed for several days.

Theft

Some mean fellow made it a practice to visit the holes, in order that if by chance the red coyote had fallen in, he would have the first chance to take it out, when he would take it to the chief and would marry the daughter of the chief. This man's name was Crow-Feathers (Coyote). While he was going around visiting these holes, he came to the place where the man had fallen through. Crow-Feathers looked down, and he saw the man in the hole. He said: "Hallo, are you down there? How long have you been there?" The man said: "I have been here for several days, without anything to eat. I fell in." When he spoke Crow-Feathers knew the man from the cap he wore on his head. He saw the woodpeckers and they made quite a noise. He said: "Do you want to get out?" The young man said: "Yes." "Well," said Crow-Feathers, "I shall help you to get out, but you must remember that I am by myself; that I cannot very well take you out with all your clothing on. First of all, hand me that thing you have on your head; now take off your moccasins and hand them to me." Each time Crow-Feathers asked for something the man handed it to him. Then the man said: "Take off your moccasins and hand them to me." The man did so. Then Crow-Feathers asked for the robe the man had on. Crow-Feathers then said: "Now wait a minute while I get my strings untied." He sat down and put on the moccasins and the leggings and the robe, and the headdress he put on his head, then he started for the village and left the man in the hole.

So the man with the things on now went and asked the chief to let him marry his daughter. It had been understood through the village that this mysterious being was to marry the chief's daughter. He had disappeared, but he had now arrived, and they knew that he had come to marry the chief's daughter. Now the chief gave his consent, but the younger girl did not like it, for she noticed that the birds, instead of hooting and singing for the boy, were pecking at his head, so that his head was getting sore. Anyhow, he married the chief's daughter and made his home with the chief.

The people in the village were now starving for something to eat, and the chief sent scouts out all over the country to find some kind of game for the people to eat, but they were unsuccessful.

One morning, about five or six days after the man had fallen into the hole, the little boy, the grandson of the Spider-Woman, was going along, and he went by the hole where the man was, and he heard a noise and looked down in the hole, and there stood a man who was in a poor condition. He never said anything to the man, but ran to his tipi and told his grandmother that he saw a man in a hole, who was very poor. She picked up her pack-strings, went to the hole, looked down, and saw this man. She said: "My son, how long have you been there?" The man said: "For several days; I am nearly starving." She now let her pack-strings down, and the man was so weak that he could not stand; so he raised himself a little, put the head-piece under his legs, and held on to the strings. The old woman and the boy pulled the man up. As soon as they got him up she put him on her back and carried him to her tipi. Then she sent the boy through the village to pick up corn, so that she could make mush for him. She fed him on this for several days, until he got a little stronger, and when he was stronger he asked the old woman to go to the timber and cut two good-sized ash poles and five or six dogwood poles. She went and brought the sticks. The boy told the old woman to make two bows out of the two ash poles, and of the dogwood she must make arrows. She made the bows and arrows, one bow for the man and one for her grandson.

Hunting Power

One day, when he was strong enough to walk, he asked the boy to go into the timber with him to try and kill small birds for food. So this young man took aim at a great pile of brush, which was a rat's nest. He shot at it, and told the other boy to run and to see what he had shot. The boy went, and he found the wood-rat with an arrow through its body. They picked up the rat, took out the arrow, and carried it home, and the old woman cooked the rat. They ate it for their dinner.

The next day they went out again. This time they killed a rabbit. They went home and cooked it. A third day they went, and they came to a thicket, and the young man shot at the thicket; they heard the scream of a fawn, and the little fellow ran and killed the young fawn. They took out the arrow, the boy threw the fawn upon his back, and they took it home. The old woman cooked it and they ate it.

On the fourth day they went again, and instead of going through the timber, he took the little fellow upon the island, and there they killed an elk. They cut up the meat, and each packed half of it upon his back and took it home. The old woman cooked some of the meat; and after the boys had come in, one of the chief's younger daughters came in and saw this young man, and thought she knew him. After that she came in and visited them every day.

Revenge

Now the young man had grown strong, and they had plenty of meat. He told the old woman to go into the timber, to cut a good-sized ash bough, and bring it to him. He told her to peel off the bark and to cut it at the ends, at one end to make a handle, and shave it down, so that a person could grasp it.

The people in the camp wondered why Crow-Feathers, who had all this fine clothing and the woodpecker headdress, did not bring game, for they understood that he had wonderful powers. When the boy rescued by the old woman had become well and strong, one morning he picked up the club that had been made for him and went to the chief's lodge; he went in, and saw his things hung up, and the man who left him in the hole was sitting by the chief's daughter and had a long piece of meat which he pulled with his teeth. So he went up to him and tapped him on the back with his club, and the fellow begged that he would not kill him, but the young man kept on pounding him; the people in the chief's tipi did not know what this was for, but the man kept on pounding Crow-Feathers until he drove him out of the lodge; then he crushed his head, killing him.

Then he went into the lodge, and as soon as he entered the lodge the birds upon the headdress and leggings began to sing, for they were glad to see the owner of the things. The other man had laid them aside, for they continually pecked at him, until they had made his head sore. The man put on the things, and the people watched him, and he entered the old woman's lodge.

Hunting Power

That night the young man, the boy, and the old woman were sitting in their tipi, when the young man told the old woman to go outside and to make a circle around the tipi, as far as she wanted to go, and as large as she wished the tipi to be. She went about the tipi in a circle. She came in, and the boy told her to put her robe over her head and to close her eyes. In a few minutes he told the old woman to open her eyes, and she did so and found herself in a nice buffalo-hide tipi; the young man told the old woman again to close and to open her eyes, and there she was, a middle-aged woman, and Burnt-Belly had also grown to be a fine young man.

The next day, when the people came out, they saw this new tipi in the west, and they asked to whom it belonged, and wondered if any new people had come to their village. Some of the people said that it was not so, but that it was the doing of the mysterious boy who used to live on the island.

When the people saw that there was plenty of meat they went there; the younger of the chief's daughters went, and the old woman was always careful to give her the best place in the lodge, for she saw that the young girl cared for the young man. The young girl and the rest noticed that the mats that were spread upon the ground in the tipi were made from flagroot tops, and the grass that was spread under the mats was sweet grass that grew upon the island, so that the tipi smelt very fragrant.

The girl now made her home with the old woman, and she finally married the young man. The chief invited the young man over to his tipi, but the young man would never go.

The young man told his servant—who, by the way, with his mother used to be made fun of, whose tipi used to be urinated on, and with whom the young man had made his home—to go and tell the old man, the crier, to come to him. The old man came to the young man's tipi and entered and sat down by the young man, who told him to go through the village, and to cry out that the men were to attack game the next day. That night the people were rejoicing that the next day they were to attack something; that they would kill, and that they would then have something to eat.

The next morning the people got together on the north side of the village, the old men with them. The young man told them to divide into two parties, one pary to go through a lake and to get on the west side of the island, and the other party to cross the lake to the island on the east side. When the two parties were on each side of the island the young man was to give the war-whoop; after that, all the men were to give the war-whoop, with hooting and all kinds of noises, and each party was to walk straight through the island. They did as they were directed; the young man gave the war-whoop, when there was a hallooing and hooting by the party on the east and on the west who were going up to the center of the island. When they got there they made a circle, and there were deer, rabbits, and other smaller and larger game, and the game seemed to go round in a circle, until they had killed all, and they took that home.

The second time the young man sent for the old man. He told them to surround another island as they had the first one; this time the game consisted of good-sized deer, and they took them home. The third time they took another island, a larger one, and here the people found elk, which they surrounded and slaughtered.

People thought so much of the young man that they would not allow him to go with them to help slaughter the game; but some of them would kill and take the meat to the young man's tipi, so that he had meat as well as the other.

The fourth time he told the old man to come, saying that he wanted him to tell the people that it was now time that they should attack buffalo. The people had not seen buffalo for some time, although they had gone out far away into the country. So the old man cried through the village, telling them to make preparation, and that the next day they were to attack buffalo. The next day the party got together on the north side of the village and stood there, awaiting orders from the young man. The young man came out from his tipi and led them up into the hills, and the people again divided into two parties, and attacked a certain ravine that was in sight. They were divided, some going west, some standing east. When the command was given to attack, the men ran their horses into the ravine, and all at once the buffalo jumped up, as if they had been sitting in the grass; but really there had been none, but the young man had called the buffalo for these people to kill. They slaughtered the buffalo and brought home much meat. They took a quantity of meat to the young man, and after that the people found many buffalo close to their village, so that other tribes came, for they had plenty to eat while other people were starving.

Strange Births

The people finally selected this young man for their chief, but he would not accept, for the oldest daughter of the chief had married Crow-Feathers, who had worn his clothes, and as the woman was with child, he wished her to bear, that he might learn what kind of an animal Crow-Feathers was.

This woman became sick and gave birth; as the thing came out it howled, and they knew it was a coyote. There was a woman sitting by, who struck it on the head and threw it to one side. Then another one was born, and it was also a coyote. The chief's daughter gave birth to seven, but as each came forth the old woman struck them on the head and laid them on one side. The coyotes, after being killed, were thrown outside of the village, where Crow-Feathers, the father coyote, was lying.

The young man then became chief, and once in a while, when the people were starving, would call the buffalo, so that the people got something to eat.

So ends the story, and the reason for the story is that the people were, in time, to have wonderful men among them, who were to be able to call the buffalo so that the people could eat the buffalo.[7]

This text contains the unusual birth, the garments, the theft and revenge, the contest, and hunting power. It must have been a favorite among the Pawnee, because there are four texts with the garments motif, and all are variations of that same motif sequence. The bloodclot and contest/impostor episodes without the garments motif are also found in even wider distribution. The basic plot is known as "Dirty Boy" (L113): "A supernatural being assumes a humble disguise. In a contest for the chief's daughter he wins the girl. Impostor who claims prize is unmasked. Loathly bridegroom assumes original form." This tale is found in the Plateau (Shuswap, Okanagon, Kutenai, Nez Perce) and the

Plains (Shoshoni, Arapaho, Blackfoot, Gros Ventre, Cheyenne, Assiniboine, Teton, Crow, Hidatsa, Mandan, Omaha, and Pawnee).[8] Among almost the same tribes, the bloodclot motif is known. That legend of the death of a woman, the birth of a boy from her blood, and his revenge on her slayer extends westward to California tribes, but only as far east as the Ojibwa and Menomini. In the Plains there seem to be various mixtures of the bloodclot legend, the Dirty Boy story, and the wonderful garments. These are even more complicated, though, because another figure is also involved.

There is a "Star-Boy," a child whose birth is from the remains of his dead mother who fell from the sky. This is known as the "Star-Husband" tale, well represented from the Northwest to the Northeast, but found in the Southeast only as a fragment from the Koasati.[9] In the Plains the Star-Husband is followed by a sequel in which the boy is adopted by an old woman and troubles her by killing animals that are her charges. He climaxes his deeds by killing the serpent under her bed; the giant serpent is, unfortunately, her husband, and she resuscitates him and sends him to the river for safety. Succeeding episodes vary considerably. The Star-Boy is known from the Arapaho, Blackfoot, Cree, Gros Ventre, Cheyenne, Pawnee, Arikara, Kiowa, Dakota, Crow, Hidatsa, and Mandan. In the last three, the "Plains Village" tribes, there is a detail from the garments episode: the old woman gives Star-Boy a flute.

Star-Boy ▪ ▪ ▪
MANDAN

At a place called the "Round Missouri" Granny had her home. A creek called "True Earth Creek" flowed into the Short Missouri, and around the Short Missouri was a flat on which Granny's garden patch was located.[10] Old Granny often went to look at her field. Once, just before reaching the mouth of the creek, she saw the print of a little child's foot in the soft ground, and when she reached the field she found her squashes crushed and corn broken down. "That is strange," said Granny. The next time she came to her field she saw the same things. She thought this was very strange and resolved to find out who did it. So she went home and made a "kickball," such as is used in a certain woman's game, and also a bow and arrows. All these she took to her garden and left them there. The next time she went to her garden the bow and arrows were gone and the ball and squashes were shot full of arrows. Evidently it was a boy and not a girl who was spoiling her garden. Granny decided to watch for the boy and soon she saw him coming, shooting his little arrows into the squashes.

"Why do you do that?" asked Granny.

"My mother is dead," said the child. "She is near here."

"Let us go and see," said Granny.

The child was so small that he could not tell how it all happened, but

Granny saw the dead mother and realized that there was nothing for her to do but to take the child to her house and make a home for him. This she did, and as the child grew older he was sometimes allowed to go hunting alone. Granny said, "Be careful, something may happen to you."

Now the boy observed something which he could not at all understand. He noticed that Granny always put a kettle of "stir-about" in her bed, and that the kettle was empty when she took it out. He investigated and found a big snake. "So this is what eats Granny's stir-about," said the little boy. He thought about it a great deal, saying to himself, "That big snake has been eating Granny's stir-about." At last he took his bow and arrows and shot the snake. When Granny came home he told her what he had done. The snake was her husband; but she did not like to tell this to the little boy, so she said, "Good, I will go and bury him." So she took the big snake outdoors and talked to him, saying, "Husband, the boy is foolish. Sometimes I am almost afraid of him myself. He killed you, but I will put you in a good place." She took him to the Missouri River, but he didn't like that, so she took him back to the round lake. He liked that place and said that if she would put him there the lake would never be dry. She put him there, and to this day the lake has never been dry.

Granny again warned the boy that he must be very careful when he was traveling about the country alone. One day the boy started out by himself and came to a place where two men were butchering a buffalo cow with an unborn calf. One of the men was a rough fellow and he followed the boy, carrying the calf and calling out: "Take this to Granny and tell her to cook it for you." The little boy was afraid of the man, and in trying to escape he backed against a leaning tree, then he backed up the tree and along its branches to the farthest end. The men put the calf in the crotch of the tree and they went on butchering the buffalo cow. After this they went away, leaving the boy in the tree. He stayed there a long time. At last the two men came back, and the more sensible of the two said to his companion, "I told you not to scare that little boy. He is still in the tree." He went near and called to him, saying, "Why do you stay in the tree?" The little boy replied, "I'm afraid of the calf." The man said, "If you will take a message to Granny, we will take down the calf and go home." The little boy consented to do this, and the man said, "Tell Granny that we want her for our daughter-in-law."

When the little boy came home, Granny pretended to be much pleased, though she had been hoping that he would never come back. She said, "I thought surely you were lost." The little boy told his strange experience and said, "The only way I could get back was by promising to tell you that these men want you for their daughter-in-law." Of course this meant that they wanted the gifts, such as robes and meat, which would accompany a daughter-in-law. Granny said, "You did exactly right. Go back to the men and tell them we have decided to do as they say. We will feed and clothe them well, but in return we ask for one of their bows and arrows."

The boy went back to the men and gave Granny's message, saying that they were good hunters and he also hunted a good deal, so he would like one of their bows. They gave him one, but as soon as Granny saw it, she said: "That bow is not good. Their medicine bow is patched with string and hangs opposite the door. Go back again and say you have wounded a deer and that the string on your bow is broken. Say that you want a bow to kill the deer, then snatch the medicine bow and run as fast as you can. They will not stop you, for you have already given part payment for it."

The boy did as Granny told him, and brought back the bow. She said, "They made you suffer, now we will make them suffer a little."

Granny went into the field and got a large sunflower stalk. She took a long section of this, bored a hole lengthwise through it, and cut seven holes in one side of it. She said the seven holes represented the seven months of winter, and told the boy that when he blew in it something would come out of it which would resemble snow. It was her intention to bring the snow to punish the two men for frightening the little boy. She told the boy to blow in the end of the sunflower stalk and taught him to play a certain melody on it.

Granny clothed the boy from head to foot in smoked buffalo hide and told him exactly what to do. She told him to travel in four circles, each smaller than the other, and to play his flute all the time. The first circle was to be at the foot of the clouds (horizon), the next a little smaller, until the fourth would bring him near the hunters. Granny said, "When you come near to your fathers, they will know it." The boy started out and traveled in a circle at the foot of the clouds, playing on the cornstalk flute which Granny had made for him. The two men were hunting as usual, and when the boy began to play, the snow began to fall. The two men said, "Something is wrong." They made a lodge to stay in until the snow should stop falling, but the snow came faster and faster, covering the lodge until only the peak was above the snow. Their medicine bow was gone, and they could kill no game. Then the more sensible of the two men said, "Someone is causing this." And the other said, "It must be so."

The boy kept circling closer and closer, playing on his flute, and the snow kept falling. The hunters had no food, and they had only melted snow to drink. When the boy came in sight, they said, "Son, we are having a very bad time." The boy replied, "That is what you gave me when I was up in the tree. Now it is my turn to make you do something for me." They said that they would, and, after talking it over, they decided to transpose their relationship, so that he would be their father instead of their son. The boy said, "All right." He stopped playing on his flute and the snow stopped falling. The boy made all the snow disappear. The men were too weak to hunt, so the boy got plenty of game for them and made them comfortable. Then he went home.

When he reached home the old Granny said, "What have you done?" The boy told her all about it, and she said: "That is good. You gave them some of their own treatment." After that the two men had to get food and gifts of clothing for the boy, because they had agreed that he should be their father. When the two men had secured these gifts they came to the lodge and told Granny and her grandchild that they had everything to satisfy all requirements, and that they would return with the articles in four days.[11]

Again we see the basic elements of the story of the wonderful garments. The complexity of this legendry among the Plains tribes seems impossible to unravel, for there was a blending of the motifs as stories were told about Dirty Boy, Bloodclot Boy, Star Boy, and the Boy with the Wonderful Garments. It is enough for us to see that the Creek legend belongs to the Plains group— Pawnee, Arikara, Hidatsa, Mandan, Omaha, Ponca, and Iowa. What sets the Creek version apart from the Plains forms is that the bloodclot birth is a minor motif and that the contest is missing, replaced by the fish and split-wife competitions with Rabbit. When we consider that Rabbit is the Southeastern trickster, as is Coyote for the Plains, and that poisoning the fish may be the Southeastern equivalent of the Plains circle drive for game, then the versions are readily seen as local adaptations of the same story. The nature of the youth is the same in both—a "child of the animals" who has great power, demonstrated in his birth, his garments of living animals, and his ability in hunting/fishing. The similarity to the wild boy of the Twins is strong, but there seems to be more of the "culture hero" about the single-hero, who uses his power for the benefit of the tribe. That the Southeastern maize legend should be connected to him in the Muskhogean world seems reasonable, for the gift of maize is the act of a culture hero rather than a trickster.

The Grandmother figure of the Creek text takes on stature, as we realize from our comparative study that she is the Maize-Earth-Moon Woman known to the Mandan as Old Woman Who Never Dies. Since we already know that the maize legend in the Creek text is a Southeastern one, we can see that the story is a reasonable synthesis of the Plains Grandmother and the Southeastern theme of maize from her grave. When Old Woman went south with the Creeks, she died.[12]

CHAPTER TEN

The Bead-Spitter/Marooned Hero

In the Southeast was told an unusual legend. Called "Bead-spitter" from its opening motif, it is represented only among the Alabama, Koasati, and Creek, but it is a thought-provoking occurrence.

Bead-Spitter ■ ■ ■
CREEK

Bead-spitter (Konapkeso'fka) lived in a certain place. Two young women heard the name and, thinking that it must belong to some person, started out to find him. They traveled an entire day and when it was getting dark met Rabbit.[1] "Where are you going?" he said. "We are going to Bead-spitter's." "Ku ku ku ku," he exclaimed, "you are naming somebody." "We do not know him," they replied, "but we thought there might be such a person and so we set out to find him." "What do you want of him?" "We want some beads." "You can't go until morning," said Rabbit. "Remain here all night." They did so, and Rabbit slept with one of them. In the morning he had disappeared, but when he came back he had a mouthful of beads which he blew all about. The one he had slept with gathered them up and began stringing them, and she said to the other, "You string some of these beads also," which she began doing.[2]

Rabbit had taken these beads from the young buzzards while their mother was away, and when she came back they told her what he had done. At that she became angry and started off to Rabbit's house. There she called out, "Pasiko-'lya' (a story name of Rabbit), what have you done to my children? You have done them great injury."

When the young women heard these words they pulled off their beads, dropped them upon the ground, and started away. Late that evening they came upon Ground Squirrel (Tcithloktco), and he said to them, "Where are you going?" "We are going to Turkey-killer's (Pin-li'dja's)," they answered. "It is a long distance," he replied. "You had better stay all night." They replied that they had been deceived before and hesitated to do so, but he answered that he was no "underminer," and he urged them to remain because it was late. "As you come near the dwelling of Turkey-killer, you will begin to find turkey feathers, at first only a few and as you go on more and more. They will be deeper and deeper and when they are over your heads you will have arrived at his house." "Then, we think we will stay with you," they answered. They did so, and set out again in the morning, but found that during the night Ground Squirrel had gotten inside of the dumplings *(odjo'tadja-haga)* they carried and eaten them all out.

By and by they came to the feathers which lay deeper upon the ground as they proceeded, and when these were over their heads they came out into the yard of Turkey-killer's house. "Whither are you traveling?" said Turkey-killer. "We heard that there was a Bead-spitter and we wanted some beads. That is why we came." "I am the one," he answered, "but I cannot provide the beads until tomorrow morning and you must remain all night."

So the young women spent the night at that place. After daybreak the man came to them and said, "Was anything wrongful done to you while you were on the way?" The one with whom Rabbit had slept denied it. "Then everything will be all right," he said. He gave a new sofki riddle (a woven basket) to each of them and continued, "Go to the creek and dip up water and if your story is true you can bring them back full but if it is false the water will run through." So they went down to the creek and dipped their riddles into it, but when they took them up the water ran through the riddle of the woman with whom Rabbit had slept, while that in the other remained.[3] When she brought it to the house the man told her to sift, and as the water came through it turned into beads. Then he told both of them to string these beads, but while he kept the one who was honest as his wife, he sent the other back. [*The text continues into Lodge-boy and Thrown-away.*][4]

This is a complicated and delightful legend. It has a trickster incident with Rabbit seducing one of the women, and another one with Ground Squirrel as trickster. Bead-spitter turns out to be "Turkey-killer," and he doesn't spit beads, but makes them magically with a basket after a truth-test. In the larger picture it seems to be a variant peculiar to the Creeks. A form which bears closer comparison with non-Southeastern texts is found in the Alabama and Koasati collections.

The Killing of Bead-Spitter ■ ■ ■
KOASATI

Two girls living in an Indian village wanted beads and said, "Let us travel to see Upward-shooter who throws down beads." They started on. As they were going they came to an Owl by the trail hunting for something in a water hole. "Where are you going?" he said. "To the home of Upward-shooter," they said. "Where is the trail to Upward-shooter's house?" "This good trail goes to my house," he said to them. "Go along the bad trail." "What are you hunting for?" they said. "I have lost in the water a sapia which I always carry on my back," he said.[5]

Then they started along the bad trail. The Owl flew around ahead, reached his house, broke a necklace of beads that was about his sister's neck, and threw the beads on the ground. Then he picked up some of the beads, put them into his mouth, and sat down. When the young women got there the Owl tried to cough as he sat and scattered beads about his yard. Then the girls picked some of them up, but there were not many.

At sundown Owl was invited to a dance. They said, "Go quickly! He wants you, Owl," so he started on that same evening. "Shut those young women up in the house," he said to his sister. So she shut up the house. He said to her, "I have placed chamber pots in the house for them." But they did not want to urinate into them, and went outside to urinate. Then he said, "Prevent them from going anywhere." When he was gone she tried to watch them, but they did not want to stay there and said, "Let us try to run to that place." So they started on.

They went on until they came to the place and found Owl dancing there with entrails tied about his neck.[6] Beads were everywhere about. They arrived and picked up the beads.[7] Then Owl returned home and when he got there whipped his sister until she cried, but the young girls stayed where they were, picking up beads. Owl did not like this; he did not like it at all. He sharpened a deerhorn. After he had sharpened it, and Upward-shooter had lain down to sleep, he took the deerhorn there, inserted it in his ear, struck against it, and killed him. Then he ran off. He got home. Then all the people informed one another and came together. And the Owl wept, "I am all alone by myself, I am all alone by myself." "The one who talks that way is the one," they said. "No, indeed, I am saying that I am left all alone by myself"...[*The text continues into the Marooned Hero legend; see discussion later in this chapter.*]

Here the Owl tries to keep the two women, a motif known as "False Bridegroom" (K1915). Owl's impersonation is found out at a dance. In contrast to the Creek text, the Bead-spitter is murdered. It is instructive to see what this legend is like in other parts of North America. Strangely, it does not appear often, and the distribution is far from the Southeast. Here is the way it was found among the Dakota of the northern Plains, formerly of Minnesota.

DAKOTA

There was a Boy-beloved (eldest son of a chief) whose spittle was all kinds of beautiful beads. So abundant were they that his people arrayed themselves therewith. As the fame of this spread abroad, the young women of surrounding tribes were all anxious to have him for a husband. And as a certain maiden was going to make him her husband, if possible, she heard behind her someone laughing. She stopped, when lo! two women came up and said, "Why, here stands Heart-killer." And they added, "Come along, Heart-killer, we are going to make the Bead-spitter our husband; let us go together." So she went with them.

These two young people were called—"The Two Women." They did not grow from the people, but grew wildly and were supernatural beings, hence their name, "The Two Women."

So Heart-killer went with them and lay down with them, as it was now night. But before they went to sleep the two women said, "Look here, Heart-killer, when the morning comes, at whosesoever head stands the birch-bark dish with quill work around it and filled with rice, she is the one who shall have Bead-spitter for a husband." So when the morning came it was standing at the head of Heart-killer, they say.

Then they went on and came to a large lake, whose farther shores could not be seen. Out on the water was a large canoe. And as this was where Bead-spitter's village was they called and said, "We have come to get Bead-spitter for our husband." Someone came rowing. When he arrived, they said, "We have come to make Bead-spitter our husband." To which he replied, "I do not know anyone by that name"; but at the same time he filled his mouth with beads, and then spat them out. The beads were scattered all around, and, laughing, they gathered them up. Then the two women went into the canoe, but the other they drove back, and said, "Go away, Heart-killer." So they went home with the man, but he was not Bead-spitter. Heart-killer stood there crying, when lo! another canoe came in sight. It was a very bright and beautiful one, for it was all metal.[9] It came on and arrived. This was the Bead-spitter, and, as he wore very bright clothing, the appearance was very splendid.

"Young woman, what are you crying for here?" he said. So she told him she had come to get Bead-spitter for a husband and what the two women had done to her. Then he said, "Come on, we two will go home." So she went home with him.

Let us return to the others.

The two women went home with the man whom they had met. His name was Teal-duck, and he lived with his grandmother. By and by someone said, "Teal-duck, Bead-spitter calls you to a feast." The Teal said, "Indeed, somebody has said something"; and then to the woman he said, "Do not come; they are making mystery; no woman looks at it." So he went. But the women said,

"We, too, are accustomed to see the supernatural; we will go," and so they went. When they reached the place there was much noise, and they came and looked in by a hole of the tent, and lo! the inmates were dancing on the back of Teal-duck. He saw his wives peeping in, and jumping up, said, "I, also, will join the dance on the Teal's back," and so he jumped about. They say this was the duck that is called the "Teal," and hence, to this day, that duck has no fat on its back, because the people danced on it, they say.

Then the two women started back, and, taking two blankets, they put bees in the one and ants in the other and went on. The other woman, who was called Heart-killer, was with the Boy-beloved. Her they took and thrust out, and then placed themselves on either side of him.

Then Teal-duck came home, and when he had lifted one blanket the bees came out and stung him; when he lifted the other the ants came out and bit him. Then he said, "Indeed, here is much that is strange," and so he opened out the blankets and the ants and bees swarmed out and drove everybody from the house. So he went and found the two wives of Teal-duck with Bead-spitter, to whom he said, "My elder brother, give me back the younger one." And so Teal-duck went home singing this song, they say:

"You Spitter of Pearls, give me back my younger wife;
For over the lake I always drive box-elder pegs."

And from this has come down to us this form of speech, viz: when sores come out on people and pus is formed, they said, "Teal-duck has shot them."

Now, when night came on, he took his sharp-grass knife, and finding the Boy-beloved sleeping with the two women, he cut off his head, and, holding it in his hand, took his station inside the tent.[10] When the people knew that the Boy-beloved lay headless there was a great tumult. So they went to the house of the Teal, but his grandmother had placed him on the top of his tent. They went in, but only a little brown heron came flying out. Hence the fowl that is called Little-Brown-Heron (snipe) is the grandmother of the Teal-duck. It flew away and alighted in the corner of a reed marsh. Then the people went and trod down and trampled up thoroughly the reed island. Hence, when all the roots of the reeds are red, they say this is the blood of the Teal's grandmother.

Then Teal-duck, having the head of the Boy-beloved, went and stood within the tent of the chief. And the mother of Boy-beloved cried, and said, "You bad, worthless fellow who debauched my child and had people dance upon your own back, you have impoverished me." While she cried, someone said, "Indeed, and was it I who did this thing?" Then they called Unktomi, and when his mother said, crying, "Who is it who says this aloud, 'Indeed, and was it I who did it?'" Then Unktomi said, 'Now, consider this: You say Unktomi is a fool; why, don't you understand this? It is he who stands within the tent who says this.'

Then they tore down the tent and beheld Teal-duck holding the head of Boy-beloved and the other hand having the knife, and [he arose] up high.

The head of Bead-spitter

"Come down," they said, "you shall live"; but up [he] went and stood in the moon. And so now, when the moon is full, what appears in it is Teal-duck holding the head of One-who-spits-out-pearls, and in the other hand is his sharp-grass knife.

This is the myth.[11]

The other Bead-spitter texts are single legends like the Dakota. The Menomini handsome man was "White Wampum," and he was killed by his brother "Hell Diver," a water bird.[12] In the Iowa text "Shell Spitter" and his father were both beheaded by his unidentified servant. The legend ends with a scatological joke.

Bead-Spitter ■ ■ ■

IOWA

[Beginning omitted.]

…He cut off their heads and rose up into the air with a head in each hand. Another chief ran and got Ishji'nki (the town herald) to exercise his power to bring back the fugitive, who was already away up in the air. Ishji'nki looked up and said:

"Uxwanyele, uxwanyele, uxwanyele, uxwanyele." ("Fall, fall, fall, fall.")

The servant came tumbling down for some distance. "Oh, Ishji'nki is surely bringing him," cried all the people. Ishji'nki kept right on singing, with his hands raised and his mouth open, while everybody gaped upward. All at once the orphan servant evacuated right in Ishji'nki's face and rose up out of sight. He went into the moon, and the black shadow sometimes visible in the moon is this boy standing there with a head in each hand.[13]

The common ending of the Dakota and Iowa texts—the translation of the murder and the head of Bead-spitter to the moon—suggests mythological status for this legend. Moreover, the peculiarity of Bead-spitter's sitting or dancing on the murderer sounds like a reference to ritual activity. The Arapaho text strengthens this possibility, for there it is specified that the dance takes place in the Sun-dance lodge. "Split-rump" was laid on the ground as a ground cover for Spitting-Horn-Shell's dance. "This Spitting-Horn-Shell danced on the backside of this little bird, because it was soft. The constant dancing made the rump split."[14] One of the few items collected from the Quapaw indicates their knowledge of Bead-spitter. "When the moon is full, the Kwapa say that a man stands within it holding the head of another man."[15]

Thus we find that the Creek, Alabama, and Koasati in the Southeast knew a legend which was known also by the Menomini, Iowa, Dakota, Arapaho, and Gros Ventre. For those peoples it was a myth of the moon related to the Sun-dance, and we can only speculate as to what it meant in the Southeast. Once again, we should note, the Creeks are related to the Plains group, while the earlier Southeast is not represented in the distribution of the Bead-spitter.

Just as the Seneca used the motif of spitting beads without the legend, it is possible to have the False Bridegroom legend without the Bead-spitter. This is how the Caddo separated them.

False Bridegroom ▪ ▪ ▪
CADDO

One time there lived an old man and woman who had two beautiful twin daughters. These girls heard of a chief who lived in another village, and rumors of his great wealth and his fame as a great chief had traveled far. The girls asked their parents if they might not go to the chief and offer themselves in marriage. Their parents consented, and so the girls started to the chief's village. They did not know just where the village was, but they started in the direction that they thought it was, and decided to ask the first person they met to direct them. They traveled along for a time and then met a man with a turkey in his hand coming down the road. They stopped him and began to talk to him. "We want to marry this famous chief, for we hear that he is good and very wealthy, but we do not know him. We have never seen him, we have not even been to his village, and perhaps we would not know him if we should see him." The man grinned to himself and said: "I am the chief and I live just a little way from here; I have been away attending a council. Well, I must say that I am willing, but wait here while I run on home and tell my grandmother."

The girls waited. They thought it strange that so great a chief should have to tell his grandmother, but they said nothing. The man, who was no other than Owl, ran on to his home, and calling his grandmother, said: "Clean up the lodge and put it in order. I am going to bring home two girls whom I am playing a joke on. They think I am the rich chief and want to marry me." After they had cleaned the lodge, for it was very disorderly, Owl said: "I am going to put this turkey which I have brought home over my bed; when you get up in the morning ask me which turkey you shall cook and pretend to point to one, and I will say, 'No, take this.' Then the girls will think that we have many turkeys and many good things to eat."

Owl went back for the girls and brought them to his grandmother's lodge. They were pleased, for everything looked neat and nice, and so they married Owl. Every day Owl came in with a turkey, and he always pretended to have been out hunting. Really he had been at the council, and the chief gave him the turkey for allowing him to sit on his back. At all the councils the chief always sat on Owl's back, and so he gave Owl a turkey every time to repay him for his trouble and the pain of holding him so long. After many moons the twins grew weary of nothing but turkey and they began to suspect something, so one day they followed Owl when he went away. They followed and saw him go to a large grass lodge. They peeped through an opening, and there they saw Owl sitting in the middle of the lodge with the chief sitting on his head. They gave a scream. Owl recognized their voices and jumped up, throwing the chief off his head, and ran home. He gave his grandmother a terrible scolding for letting the girls follow him and find him out. The girls felt so ashamed when they discovered how they had been fooled, that they slipped off to their home and told their father and mother their experience...[*Continues into a legend of impounded water.*][16]

"Bead-spitter" served as the introduction for another longer legend for the Alabama and Koasati. That legend, a complex one in its own right, we may call the "Marooned Hero." An intricate version has been collected from the Biloxi.

Marooned Hero ■ ■ ■
BILOXI

The uncle of Tuhe, the Thunder being, confined his nephew in the house and went to get medicine to administer to him. The man's wife, while going to the stream to dip up water, found a squirrel. When she returned home, she said to Tuhe, "Shoot that squirrel for me." He replied, "I cannot shoot it." But the woman said, "It is lodged in the brush."

"I cannot shoot it," repeated the youth. Then Tuhe's sister pushed an arrow through a crack in the wall of the house, and Tuhe shot through the crack, killing the squirrel. Then his sister ran thither and picked up all the claws, as she supposed, but she overlooked a very tiny one.

Whereupon the woman went thither, seized the tiny claw, and scratched herself in many places, drawing much blood; and being very bloody she lay by the fireplace, grunting there till the return of her husband. In response to his inquiry, she said, "Your nephew whom you confined in the house for the purpose of giving him magic power scratched me again and again, and so I lie here in this condition."

The enraged man said to his nephew, "Since you have been going out, you can now remain out. Fetch me arrow shafts." Then Tuhe went to gather arrow shafts. On his return with them, the uncle said, "These are not the right kind. Fetch spotted arrow shafts." So Tuhe departed again. He took some food with him, and put it down on the ground while he continued walking about. While he was seeking the spotted arrow shafts the Ancient of Rabbits found the food and sat there eating it. Just then Tuhe returned, and the Ancient of Rabbits questioned him, saying, "Why are you walking about?" "I am going about because my uncle ordered me to get him some spotted arrow shafts," replied Tuhe.

"Cut a black rattan vine into four pieces and bring them to me," said the Ancient of Rabbits. This was done by Tuhe. The Rabbit rolled the pieces of the rattan vine over and over, and, behold, they became rattlesnakes that chased one another. But they soon resumed the form of spotted arrow shafts, which Tuhe carried home on his back. On reaching home he began to make the arrows, but the uncle ordered him to go to seek turkey feathers.

He found the turkeys and gathered many feathers, which he carried home. But the uncle said, "These are not the right kind. Fetch white turkey feathers." So Tuhe had to depart again. He reached the edge of a lake, where a very Aged Man sat trapping ducks. Tuhe's dog scared off the ducks, which went out into the middle of the stream where they sat on the water. "Oh!" said the Old Man. "Someone has been coming here, and he has scared off my ducks. See! I will kill you and throw you away." Then rising to his feet he moved along. Tuhe approached him, and the Old Man said, "Why are you walking about?" "My uncle ordered me to procure the feathers of white turkeys; therefore I am walking about," replied the youth. "I will go home and eat," said the Old Man, "and then I will whip you at the place where they roll logs, in which event there will be plenty of white turkeys everywhere." So the Old Man took Tuhe to his home. When he got there, the Old Man cut a bamboo brier in four pieces, with one of which he whipped Tuhe as he moved along. On reaching the end of the course the Old Man took another piece of the brier, continuing the castigation, whipping Tuhe back to the starting point. Then he used the third piece, and finally the fourth, and then left him.

Tuhe then sat down, being very bloody. His dogs trailed him and were yelping as they came. He whistled, and the dogs came to him and licked off the blood. Then the youth arose, called his dogs, went to the house of the Old Man, and when he found him he killed the Old Man. The dogs seized the Old Woman, who cried out, "I fed him," hoping to find mercy. But they killed her. Tuhe climbed up into the loft, where he found a great quantity of dried duck meat, which he threw down, sharing it with his dogs. When he finished eating and was preparing to go home, his sister, who thought that he was dead, was coming toward him, following his trail. The dogs just then were chasing white turkeys, and the latter flew toward the approaching girl, who leaped up with arms above her head, trying to catch the turkeys. She fell to the ground with one just as her brother reached her. He picked off the feathers and carried them home to his uncle.

"Fetch deer sinew," said the uncle. So the youth departed again. He shot a deer, picked off the sinew, and carried it home to his uncle, who said, "This is not the kind. Get the sinew of a white deer." And when the youth had departed for that purpose and was walking about in search of that kind of sinew, the White Deer found him, and said, "Why are you walking about?" "My uncle said that I was to bring him the sinew of a white deer, so I am walking about," said Tuhe. "Take my sinew," said the White Deer. "Replace it with the peeled bark of the mulberry tree." And the youth did so. "He told you that because he wished your death. But he shall see you return alive," said the White Deer. Then they separated, the youth returning home.

When he got home, his uncle said, "Fetch a small bird, so that the child may have it for playing roughly." The youth departed, and when he had almost captured the young bird, the old mother came back and was flying round and round her nest. As she was thus flying, she addressed Tuhe: "What is your business?" "My uncle said that I was to fetch the young bird as a playmate for the child; hence I have been going about," replied Tuhe. "Well! wait till I go first to the village to examine it and then return hither," said the mother Eagle. She took some pokeberries in her claws and departed. When she reached the house she flew round and round above the house, and when she squeezed the pokeberries the red juice was falling into the yard.

When the people noticed this, they said, "He is dead," and they were very glad. While they were acting thus, Tuhe's sister was crying. The Eagle noticed her, and then departed homeward. On reaching home, she asked, "How large is the child?" "It is large enough to sit alone," replied Tuhe. "Well, my youngest child is always hungry," said the Eagle, as she handed this young one to Tuhe. "If the child is sitting alone when you reach home, say, 'This is the small bird about which you were speaking,' and pitch it on the child. They have done so to you just because they wish your death, but you shall not die; they shall see you home," said the Eagle.

When Tuhe reached the house with the eaglet, he pitched it on the child, and said, "This is the small bird about which you were speaking." Away went the eaglet, clutching the child in its talons, and all the people ran in pursuit of it.

Up went the eaglet, and as he flew, nothing but the bones of the child fell to the ground. Therefore since that time eagles have wanted children badly: they are fond of eating them, so say the people.

When the uncle had finished making the arrows, he made Tuhe enter a boat with him, in which they crossed the great water for the purpose of setting fire to the grass on the opposite side. "Set fire to the grass," said the uncle to Tuhe. Then the nephew went ahead firing the grass, the uncle following him. When the fire went out, the youth thought, "He must have started home," so he ran back to the bank. On reaching there he found that his uncle had the boat out in the middle of the great water; so he unstrung his bow, took off the string, one end of which he threw toward the boat. It caught on the boat, and Tuhe began to pull the boat ashore. But when it had reached the edge of the water, the uncle cut the string and it returned to the middle of the water. Then Tuhe made a loop in the string, and threw it again. Again it caught on the boat, and Tuhe began to draw it ashore. But when it had neared the edge of the water, the uncle cut the string, and away went the boat back to the middle of the stream. This was repeated with a like result. The fourth time that Tuhe threw the string, it did not reach the boat, and the uncle left him and went home.

Then Tuhe thought, "I can go around the bank of the stream." So he was walking along till it was getting dusk. Just then a Sapsucker cried out, *"Tin!"* "O pshaw! what does such an ugly bird as that amount to?" said Tuhe. "I can extricate you from your trouble," said the Sapsucker. "If you can do anything for me, please do it," said Tuhe. "You must first sleep in my house," replied the Sapsucker. "How can I climb thither?" inquired Tuhe. Whereupon the Sapsucker thrust out its tongue, which became long enough to reach to the ground, and Tuhe caught hold of the tongue, and thus climbed up the tree into the nest. While he was reclining there, the Old Woman was coming in the distance. On reaching the tree, she said, "O yes! does he not lie right here?" And she remained there hitting against the tree till day, when she disappeared.

Then Tuhe came to the ground and resumed his wanderings, traveling till dusk. Then he heard the cry of the Ancient of large black Woodpeckers. "O pshaw! what can such an ugly bird as that accomplish?" "I can extricate you from your trouble," replied the Woodpecker. "If you can do anything for me, please do it," said Tuhe. "You must first sleep in my house," replied the Woodpecker. "How can I climb thither?" inquired the youth. Whereupon the Woodpecker thrust down his tongue, which was long enough to reach the ground, and Tuhe caught hold of the tongue and thus climbed up the tree into the nest. While he was reclining there, the Old Woman was coming in the distance. On reaching the tree, she said, "O yes! does he not lie right here?" And she remained there hitting against the tree till day, when she vanished.

Then Tuhe came to the ground and resumed his wanderings, traveling until dusk. It was then that he heard the hooting of a Swamp Owl. "O pshaw!" said he, "what can an ugly swamp owl accomplish?" "I can extricate you from your trouble," said the Swamp Owl. "If you can do anything for me, please do it," replied Tuhe. "You must first sleep in my house," said the Swamp Owl. "How can I climb thither?" replied Tuhe. Then the Swamp Owl made some steps of toadstools, one of which he barely stuck on the tree, and against which he warned Tuhe, who stepped over it and climbed the tree by means of the other steps. Again was the Old Woman coming in the distance. Well, she reached there, and said, "Right here does he lie." And addressing the dogs, she said, "You must catch him when he falls, as I will climb the tree and knock him down. Though he should say, 'It is I,' do not release him." Then she started to climb the tree, putting her foot on the toadstool that was barely sticking there. It gave way, her foot slipped, and down she fell to the ground. And then the dogs seized her. Though she cried, "It is I! It is I!" they would not release her. When it was daylight the dogs released her and she disappeared.

Then Tuhe came to the ground and resumed his wanderings, going till dusk. He had gone along without anyone saying anything to him until he found a hole in the ground which he entered, and there he lay down to rest. Again was the Old Woman coming in the distance. "Right here does he lie," said she. She reached the hole and peeped down into it, but, as it lightened, she went off and fell down. So she kept on doing till day. And then she disappeared.

Then Tuhe came out of the hole in the ground and was traveling till noon, when he found a ford. He climbed a tree which stood near and was sitting up there when two women were coming to get water. On reaching the stream they peeped down into it and saw the shadow of the youth. "A very handsome man is there," said one, and she entered the water and caught at the reflection, but she brought up nothing but leaves. Thus the two continued for some time, getting very cold. At length, when Tuhe observed their condition, he spit down on them. As they raised their eyes, they beheld him, and cried, "Get down!" Then he got down, and they took him to their house, where they fed him, first offering him stewed human flesh. "I never eat such food," said he, so they gave him stewed venison. When he had eaten that, they said, "Mother is very bad." They referred to the Old Woman, whose daughters they were. They laid him in a long box, which they locked. By the time he had lain down in this box, the Old Woman had come home. Then she began to eat, and was sniffing the air. "There is food here which has a strong odor," said she. To which her daughters responded, "If there is really any food here, it must be that which you are eating." "But this has a fresh smell," said the Old Woman. "If there is anything here which has a fresh, strong odor, it must be that which you are eating," replied her daughters.

"Tcidikuna," said the Old Woman to her son, "pull that box toward me." And he pulled the box; but when he had drawn it to her and she opened it, it was empty. Then she said, "Bring the other one." That too proved to be empty, and so did a third. Then she said, "Bring that long box." When he began to pull it, he said, "O mother, it is very heavy." "Let it alone!" said she, as she ran toward it. When she reached there and opened the box, it lightened so that she retreated some distance and fell to the ground. On rising to her feet, she said, "I said that this was the way, and so it is. Make a fire in the back room." So they were making a fire there. "Tcidikuna, say to your sisters' husband (i.e., Tuhe) that he is to take a small bird and bring it to me, that I may swallow it whole." So Tcidikuna went to Tuhe, and said, "Mother says that you are to seek the small bird and bring it to her that she may swallow it." And the two daughters said to Tuhe, "If you take hold of the small bird, and it flies upwards with you, let it go and return hither." He went and grasped the small bird, which flew up into the air with him. Though they had said to him, "Let it go and return hither," he decided to retain his grasp, and so he was going higher into the air. When he had gone very high, the Old Woman said, "O Tcidikuna, go and see how they are. He may be up very high." Then Tcidikuna departed, and when he saw that Tuhe and the bird had indeed gone very far, he cried out, "O mother!" Whereupon the Old Woman took some fire, and when she reached there she set fire to the tree on a high branch of which Tuhe was lodged.

Then Tuhe began to sing a magic song, which caused a great rain, and that drove the Old Woman away and put out the fire. And then Tuhe descended to the ground and resumed his travels.

When the Old Woman reached home, she said, "O Tcidikuna, go yonder and invite your brother-in-law to run a race with me." So Tcidikuna departed, and when he found Tuhe he gave him the invitation. But the daughters gave Tuhe another warning: "There is a hole in the ground close to the goal, and when you reach there, she will try to throw you into it. But when you reach there before her, jump over the hole, and on her arrival, push her into it." When Tuhe reached the starting place, the Old Woman said to him, "Let us go," as she stood there pretending that she was about to start. "O yes," said she, "you are all scared." As they went, Tuhe reached the hole in the ground over which he jumped, and as he stood on the other side, up came the Old Woman, whom he pushed, causing her to fall into the hole, down which she disappeared, making a series of rattling sounds. Tuhe then returned to the young women, but Tcidikuna sat a while by the hole in the ground, weeping over his mother's disaster. Checking his tears, he tied together several vines of the "devil's shoestrings," lowered them into the hole to his mother, who climbed the vines and reached the surface of the earth again. Her son took her home, and when they reached there she sent him again after Tuhe. "When I conjure a deer to him, he must shoot it," said the Old Woman. But her daughters warned Tuhe again: "She is saying that because she wishes her pet deer to chase you. Do not stand in the yard." So he took a doll shaped like a man, stood it up in the yard, and hid himself. Not long after the very aged deer arrived there, rushed on the man doll, gored it, and was about to throw it down when Tuhe shot him, wounded him, and made him fall to the ground. And then Tuhe went back. When he reached home, the Old Woman sent to him again. "I have made a deer trap. Let him go and see it," said she. So Tcidikuna went and delivered the message. But the daughters said, "When you see the small string there, do not touch it." But he thought, "What harm can so small a string do?" and when he touched it with his foot, he was caught in the trap, and Tcidikuna came again to the place. When he saw that Tuhe had been caught, he called out, "O mother! O mother! halloo! he has been caught!" Then the Old Woman caught up her sledge hammer, kettle, and some fire, and went to the place. She made a fire, and put some water in the kettle to boil, and then as she wished to kill him she seized the ax, and said, "You are very foolish to act in that manner." "Where ought one to hit you in order to kill you outright at one blow?" "On my head," said Tuhe. "I do not think that is it. Where ought one to hit you in order to kill you outright at one blow?" repeated she. "On my head," said he. "I think that that is not the place," replied the Old Woman. "On my ankle," said he. "I think that that is the place," said she, and as she was wishing to hit him, she raised her arm to give the blow, but when she struck at him he leaped aside, and the weapon descended on the little string and cut it in two without hurting Tuhe, who snatched the ax from her, hit her with it, and killed her. He put the body into the kettle of boiling water, pressing it down into the kettle. "O Tcidikuna," said Tuhe, "sit here and keep up the fire in order to boil your mother's body, and when it is cooked, eat it and depart home." After saying this Tuhe went home, leaving Tcidikuna there alone, crying aloud.

Well, when Tuhe reached home the two young women said, "You thought that you had killed her, but she will return." And not long after they had spoken, their mother returned. Then one of her daughters sat by her to examine her head. There was a hole in the top of the Old Woman's head, and the daughter cleaned the hair away from the hole. The other daughter was heating an iron rod, and when the first daughter had cleaned the hair away from the hole in her mother's head, she waved her hand toward her sister, who carried the hot iron to her, thrust it into the hole in the head, causing the Old Woman to throw her head back several times before she really died. The death of the Old Woman having removed the sole obstacle, the two young women became the wives of Tuhe.

After they had been married for some time, Tuhe wished to return to his boyhood's home, so the women prepared a supply of food for the journey, and he made a number of arrows. When the preparations were completed, the elder wife went close to the stream and began to sing a magic song, which caused an immense alligator to appear. This alligator served as a boat, and on him they piled their food and other possessions, after which they got upon him, and off he started toward the other side of the stream.

Then each of the women said, "So long as he hears me sing, he will continue to go rapidly, but when he does not hear me sing, you must throw some of the food in advance of him. The alligator swam toward the food, and seized and devoured it. Tuhe continued throwing the food beyond the alligator until it was all gone. Then he took his dog and threw it into the water. The alligator overtook the dog, caught it, and swallowed it. Not long after Tuhe threw the otter into the water, and he too was devoured by the alligator when he had almost reached the other side. As a last resource Tuhe began to shoot his arrows ahead of the alligator, but when an arrow alighted on the ground, the alligator stopped swimming. At last Tuhe fastened to the arrow a string with a loop at one end. He took his seat in the loop, and shot the arrow with great force, causing it to reach the ground, and so he alighted on the other side.

Then Tuhe was going toward the house of his uncle. At the same time his sister was approaching. When he noticed her approach, he shot an arrow far into the air, and when it alighted the sister took it up. "Whoever has been making arrows? My brother used to make arrows just like this. But no matter who made this I will break it," said she. She was just about to break it when he said, "Do not break it. It is mine." At once she discovered his presence and was very glad. She caught hold of him and cried aloud. "What are you desiring to do?" said he. "I am wishing to make hominy," she replied. "How large is my uncle's child?" said he. "It sits alone," replied the sister. "When the water boils in the kettle, put the child into it! When they wish to kill you for doing that, return to me." Then Tuhe left her, and she returned to her uncle's house. She made the water boil, and she stood by it singing. As she sang, some bystander remarked, "Ha, ha! Very-long-headed-Fish must have been told that her brother would come back today." At which she rejoined, "Do you always come back after you have died?"

When the water was boiling, she said, "I wonder whether the child would die if I put it in the boiling water." Saying this she took the child and set it in the water. And then they wished to kill her, and as she had fled they went along in pursuit of her, going toward the place where her brother was standing. They were on the point of killing her, one having raised a stick on her, when her brother came in sight right there. The Ancient of Long-necked Buzzards, who was one of the party, hid a spade behind him to conceal it from Tuhe; he made it resemble a tail. For this reason the Biloxi say that the buzzard has a tail. Because of this act of the Ancient of Long-necked Buzzards, his making a tail out of the spade, the buzzard's tail is flat, they say.

When the sister saw Tuhe she was very glad. Then the people lay down all along, touching one another, forming a line of bodies extending from the place where they were about to kill the sister to the home of her uncle. "You must get home," said the sister to Tuhe, so he walked along over the line of bodies, and thus reached home. When he arrived there, he killed all the people who were there as soon as night came, and by daylight he wished to go upward. So he asked the Frog to sing a magic song for him, but the Frog replied, "I do not know how." Then the Ancient of Toads said, "I can say it." "If you can say it, let me hear you say it," said Tuhe. Then the toad began to sing. "That is it," said Tuhe. Next, addressing his sister, he said, "When I leap upward, grasp my ankle." But when he leaped she grasped at the ankle and missed it. "I shall remain here," said she. "When the deer are fat, I will collect the fat and will carry it to you," said she as Tuhe ascended. Therefore since that day they always call the bird "She-always-gathers-deer-fat" (snipe). And since then when a toad cries the people always say, "It is going to rain," because Tuhe had said to the Ancient of Toads, "When you are very thirsty, be crying out in that manner and rain shall come."[17]

This is a lengthy and complicated story. It begins with a well-known incident called "Potiphar's wife" (K2111) from its occurrence in the Old Testament. When Riggs collected a Dakota text from Michel Renville, his informant observed, "It's another Joseph," indicating he recognized the Old World analogue.[18] There is a sequence of four tasks assigned to Tuhe, all designed to kill him, but when he accomplishes them, he is marooned on the other side of the "great water," a motif known as "Marooned egg-gatherer" (K1616) from a detail in its northern form. He then has various adventures with the Old Woman and her daughters, the Two Women, who help him kill their mother. The legend ends with Tuhe's return to his original home on the back of an alligator, a motif called "Whale-boat" (R245) because of its northeastern form. Back home he completes his revenge on his uncle, then joins the sky people. The identification of Tuhe as Thunder indicates that this text was more than just an entertainment for the Biloxi. The Caddoan text suggests the same.

Marooned Hero ■ ■ ■
CADDO

A poor orphan boy lived with a large family of people who were not kind to him and mistreated him. He could not go to play or hunt with the other boys, but had to do all of the hard work. Whenever the camp broke up the family always tried to steal away and leave the boy behind, but sooner or later he found their new camp and went to them because he had no other place to go. One time several families went in boats to an island in a large lake to hunt eggs, and the orphan boy went with them. After they had filled their boats with eggs they secretly made ready to go back to the mainland. In the night, while the orphan boy was asleep, they stole away in their boats, leaving him to starve on the lonely island.

The boy wandered about the island, eating only the scraps that he could find around the dead campfires, until he was almost starved. As he did not have a bow and arrows, he could not hunt, but he sat by the water's edge and tried to catch fish as they swam past him. One day as he sat on the lonely shore he saw a large animal with horns coming to him through the water. He sat very still and watched the animal, for he was too frightened to run away. The monster came straight to him, then raised his head out of the water and said: "Boy, I have come to save you. I saw the people desert you, and I have taken pity upon you and come to rescue you. Get upon my back and hold to my horns and I will carry you to the mainland." The boy was no longer afraid, but climbed upon the animal's back. "Keep your eyes on the blue sky, and if you see a star tell me at once," the animal said to him. They had not gone far when the boy cried, "There in the west is a big star." The monster looked up and saw the star, then turned around at once and swam back to the island as fast as he could. The next day he came and took the boy again, telling him, as before, to call out the moment that he saw a star appear in the sky. They had gone a little farther than they had the day before when the boy cried out, "There in the west is a star." The animal turned around and went to the shore. The next day and the next four days he started with the boy, and each time he succeeded in getting a little farther before the boy saw the star. The sixth time they were within a few feet of the opposite shore when the boy saw the star. He wanted to reach the shore so badly that he thought he would keep still and not tell the monster that he saw the star, for he knew that he would take him back to the island at once if he did. He said nothing, and so the monster swam on until they were almost in shallow water, when the boy saw a great black cloud roll in front of the star. He became frightened and jumped off of the animal's back and swam to the shore. Just as he jumped something struck the animal with an awful crash and he rolled over dead. When the boy came upon the shore a handsome young man came up to him and said: "You have done me a great favor. For a long time I have tried to kill this monster, because he makes the water of the lake dangerous, but until now I could never get the chance. In return for what you have done, I will take you with me to the sky, if you care to go." The boy said that he wanted to go, as he was alone and friendless upon the earth. The man, who was Evening-Star, took him with him to the sky, and there he may be seen as Orphan-Star who stands near Evening Star.[19]

This mythic dimension so evident in the Biloxi, Dakota, and Caddo texts is hardly visible in the Alabama and Koasati versions. We have already noted that it is introduced in both by the Bead-spitter, but the Marooned Hero also appears as a separate legend among the Koasati. The redundancy seems of less importance than getting a feel for the range of possibilities of treatment of a common legend, so here is the separate text.

Marooned Hero ▪ ▪ ▪
KOASATI

An orphan was traveling along and other persons said, "Let us cross to the other side of this big river." They took the orphan along. They went together and reached the other side. They told him to wander off (hunting), and when he did so they got into the boat and went away, leaving him there. Then the orphan said, "Hold on, I want to go too," but they left him and went away. Not knowing what to do, the orphan traveled along by the river. He traveled, traveled, and presently a Woodpecker came close to him singing. "Hi-yi', I will knock you down and kill you," said the orphan. "Don't. I am making a noise because I have something to tell you." "All right. Tell it to me!" he said and he rubbed red paint on the Woodpecker's head. Then the latter said to him, "Something big is pursuing you. Make many arrows. And as you travel make four wooden rollers, travel on, and sit at the end of a bent-over tree. The big thing, Big Man-eater, will come there with some huge dogs."

He got there with the dogs. Then the man was sitting up in the tree. And he threw the rollers one by one far out on the water. Each time he did so the dogs jumped in after it. When he threw in the fourth one, the dogs did not want to go in after it. So Big Man-eater became angry and killed all of his four big dogs. He took out a little clay pot which he always carried in his pocket and made it large by snapping his fingers against it. He set it down right at the very edge of the water, made a fire, and put water into the pot. Then he put all of his dogs into it, cooked them, and devoured them all. He put all of their bones into the water, stood on the bank and called all of his dogs by name. One shook himself and came out. All four did the same thing. He called to them and started off and they disappeared.

Then the orphan climbed down, made many arrows, and traveled on. As he was going along he shot and killed a bird. He killed a number of them and roasted them. Then he took them with him and stood on the bank of the river. He called, "My grandfather," upon which the turtle, alligator, loggerhead turtle came out in succession. "Not you," he said. After they had gone away the Horned Snake came out. "You are the one," he said. Then it came close to him and lay still on the water. It was very pretty, having one blue and one red horn, and he sat upon them. Then he threw a bird far off. The Snake shot forward, picked it up, and ate it. When it was finished the orphan threw another far out. While he was doing this he was sawing upon the horn with a strong rope he had. He threw another far off and the Snake went on with him. Meanwhile he kept sawing upon the horn. Now the Horned Snake said, "What are you doing to my horn?" It gave him an itching feeling. "I am doing nothing," he answered. "I like it and so I am patting it." He went on in this manner until there were no more birds. Then he shot an arrow to a great distance and the Snake went on rapidly with him. When he got to the arrow he seized it by the ligaments used in fastening on the feathers and swallowed it. When he was about to sink the man shot another. The last one stuck into the ground close to the water. At that time the horn was about cut through. Holding it, he jumped and reached shore with the broken horn. The bank slid back under him, but he kept on and got out. Then he started on.

When he had nearly reached the house where his sister lived he stuck up an arrow at a spring by the road. Then his sister came for water and saw the arrow.

She said, "This looks like my brother's arrow. I think he is not in this world and has been dead a long time." Then her brother, who had hidden himself, stood up and said, "He, I am not dead. I have returned." He talked to her.

When he was on his travels they said to him, "Your sister has married Owl. They have a little owl baby." So he said to his sister, "They say you have married Owl." She answered, "I have married him. He whips me all the time." At that her brother was very angry. He said, "When I come, heat some water boiling hot on the fire. Call to Owl and when he looks toward you throw the little owl into the water and run this way."

When he got there Owl was seated fixing an ax handle. Then the woman called to Owl. When he looked toward her she threw the little owl into the hot water and ran off. Owl ran toward her, holding his ax handle; but, when they got near, her brother, who was hidden, stood up. His sister went round and stood behind him. Owl came one, intending to hit her, and suddenly saw her brother. He said, "O-oh, I was just playing with you." But the brother shot him through with an arrow.[20]

The legends in this group appear to be northern in origin, for they are widely known and are distributed from the Eskimo across the northern reaches of the continent. The three major motifs, Potiphar's wife, Marooned egg-gatherer, and Whale-boat, are also frequently associated in the same texts.[21] Two motifs, Marooned egg-gatherer and Whale-boat, are also known from Siberia, a fact which suggests that this complex is one of those ancient ones stemming from a circumpolar tradition. It is interesting to note that the Whale, if that was the original animal, became the horned water serpent in the central Woodlands; the Biloxi stand alone in their identification of it as an alligator.

By contrast, the Bead-spitter legend is not nearly so widely known, even though it is connected with the Marooned Hero in the Southeast. As we have seen, it is a Creek-Plains legend, probably taken to the Southeast by the Creeks, where it was linked to the ancient legend of the Marooned Hero to form a story peculiar to the Southeast.

CHAPTER ELEVEN

Other Adventures

One of the persistent themes we have seen is the search for knowledge and power. Heroes ventured into the Under World to receive power and gifts from the water powers, they climbed into the Above World of the thunderbirds, and they took sides in the eternal battle between the two forces. They also went to the highest level of the Above World to investigate the ultimate. The legend of that journey is a classic illustration of the many levels of myth, because it can be interpreted in several ways. It inevitably constitutes a description of the way the worlds are constructed, and it also gives insight into the nature of the Above World people. It is clearly a coded account of a shamanistic out-of-body journey, even though the various levels of esoteric interpretation are not available to us. It is, at least in some cases, a description of the path of the soul at death and thus functions also for preparation for that journey. It also gives information about culture heroes who brought back such important gifts as plants, hunting power, and medicines.

Journey to the Sky ■ ■ ■
CHOCTAW

Tashka and Walo were brothers who lived long ago. Every morning they saw the sun rise above the horizon, pass high overhead, and late in the day die in the west.

When the boys were about four years old they conceived the idea of following the sun and seeing where he died. So the next day, when he was overhead, they started to follow him; but that night, when he died, they were still in their own country, where they knew the hills and the rivers. Then they slept, and in the morning when the sun was again overhead they once more set off to follow him. And thus they continued for many years to wend their way after the sun in his course through the heavens.

Long, long afterward, when the two boys had become men, they reached a great expanse of water, and the only land they could see was the shore on which they were standing. Late that day, when Sun died, they saw him sink into the water; then they also passed over the water and entered Sun's home with him. All about them they saw women—the stars are women and the moon is Sun's wife. Then Moon asked the brothers how they had found their way so far from their home. They told her how for many, many years, ever since they were mere boys, they had followed Sun in his daily journey.

Then Sun told his wife to boil water. Into this he put the boys and rubbed them; this treatment caused them to turn red and their skin to come off.

Sun then asked them whether they knew the way to return to their home, and they said, "No"; so he took them to the edge, whence they looked down to the earth but they could not distinguish their home.

Sun asked why they had followed him, as it was not time for them to reach heaven. They replied that their only reason for following him was a desire to see where he died.

Sun then told them that he would send them home, but that for four days after reaching their home they must not speak a word to any person. If they spoke during the four days they would die, otherwise they would then live and prosper. A large buzzard was then called by Sun and the two boys were placed on its back. Buzzard then started toward the earth. The clouds are midway between heaven and earth; above the clouds wind never blows. As Buzzard flew from heaven to the clouds the brothers could easily keep their hold; but from the clouds to the earth the buzzard was blown in all directions. All reached the earth in safety, however, and the boys recognized the trees that stood about their old home.

They rested beneath the trees, and while (they were) there an old man passed by who knew the brothers. He continued down the road, and soon meeting the boys' mother, told her the boys had come back. She hastened to see them. When she saw them she began to talk and made them answer her. Then they told her that, as they had spoken during the first four days after their return, they would surely die. Knowing she had forced them to speak, on hearing this the mother was greatly worried. Then all went to the mother's home, and the brothers told of all they had seen and how they had followed Sun during many years. After they had told all, they died and went up to heaven to remain forever.[1]

Here the adventurers travel west, then follow the sun into the water, which brings them up into the sky world. They receive purification from the sun, symbolized in the boiling. Then they are brought from the sky by a buzzard. The taboo on speaking reinforces the seriousness of information about the Above World, but the brothers' breaking of it permits humans to have the information. In other texts, more is gained from Above than purification.

Journey to the Sky ▪ ▪ ▪
CHITIMACHA

One time from 20 to 22 men set out toward the north until they came to the edge of the sky. In trying to pass under this all of them were crushed except six, who continued on along the sky floor until they came to Ku'tnahin. After they had remained with him for a certain time he asked them how they would descend. One answered, "I will go down as a squirrel." He tried to do so, but was dashed to pieces on the earth. Two others chose the forms of other animals, but with no better fate. The fourth, however, declared he would go down like a spider, while the fifth chose the form of an eagle, and the sixth that of a pigeon. Each of these succeeded, and each brought back to mankind a gift from Ku'tnahin. The man who had descended in the form of a spider learned how to cure people and was the first shaman. Before he could get back to earth with his new knowledge, however, one man fell sick and died. This was the first death among mankind, and had the shaman gotten back in time to cure him there would have been no death among human beings. The man who came back as an eagle taught men how to fish, and he who came down as a pigeon taught them the use of maize, which was then growing wild.[2]

The story of the journey to the sky is widespread and is so close to universal that there is little which can be inferred from the distribution pattern.[3] Even so, the varieties of elaboration taken from tribe to tribe are enlightening, and close ethnographic examination of each might reveal something of the relations of tribal life and the adaptation of migratory legends. In some, for example, the journey itself can get very complicated, taking the form of tests that have to be negotiated by the heroes, presumably to demonstrate their worthiness to reach the sky.

Journey to the Sky ▪ ▪ ▪
ALABAMA

In the beginning four old men walked toward the west. They heard a sound—boom, boom. The sky opened and they went up. One after another they ran through the sky.[4]

One said, "I am the panther, running through." Another said, "I am the wolf, running through." Another said, "I am the wildcat, running through." The last one said nothing, but he got caught and killed. The others went on until they came to a place where an old woman lived by herself. There was a river near by. The old woman told a boy to make a dipper and give it to these men. One after another they dipped up water and threw it in different directions. Then they crossed the river on dry ground.

They went a long way and found some people fighting; so they could not pass. The three men made cigarettes and smoked, and blew the smoke all over the land. It became such a thick fog that the people could not see to fight, and the men passed through.

They came to a great many snakes piled up—about a mile of them. The men tied slippery elm bark all over their legs and then they could walk among the snakes. Afterward they took off the slippery elm bark and threw it away.

They went on and on. At last they came to another old woman. They had eaten nothing and were hungry. The old woman cooked squashes and put three on each plate. As soon as a man had eaten these squashes three more appeared on his plate.[5]

The woman said, "You are dirty." She said, "Go fill a bucket with water and put it on the fire." When the water was boiling, she made them stand in a row with their backs to her, and she poured the boiling water on their backs and scrubbed them hard. They felt light after this and went on and on.

They went up on high to the Lord's place. The Lord asked, "Do you think you came a long way?" The Lord had a big telescope and said, "Come, look in here." They looked and saw their old home down below. The Lord said, "Do you want to go back?" They said, "Yes." The Lord gave them all kinds of seed—corn, sweet potato, and so forth, and made them sleep that night. In the morning they waked up in their old home and had all this seed with them.[6]

This was told by Charles M. Thompson, chief of the Alabama in Texas, who died in 1935. This was apparently a favorite legend of his, because it was recorded many times. Thompson served as interpreter for Swanton in 1911 and 1912, when Swanton collected a text of "journey to the sky" from him and two others from other informants, probably Celissy Henry and George Henry.[7] Thompson became chief in 1928, and in 1932 Frances Densmore collected from him the text just given. Elma Heard collected another text a year later.[8] Finally, Howard Martin collected more than a half-dozen tellings of it from him before his death, and he later published two of them.[9] All of that collecting makes Thompson's version of this legend a valuable source for the study of a single narrator and the changes legends undergo through the life of a single informant.

If the three Alabama and one Koasati texts collected by Swanton are examined, it is obvious that there is an important disagreement. Thompson's version is the journey we have seen so far, but the other three have a different outcome—the dead are brought back to earth where they are revived. This is known as the Orpheus myth from its European distribution, but it is so widespread in North America that there seems no question that it is pre-Contact; "...it is sufficient to be able to observe that the Orpheus tradition was probably spread from tribes with hunting culture." According to Hultkrantz, the North American Orpheus tradition arose out of the shamanistic experiences of hunting cultures and thus antedates the arrival of corn and the development of agrarian societies.[10] Attempting to separate the Journey texts from the Orpheus tradition seems hopeless, and Hultkrantz found it easier to lump the Eastern Woodlands together regardless of the variation.[11] Here is how the Orpheus legend appears in a Southeastern collection.

Orpheus ■ ■ ■
YUCHI

Four Yuchi who had wives decided one day to kill them. So they killed the four women. "There is no such thing as death. So let us go and hunt them," said they.

Accordingly the four husbands set out to find their wives. They said, "Let us go where the Creator is." They set out westward and traveled a long while, coming at length to a place where there was a great cave. Before its mouth swayed a great cloud, in such a manner that they could not get by it or around it, for it was moving up and down. They saw that their journey would end here unless they could devise some means of passing the cloud. It was decided that they would imitate something very swift and get in that way. Said one of the men, "I'll be a deer." So he became a deer, and when the cloud raised up the next time, he jumped in. The next said, "I'll be a panther." And when the cloud raised up, he jumped in. The third man said, "I'll be a bear." And the next time the cloud raised up, he too jumped in. They had jumped at the right time, and had succeeded. Now the fourth man said, "I am a man, and I'll be a man." And when he tried to get in, the cloud fell on his head and crushed him.

Then the three men who had reached the inside of the cave took their natural shape as men, and began to climb up the back of the cloud within the cave. After they had been some time climbing, they came to a wonderful scene, and as they went on they beheld an old woman seated there. The old woman was the sun. When she saw them she spoke to them.

"My sons, you are come. Are you not hungry?"

And the men said that they were hungry. Accordingly she planted a hill of corn, a hill of beans, and a hill of squash for each man. Now when they saw her doing this, they thought, "Well, as we are so hungry shall we have to wait for these things to grow before we can eat?" But the old woman knew their thoughts, and replied as though they had spoken out loud. She said, "You think you won't eat very soon, but you won't have long to wait."

Even then the plants began to sprout and grow up, and soon they fruited, and it was not long before they gathered the corn, beans and squashes, and were ready to eat. The old woman then put a small quantity of the vegetables before each man. But they said, "Do you think that that little will fill us?" In reply, she said to the, "There will be some left over."

When they had finished eating, it was as she had said. There was some left over. Now the old woman spoke to the men again.

"What did you come here for? What do you want?" she asked them.

"We had four wives who are dead. We lost them, and they told us to hunt for them. So we are here."

"Well, they are here," said the old woman, "we are going to have an all-night dance, and the women will be there. Then you will see them."

Now the men were deciding whether to stay for the dance, or to go on. And while they were thinking over it, a panther monster came up, and they were very much afraid. But as soon as they saw him, the old woman lifted up her dress and told the men to come and get beneath it; they went under and she protected them. When the great monster came near, he said to her, "I smell people." But the old woman said, "You smell me." The monster was deceived and went away. Then when it became time the men went to the dance. They arrived at the place where they were dancing, and the men could hear the dance but they couldn't see anything. They said to the old woman,

"We can hear, but we cannot see. So give us a sign so that we may know that our wives are here."

Then the old woman got a coal from the fire and put it on the hip of one of the women who was now dancing with the rest. She did the same with each woman until the four had coals of fire on their hips. Now all that the men could see was the coal, when the women were dancing. But they stayed there watching. Soon the old woman said to them,

"If you cannot see, lie down and go to sleep."

So they did as they were told, and went to sleep. The old woman left them, and getting four large gourds, made holes in them and put one woman in each gourd. Then she carried the gourds to where the men were, and woke them up, saying, "Here are your women." She laid the gourds down, one near each man, and said,

"Now lie down and sleep again. When you wake up you will be back on earth. But when you wake up, don't open the gourds." She told them, "When you get back to your people, go to a dance and take these gourds with you."

Then they went to sleep again, and after a while woke up. They were back on the earth. They went on until they reached their people. But on the way, one of the men became impatient, and opened his gourd. Immediately a great wind came out and went up in the air. So the other three kept theirs and didn't open them. At last they reached their own land. When the time for a dance came around they took their gourds with them. While they were dancing they hit their gourds on the ground and broke them. The women jumped out and joined them in the dance. But the man who broke his beforehand, when he saw the other women restored to their men, wept. Now that's the way it was done.

The three who had done as the old woman told them, had a good time and were afterwards called by the others "the people hunters." They were considered to be very wise, and in a short time they all became great chiefs and councillors in their tribe.[12]

Finally, let us look at a few more adventure tales without comment, for they give a more complete idea of the range of adventure themes in the Southeast.

The Rescue of the Brothers ■ ■ ■
TUNICA

(Once there) were four orphan boys. One day the oldest (of the brothers) took them and went hunting in the woods. When he got near (the place) where he hunted in the woods, he sent the rest of his brothers ahead (to the place) where they went to hunt. "If I go into the woods and kill something, we shall eat well tonight," he told them. While his brothers were watching him, he went into the woods.

He went on into the woods. "If you come (to the place) where (we camp), gather some wood, and kindle a fire, it will be a good thing," he told them. They came (to the place) where they camped. When they arrived, they gathered the wood. They gathered (it) and when they had kindled the fire, they kept watch. They kept watch until they went to bed. (Their brother) did not come (back) at any time during the night.

The oldest of the remaining brothers spoke to his two brothers. "If you stay and guard the fire while I go into the woods to see where our brother went, it will be a good thing," he told them. When he had finished speaking to them, he went into the woods. They were watching him (to see) where he went into the woods.

He too did not come (back) at any time during the day. At night they kept watch. Then they went to bed. He too did not come (back) at any time during the night. The next day there were (only) two brothers left. They got up early and the older one spoke to the little one. "If you guard the fire, it will be a good thing," he told him. "If I go to see where our two brothers went, it will be a good thing," he told him. Then he too went into the woods. The little one watched him (as he went).

He went on and on into the woods. He too did not come (back) at any time during the day. When night came, the little one was frightened. He was crying. (Then) when he had made a good bed, he lay down.

Now the fire turned (itself) into a person, an old man. When he had transformed (himself) he sat down and spoke to the little one. Then the old man put a little pot in the fire. When he had boiled the little pot (long) enough, he took it and put it to his mouth and sipped the liquid. Then (he went over to the place) where the little one lay and started to spit in his face. The little one hid his face. But in spite of this, he spat in his face. Then the old man spoke to the little one. "Get up early in the morning. (Go and) whoop (by) the pecan tree which stands (there). Jump and catch hold of it and when the pecan tree bends and splits, take one (of the) limbs and make a bow. (Then) feather some arrows. (After that), if you (will) go to see where your brothers have gone, it will be a good thing," he told him.

The little one got up very early, whooped, and jumped catching hold of the tree. The tree bent and split. Then he cut one (of the) limbs. (From this) he made a bow, (then) cut (some) arrows, made (them) straight and feathered (them). After he had finished making everything (as) good (as possible), he went into the woods. He was walking along.

Then a limb cracked. When he looked right there, a deer was standing there. He shot and killed it. When the deer fell, he went (over) beside it and circled (it) in order to skin it.

Then (another) limb cracked. When he raised his head and looked, (he saw) the Clawed Witch coming. She had a basket hooked over her arm. She came carrying a hatchet in the basket.

She looks like a person. When she starts to run, she throws her breasts to either side over her shoulders. Her claws are sharp. When she catches hold of something, she snares it by hooking it (in her claws).

Now she was coming up (to him). She spoke to him. "I am very hungry," she said. "Make haste; finish skinning it; (then) give me the blood; (for) if I drink it, it will be a good thing," she said.

Then (as) he circled the deer in order to skin it, she was creeping up on him. When she came too near, he would step over to the other side of the deer. (As) he went around the deer, she crept up on him again. She was speaking to him and creeping up on him. She (kept) acting in this manner, and (when) she came close and took her hatchet out of her basket, (she) held it ready to hit him. Then he stood up. He seized the hatchet and took it out of her hand. Then he hit her (with it). He hit her and killed her.

After he killed her, he went there (to the place) whence she had come. As he was walking in the woods, he saw smoke. When he got there, two girls were standing there. He went up (to them) and questioned them. One (of them) answered him. "My grandmother has brought (some) people. They are cooking (over) there on the fire," she told him.

When he went (over) and looked, his brothers were cooking there. He picked up all of the bones. He placed them all together. When he had put them together properly, he spoke to them. When he (had) spoken, they rose and sat up.

He spoke to them again. When he finished speaking, they stood up. Then he spoke to them. "I (shall) walk ahead. If you look at my heels and (let) me lead you home, it will be a good thing," he said. He stood ahead and they went (toward) their home. They were going (along) somewhere in the woods (when) the one in the rear looked to one side. When he looked to one side, he turned into a hoot owl. He rose up and perched on a limb.

Now (the leader) stopped and spoke. (Only) two were left. When he finished speaking, he went (on) leading them. They were walking (and) going to their home. As they were walking, the one in the rear looked to one side. He went up and perched on a limb. He turned into a horned owl.

Now only one was left. The leader stopped again. He still spoke to his brothers. He went (on) leading only one. As they were walking (along), he, on his part, looked to one side. He went (up) and perched on a limb. He turned into a screech owl.

Then (the youngest brother) went home by himself.[13]

The next adventure is grim, but it contains a truly great understatement by the Choctaw informant.

Owl Murders a Man ▪ ▪ ▪
CHOCTAW

Late one afternoon several children were playing near their house when suddenly they saw a woman approaching. She was very old and stooping, and her hair was white. The children were greatly frightened and ran into the house, but soon returned to the old woman, who said to them: "Children, do not be afraid of me, for nothing will harm you. I am your great-great-great-grandmother, and neither you nor your mother has ever seen me. Now, go to the house and tell her that I have come." The children did so. Then they took a deer skin and spread it on the ground for the old woman and carried her food and drink. She then asked the children when their father went to sleep and in which part of the house he lay, and the children told her all.

That night, after all had gone to sleep, the old woman entered the house and cut off the man's head, which she put into a basket and quietly left the house. The next morning the man's wife was surprised to find him asleep, since it was his custom to go hunting before sunrise. So she spoke to him, and as he did not answer she pulled off his blanket. When she saw that his head was missing she became greatly alarmed.

After cutting off the man's head Skate'ne, the old woman, immediately left the house and started down the road. Soon she met a large bear, who said to her, "What have you covered up in your basket, old woman?" "You must not see it," said she, "for if you look on it you will lose your eyes; it is poison and bad." The bear was contented and went on his way.

Then she met many other animals, and at last came two wildcats. "Stop, old woman, and show us what you have in your basket," called one of the wildcats; "we must see what you carry." The old woman repeated what she had told the bear and all the others. "But we must look inside your basket, even if we do lose our eyes," replied one of the wildcats, at the same time seizing the basket and raising the cover. When they saw the man's head they knew it was the old woman who prowled around during the night, killing men and animals and birds, so they determined to kill her. While one held her the other went to find a large club. When he had gone she said to the wildcat holding her: "Over

217

there is a large club. You would do well to get it and kill me before your companion returns, for the one that kills me will always have good luck, and I like you." So the remaining wildcat went to get the club, for he believed what the old woman had told him, and hence wanted to kill her. On his return with the club he could not find the old woman, for she was Skate'ne, an owl, and had flown away.[14]

An Underwater Hero ■ ■ ■
KOASATI

Six Indian brothers lived under the water. The youngest was unmarried. All of the older brothers had wives; he was the only one without. Women wanted to get him, but he did not want any of them. He thought, "I will wander off somewhere and die." So he traveled on until he heard someone chopping wood. He went on and when he came to the place he found a girl there chopping wood. When she saw the man, she said, "They make me stay here and watch the field lest raccoons steal some of the corn. Will you stay here and comfort (i.e., marry) me?" And they stayed there together.

By and by she said to him, "Let us go to see my uncle; he lives not far away. My father," she said, "lives at a distance." So they set out to see the girl's uncle. When they got to the place he looked out and said, "Ohoho' ho', my niece, that is a good young man." He said, "Let the young man who has just come kill some ducks for me." He gave him a strong cord, and he took it and went on. When he got to the water he took off his shirt. There were many ducks on the water, and, taking his strong cord, he dived under, reached them, and diving about he tied up their feet and brought them back. While he was on the way and before he had gotten back the old man looked out and said, "Oho, go back!" Then he went back and disappeared under the water. Upon this his wife wept, ran to the water, jumped into it, and disappeared.

She went weeping to him and stayed there. He could not get out but his wife came up, tied his clothes together and carried them back. When she got to her house she wept all day. She wanted very much to see him and at night when she lay down to sleep she did not sleep much. During the day, while she was sitting down, she would think she saw a person coming but when she looked all around it was nothing. It was that way all of the time, until on the third day when she was lying down she dreamed that she should cook. She finished cooking and placed the food on the table, and sat looking down (toward the river). She thought something in the shape of a man was coming but when she looked out nothing was there. That was the way it continued always. When night came and it was dark she lay down but slept little, and in the early morning while it was still dark she started off. She went straight on, took off her clothes, and jumped into the water. She dived until she reached the bottom. He was lying inside of a locked trunk, and she stayed there a while feeling of it and then went back out of the water and came home.

She sat down on one of two cane scaffolds which were near the house, looked about, and thought she saw a man coming. In a little while she wanted to look out, and at noon she thought a man had come. She looked around and her husband sat on the platform. When she saw that he had returned, she was very happy. And they ate together.

They lived there for some time and after many days he made a club. He made a red club. Next day he said, "Let us go to see him." He teased very hard until he persuaded her and they set out. Arrived at her uncle's house, he struck him, knocked him down, and killed him, and he flayed him. After he had flayed him he threw his bones into the water. His skin he carried down and filled with white tree moss, and when it was done hung it in the sunshine until it was dried. When it was completely dry he said to her, "Let us go to visit your father."

They set out. He took the skin and went on and when they were nearly there he put on the skin of the old man and took a walking stick and his wife walked on ahead laughing. When they got to the place they looked at him and said, "Ohoho, I thought he was a young man; he is a very old man." "Is he not really a young man?" they kept saying to her. Her husband had charged her, however, to say that he was an old man.

After some time they said, "Let the man who has just come kill squirrels for us to eat." So they loaned him a gun, and he got into a canoe, crossed, and traveled along on the other side. Presently he came back and recrossed the river. He said, "A red-tailed hawk killed some squirrels and brought them to me and I put them into the canoe. Tell them to go down and look." Ao they went to look and when they got to the canoe they found that it was full of squirrels. Then they gathered them up, carried them home, cooked, and ate them and were very glad to have them. After they had eaten all the squirrels, they said, "Let him go to kill deer next." Again he got into the canoe, crossed the river, and started off. After he had hunted all about he came back and said to them, "A panther killed the deer and brought them to me and put them into the canoe. Let them go and look for them." They went there to look, and the canoe was full of deer which they took and brought up to the house, cooked, and ate.

By and by he said to his wife, "Let us go back home." Then they questioned her about the man. "Is he not a young man?" they said. "Yes," she said to them. Upon this he took off the skin and threw it away. After that his wife's brothers wanted to play ball and took him along to help them. When they began to play he stood helping them but he did not want to catch the ball. By and by, when the other side had half won, he caught it and threw it a long distance. He kept throwing it in this way until his party won. Then he stopped and came back home.

After that the man went back to the place from which he had first come. His wife wept and wanted to give him food for the journey but he refused it. He took only his clothing, set out, and disappeared. This was because she had let them know that he was a young man.[15]

The Obstacle Flight ■ ■ ■
ALABAMA

Big Man-eater had a wife but stole another woman and carried her to the place where his wife lived. Next day he started off. After he had traveled about hunting for a while he came back without having killed anything. Then he said to his wife, "Cut off a piece of your body and roast it for me." She roasted a small piece of her body and gave it to him, and he ate. That went on every day. Big Man-eater came back every time and just the same thing happened over again.

Then the woman who had been carried away was afraid that her body would be eaten up and she ran off. She started for the home of her three brothers. Big Man-eater came back and called for her but she was gone. Then he set out in pursuit of her on the trail just like a dog.

Before she started the first wife broke off four huckleberries and gave them to her (along with some canes). And when Big Man-eater followed her and had almost caught her she threw the huckleberries down on the ground and Big Man-eater stopped behind the bushes and ate them. When he came on again and got close she dropped canes on the ground, and canes grew up high and thick and it became boggy. Big Man-eater started in slowly, and meanwhile the woman got to where her brothers lived and they took her in. Her brothers shut her in the house. When Big Man-eater came along to the house they shot him. Some of them struck him from behind on the ankle with a stick and knocked him down. They shot at him and killed him. Then the men hunted up wood, piled it upon him, and burned him up. It took a long time, but his body was finally consumed. Then the men picked up the ashes and threw them up into the air. When they threw up the ashes they turned into bees and flew away. When they threw them up again in the same manner blackbirds flew away. The next time crows flew away. Then hornets flew away, next wasps, then yellow jackets. It kept on so until all sorts of winged insects, including mosquitoes and flies, had been created.[16]

The final motif, "Insects from burnt monster's body " (A2001), is another universal motif found from the Northwest to Central and South America.

As might be expected, important myths sometimes produce offspring, or attract related legends. Here is an example—our final adventure—that stems from the Cherokee "Thunders" myth which we have already seen. Somewhere along the line, a lone adventurer became elevated to the level of the Twins. Here is his story.

The Third Thunder ▪ ▪ ▪

CHEROKEE

Once a young man fell in love with a strange girl at a dance and followed her home. He caught up with her and she agreed to marry him. They went a long way up into the mountains to her house, and were welcomed by her mother.

The next day they told him they were expecting the girl's two brothers. Later he heard a terrible thundering and roaring and the Thunders rode up mounted on huge rattlesnakes. They seemed pleased to have another man in the family and said that he could help them with their work, but they looked uncomfortable and complained that something smelled in the house. They were not human and so were very sensitive to the odor of a man. However, they assured him that he would very quickly lose his human scent, and invited him to play ball with them the next day. They asked him to stable their "horses" for them in order to try his courage. He was very frightened, but he managed to lead the snakes off and put them away without showing fear.

Early the next morning they told him to get onto a third snake and come with them. He was terribly frightened but he climbed on and rode a long way with them until they came to a ball-ground. Here they got out their sticks and began a ball-stick game. This was his third trial for they used a human skull as a ball. When he saw it come flying at him with its jaws agape he was afraid, but he thought of his wife and played well. So he proved his courage and became the third Thunder. He can be heard sometimes traveling across the sky with his brother-Thunders, who make a louder noise than he does.[17]

221

CHAPTER TWELVE

Tricksters

For the Euro-American, the trickster tale is probably the most confusing kind of oral literature to comprehend. It is a universal genre, with the exception of Europe and Euro-America, but there are indications that it used to exist there too up until a few centuries ago. The Greek Hermes and the medieval fool, the popular stories of Jesus and Peter in the Middle Ages—all have vanished, replaced, perhaps, by movie cartoons. Why the trickster tradition should have ceased to be important for Europeans is a much debated point, with no clear answers, but the question is a significant one, particularly in the light of the importance of the trickster in other cultural traditions.

Among Native Americans the identity of the trickster varied from region to region. In many nations more than one trickster was present; one was usually predominant, but other persons, normally non-humans, also figured in trickster incidents. The most widespread character was Coyote of the Plains and the West, but Raven played the role in the Northwest, Rabbit was the major trickster of the Southeast, and there were various others. Coyote appeared in the Southeast only among the Caddo on the western edge.

"Trickster" can be a deceptively simple label, for the trickster does far more than just play tricks on people. If he were just a practical joker, he probably would not be a very important person in the folklore of the world. The trickster is also a creator, so much so that early folklorists preferred to speak of the "trickster-transformer." He creates good things by whim or by accident, but he also blunders, bringing difficulties for humans. As has been pointed out many times, the trickster is the dark side of all of us, freed from the social and personal rules that direct our normal behavior.[1]

The humor surrounding him far surpasses the level of slapstick, but understanding the humor of other cultures can be a most difficult task. Nonetheless, even the attempt can give us valuable insights into the thinking of people for whom the trickster is a beloved person. Let us look at some of the dimensions of this most complicated of all characters by examining some of the many trickster tales found in the Southeast.

Coyote Challenges the Snake ▪ ▪ ▪
CADDO

One time while Coyote was out hunting something to eat he decided to go where Snake lived. He started in the direction he thought Snake lived and went to many places, but he could not find him. He went along talking to himself, saying, "I thought so; Snake is not so poisonous as people think, and if I ever find him I will show him my power." He kept going from place to place. Finally he came to one place and thought he would stop and rest for a while. He was not there very long when he heard someone calling him. When Snake came up to him, Coyote asked him how he was getting along in the world, since he had been made so small. "You look so small that I do not think you can do very much harm to anyone, though I have heard many times that you have much poison. They say that you are more dangerous than I, and so that is the reason I have gone from place to place looking for you. Now that I have met you I want you to show me in what way you are more powerful and dangerous than I am." Snake said: "Yes, I look very small to you, but you know that although I am small I am given power by your Father, and by his aid I have done many things in this world. I have killed many animals, large and small. Now you have come to see me, and whatever you want me to do I will do it; but first tell me what you want me to do." "Well," said Coyote, "I want to see which of us has the most power." "All right," said Snake, "you may bite me just once anywhere you like, and I will bite you, too, and in that way we will see who has the more power." "But you have to bite me first," said Coyote. "All right," said Snake, and went up to Coyote and bit him on the top of his nose, and then said: "That is all I can do." Coyote stood there as though he was not hurt at all. He asked Snake if that was all he could do, and Snake said: "That is the best I can do to show you my power." Coyote said: "Well, it is my time to show you my power." "Yes," said Snake, and so Coyote came up to Snake and bit him nearly in two. Snake cried out and begged Coyote to let him go. "Now," said Coyote to Snake, "you lie there and I will lie here. We will call to each other every now and then, so that we can see who will live the longer." Snake went a little way off and lay down, acting as though he were about to die. Coyote also went off a little way and lay down. He was thinking Snake would die in a little while, and so he called out to him. Coyote could just hear him answer in a weak voice, as though he was almost dead. After a while he heard Snake calling him and he answered with a big voice. They kept on calling to one another all night. Toward daylight Snake called Coyote, but no answer came from him. He called again, but still no answer. The third and fourth times he called, but there was no answer. Snake went over to see what was the matter, and when he got there he found Coyote all swollen and dead. Snake was more dangerous than Coyote.[2]

First off, we need to be reassured about the fatal consequences of Coyote's stupidity. The trickster is immortal. He will reappear in the next tale as if nothing had happened. For him, death has no permanent meaning; it is just the frequent consequence of his strange behavior. In fact, he usually dies, and that evokes laughter, because he deserves it.

A pervasive characteristic of the trickster is his lack of understanding of the way things are. Any child knows that the rattlesnake is due respect. In the Southeast snakes were greatly respected, if not honored, and most nations had a strong taboo on killing them. The lethal power of the serpent demanded that humans establish good relations with snakes, in contrast to the Euro-American tradition of carrying on war with them. After all, from the Native American perspective, any small creature with that much power can be of great service, if the serpent chooses to give some of his power to a human. In fact, the only people who could rationally challenge a venomous serpent are those who have reason to believe that their power is equal to that of the snake—shamans, medicine men, or heroes who have been given special power.

Coyote, of course, is not one of those people, and for him to challenge a snake to a biting contest is an act of supreme arrogance and stupidity at the same time. Any rational person constantly assesses the power levels of the people with whom he deals, for things are rarely as they seem on the surface; Coyote demonstrates that he has no idea of the power of the snake, and that makes him both arrogant and stupid. And he pays the price. He thus also points a moral lesson: do your homework before you challenge people to a test of power. Humility and understanding are important virtues in the Native American world.

The Bungling Host ■ ■ ■
HITCHITI

Bear and Rabbit were traveling about together. They had become friends. Bear said to Rabbit, "Come and visit me. That red house way off yonder is my home." He went off. At the appointed time Rabbit set out and came to where Bear lived. Bear's home was a hollow tree. At the bottom of the tree was a hole. There was where he lived. When Rabbit came Bear said, "Sit down." So Rabbit sat down and both talked for a while.

Bear went around back of his house while Rabbit sat watching him. He went out of sight. When he came back to where Rabbit was sitting he had a lot of good lard. He put the lard into some beans which were cooking and when the beans were done he set them out for Rabbit, who ate all he could.

Now when Rabbit was preparing to go home he said, "Come and visit me, too. I live way over yonder where you see that white house. That is my home." Bear said, "All right." By a white house Rabbit meant white grass.

On the appointed day Bear started to visit Rabbit and reached his place. His house was made of dry grass. When Bear got there Rabbit said, "Sit down." So Bear sat down and they talked. Then Rabbit stood up and went round back of his house. Bear saw him and thought, "He may hurt himself." While Bear was sitting there he heard Rabbit cry out, *"Dowik."* He started out and when he reached Rabbit found he had cut his belly and sat with a little blue hanging out of it. "Oh, I alone can do that. You have hurt yourself," he said. He took Rabbit and laid him down in his house.

The False Doctor

Then Bear went out to look for a doctor. Finding Buzzard, he said to him, "My friend, Rabbit has hurt himself badly. I am looking for a man able to treat him." "I make medicine," said Buzzard. So Bear led him back to the place where Rabbit was lying. When Buzzard saw him he said, "Make some hominy and place it near by and I will treat him." The hominy was prepared. "Now shut up the house and make a hole in the roof and I can treat him," he said. So the house was shut up and a hole was made in the roof. Then Buzzard sat in the room where Rabbit lay eating hominy. Presently Rabbit said, *"Dowik."* "What are you doing to him?" they called out. "He is afraid of the medicine," said Buzzard. As he sat there with Rabbit he struck at him, killed him, and ate him. He ate him all up and flew out through the roof. Then he said to the people, "He is lying there waiting for you," and he went away. Bear entered the house and found only Rabbit's bones lying there.

When Bear saw this he was very angry. Just then an orphan with a bow who was traveling around came to the place and Bear said to him, "We asked Buzzard to doctor Rabbit but he devoured him and has flown away. Shoot at him and see if you can hit him." He orphan shot at him and brought him down. Bear beat him and killed him, and hung him up. He lighted a fire under him and smoked him, and Buzzard hung there many days. He came to look yellowish, it is said. Therefore, because the little boy shot him and they hung him in the smoke, he is yellow.

This is how they tell it.[3]

The first motif, "Bungling host" (J2425), is universal throughout North America. Another episode of that story is a competition in diving for fish, which found its way into the Creek version of the Wonderful Garments myth and is the only Southeastern representative of this Plains–Central Woodlands episode. The second part of the text, frequently told separately, is "Sham doctor" (K1955), universally known in the Plains and Eastern Woodlands. One message of the beloved "Bungling host" is the same as the encounter with the snake—a person should know and use his own abilities rather than copying others. Rabbit is not a bear, and to pretend otherwise is to court death. The addition of the sham doctor to it works nicely in this case, for Rabbit's death comes about because Buzzard is also deceitful about his abilities.

While in the Bungling Host the Bear is innocent of any ill will, some trickster stories incorporate streaks of sheer malice.

Deer Butts a Tree ■ ■ ■
CHOCTAW

It had been a dry season and there was very little food for Deer, consequently he had become thin and rather weak. One day Deer met Possum and exclaimed: "Why! Possum, how very fat you are. How do you keep so fat when I can not find enough to eat?" And Possum answered, "I live on persimmons, and as they are unusually large this year, I have all I want to eat." "But how do you get persimmons, which grow so high above the ground?" "That is very easily done," replied Possum. "I go to the top of a high hill and, running swiftly down, strike a persimmon tree so hard with my head that all the ripe persimmons fall to the ground. Then I sit there and eat and eat until I can not hold more." "Indeed, that is easily done," answered Deer; "now watch me."

So Possum waited near the tree while Deer went to the top of a nearby hill. And when Deer reached the top of the hill, he turned and then ran quickly down, striking the tree with so great force that he was killed and all his bones were broken.

When Possum saw what Deer had done, he laughed so hard that he stretched his mouth, which remains large even to this day.[4]

That is bad news for Deer, but Deer, despite his power, was fated for the dinners of humankind. It should be noted that the trickster in this case is Possum, which indicates that a people's recognition of a major trickster does not preclude others from taking on the role. Sometimes a trickster can just be amusing himself and still get into trouble.

Learning to Fly ■ ■ ■
CREEK

Once when Rabbit was traveling along he came to a lot of ducks swimming in a pond. Presently he went to them with a cord tied about his waist, dived under the place where the ducks were and, when he reached them, tied all of their legs together. When he had finished he came up in their midst and the ducks flew away; they carried Rabbit along hanging in the middle.

Rabbit's grandmother had just been rubbing a pot smooth and had set it

226

down when they flew over her. He called to his grandmother and he saw him. When he got just above her, she threw the pot over him and it cut the string so that he fell down.[5]

The Koasati present his flying exploit as a simple miscalculation, but the Natchez, despite their disguise of Trickster as "cannibal," portray him as a complete fool, for he ties the birds to his privates.

Flying into Disaster ■ ■ ■
NATCHEZ

A cannibal found a large number of ducks swimming about in a certain lake or river. Then he procured a great quantity of hickory bark, dived under water toward them, and when he was among them he stood with his nose sticking out of the water and tied the ducks to his body one after the other by means of the bark, until all of it was used up. Afterwards he dived under water again, came to the surface a short distance away, and began singing. He thought that they could not fly. He sang:

"Agu'shuwe'bangini, Agu'shuwe'bangini
Ada'gitsa'gitsak a'tsaga'gitsagitsak,"

meaning that he had tied the ducks up and that he had tied them to himself. Then the ducks said, "What is he singing?" After a while he sang the same thing again. *"Agu'shuwe'bangini, Agu'shuwe'bangini Ada'gitsa'gitsak a'tsaga-'gitsagitsak."* The ducks said to one another, "He has tied the strings to his body," and all flew off up into the air carrying him with them, singing. As he went up he kept catching at the strings, but they flew on until at last his member broke off and he fell down, landing in a hollow tree. After he had sat inside of this tree for seven days a woodpecker began pecking at it. Then he told this bird to collect the rest of the woodpeckers and cut the tree down, saying, "I shall be very thankful to you all." Presently a flock of these birds came, settled around the tree and began pecking at it. As they pecked they sang, *"Tom-'shithlho'nho'nogua shu'uhuts gai'tsii ni'yi ni dogotilu'shik,"* meaning that they were pecking at a hollow tree in which there was a cannibal. They repeated this over and over and shouted again and again until they had pecked the tree down. Their song and the clamor they made over him had made the cannibal angry, so, as soon as he had gotten out, he sat down on a log and said to them, "Just now I cannot reward you in any way. But gather near and I will tell you something strange." So all collected close to him, and when they had done so he suddenly seized them and ate a great number. Some of them flew away, however. When he had finished he said, "Now let them shout and carry on." Then he left that place.

By and by the cannibal heard someone ahead of him singing in a low voice, *"Tom'shithlhonho'nogua dahaba'li gabi'shgua gabukta,"* meaning, "Kill that

227

cannibal and let us eat him." "What is that?" he thought. Then he went into a little bushy place from which the sound came and found a redbird's nest with a number of young ones in it with their feathers just starting out. He seized it and began eating them, nest and all. Then he said, "Sing on. Sing on again." Then he started westward once more.[6]

This motif, "Trickster carried by birds and dropped" (K1041), is known universally in the Plains and throughout the Eastern Woodlands, but it is remembered in the Southeast only by the Hitchiti, Natchez, and Cherokee. The mythic exploits of the Central Algonkin trickster Rabbit are easily recognized in these texts.

Sometimes the Southeastern texts suggest the mythic significance of the trickster by including trickster episodes in otherwise solemn myths. Sometimes in a trickster tale, there is just a hint of the creative activity of the trickster, as in this narrative:

The Spitting Fire ■ ■ ■
CREEK (TASKIGI)

Rabbit and Panther were friends. They were traveling together. After a while they came to a place where there was a creek with a bad name. It was "Dofogaga hatchi." Now, Rabbit wanted to go on and said that, as the creek had a bad name, it would not be good to camp there for the night. He said, "This creek has a bad name."

"Why is that?" asked Panther.

"Because everybody who camps here at night gets burned up." That is what Rabbit told him.

"Well, I think it will be all right," remarked Panther. "We will camp here anyway."

But Rabbit did not want to, so he said. But at last they made ready their camp for the night, as Panther would go no farther.

So when it got late they prepared to sleep. They had talked all the evening about the place and other things. Now Rabbit asked Panther, "What kind of a noise do you make when you are asleep?" He meant how did he snore.

"Why, I say, 'Nutslagum! nutslagum! nutslagum!'" said Panther. Then he asked Rabbit what kind of a noise he made when he slept.

"I say, 'Nuts! nuts! nuts!'" replied Rabbit.

Now, they went to bed and in a short time Rabbit pretended that he was asleep. He began to snore, saying, "Nuts! nuts! nuts!" And Panther thought that he was surely asleep, so he went to sleep himself, snoring, "Nutslagum!" Now, when Panther was sound asleep Rabbit got up and got a piece of bark and shoveled a lot of coals from the fire on it. Then he threw the coals on Panther, and fell down quickly, lying as though he had been asleep all the time. Panther jumped up, howling with pain, and woke Rabbit. He told him that he was right, that he had been nearly burned to death. Rabbit would only say, "I told you so. I told you so." Pretty soon they settled down to sleep again. As soon as Rabbit heard Panther snoring he thought that he was asleep and got up and played the same trick on him again. But this time Panther was only pretending to be asleep, and he caught Rabbit in the act and jumped up to kill him. Rabbit barely escaped his claws and ran as fast as he could. Then Panther gave chase. Several times he nearly caught him, but Rabbit managed to keep ahead. But soon he began to lose strength. Then to save himself, he made an ocean spring up between himself and the angry Panther. Panther could not get across that. And that is why there is an ocean.[7]

Mixed into the Southeastern trickster tales with no indication of distinctiveness is a large group of stories taken by Native Americans from Africans. How the transmission occurred is not known, but Africans were living with Native Americans from early historic times. A slight difference between the two groups should be noted. The North American trickster tends toward innocent stupidity, while the African trickster is known for his cleverness over stronger adversaries. This trait made the African trickster a useful model for the survival lore of an oppressed slave class in the New World. For the Southeastern tribes, the attraction was probably the sheer quality of the African material. African folklore is a rich body of narratives, and the African tricksters are humorous from anyone's viewpoint. Moreover, the Southeasterners already had a diverse body of trickster tales, making it possible for them to add new materials to their lore without serious disruption. In fact, the African tales have become so thoroughly Southeastern that only comparative study can now reveal the source of a legend.[8] Here is a sample, with the African narrative given first, then the Southeastern derivative.

The Tasks of the Trickster ■ ■ ■
Ashanti (Gold Coast)

Kwaku Ananse the spider once went to Nyan-konpon, the sky god, in order to buy the sky god's stories. The sky god said, "What makes you think you can buy them?" The spider answered and said, "I know I shall be able." Thereupon the sky god said, "Great and powerful towns like Kokofu, Bekwai, Asumengya, have come, but they were unable to purchase them, and yet you who are but a mere masterless man, you say you will be able?"

The spider said, "What is the price of the stories?" The sky god said, "They cannot be bought for anything except Onini the python; Osebo the leopard; Mmoatia the fairy; and Mmoboro the hornet." The spider said, "I will bring some of all these things, and, what is more, I'll add my old mother, Nsia, the sixth child, to the lot."

The sky god said, "Go and bring them then." The spider came back and told his mother all about it, saying, "I wish to buy the stories of the sky god, and the sky god says I must bring Onini the python; Osebo the leopard; Mmoatia the fairy; and Mmoboro the hornet; and I said I would add you to the lot and give you to the sky god." Now the spider consulted his wife Aso, saying, "What is to be done that we may get Onini the python?" Aso said to him, "You go off and cut a branch of a palm tree, and cut some string-creeper as well, and bring them." And the spider came back with them. And Aso said, "Take them to the stream." So Ananse took them; and, as he was going along, he said, "It's longer than he is, it's not so long as he; you lie, it's longer than he."

The spider said, "There he is, lying yonder." The python, who had overheard this imaginary conversation, then asked, "What's this all about?" To which the spider replied, "Is it not my wife Aso who is arguing with me that this palm branch is longer than you, and I say she is a liar." And Onini the python, said, "Bring it, and come and measure me." Ananse took the palm branch and laid it along the python's body. Then he said, "Stretch yourself out." And the python stretched himself out, and Ananse took the rope-creeper and wound it and the sound of the tying was nwenene! nwenene! nwenene! until he came to the head.

Ananse the spider said, "Fool, I shall take you to the sky god and receive the sky god's tales in exchange." So Ananse took him off to Nyame, the sky god. The sky god then said, "My hand has touched it, there remains what still remains." The spider returned and came and told his wife what had happened, saying, "There remain the hornets." His wife said, "Look for a gourd, and fill it with water and go off with it." The spider went along through the bush, when he saw a swarm of hornets landing there and he poured out some of the water and sprinkled it on them. He then poured the remainder upon himself and cut a leaf of plantain and covered his head with it. And now he addressed the hornets, saying, "As the rain has come, had you not better enter this, my gourd, so that the rain will not beat you; don't you see that I have taken a plantain leaf to cover myself?!" Then the hornets said, "We thank you, Aku, we thank you, Aku." All the hornets flew, disappearing into the gourd, fom! Father Spider covered the mouth and exclaimed, "Fools, I have got you, and I am taking you to receive the tales of the sky god in exchange."

And he took the hornets to the sky god. The sky god said, "My hand has touched it; what remains still remains."

The spider came back once more, and told his wife, and said, "There remains Osebo the leopard." Aso said, "Go and dig a hole." Ananse said, "That's enough, I understand." Then the spider went off to look for the leopard's tracks, and having found them, he dug a very deep pit, covered it over, and came back home. Very early next day, when objects began to be visible, the spider said he would go off, and when he went, lo, a leopard was lying in the pit. Ananse said, "Little father's child, little mother's child, I have told you not to get drunk, and now, just as one would expect of you, you have become intoxicated, and that's why you have fallen into the pit. If I were to say I would get you out, next day, if you saw me, or likewise any of my children, you would go and catch me and them." The leopard said, "O! I could not do such a thing."

Ananse then went and cut two sticks, put one here, and one there, and said, "Put one of your paws here, and one also of your paws here." And the leopard placed them where he was told. As he was about to climb up, Ananse lifted up his knife, and in a flash it descended on his head; gao! was the sound it made. The pit received the leopard and fom! was the sound of the falling. Ananse got a ladder to descend into the pit to go and get the leopard out. He got the leopard out and came back with it, exclaiming, "Fool, I am taking you to exchange for the stories of the sky god." He lifted up the leopard to go and give to Nyame, the sky god. The sky god said, "My hands have touched it; what remains still remains."

Then the spider came back, carved an Akua's child, a black flat-faced wooden doll, tapped some sticky fluid from a tree and plastered the doll's body with it. Then he made eto (pounded yams) and put some in the doll's hand. Again he pounded some more and placed it in a brass basin; he tied string round the doll's waist, and went with it and placed it at the foot of the odum tree, the place where the fairies come to play. And a fairy came along. She said, "Akua, may I eat a little of this mash?" Ananse tugged at the string, and the doll nodded her head. The fairy turned to one of the sisters, saying, "She says I may eat some." She said, "Eat some, then." And she finished eating, and thanked her. But when she thanked her, the doll did not answer. And the fairy said to her sister, "When I thank her, she does not reply." The sister of the first fairy said, "Slap her crying-place." And she slapped it, pa! And her hand stuck there. She said to her sister, "My hand has stuck there." She said, "Take the one that remains and slap her crying-place again." And she took it and slapped her, pa! and this one, too, stuck fast. And the fairy told her sister, saying, "My two hands have stuck fast." She said, "Push it with your stomach." She pushed it and her stomach stuck to it. And Ananse came and tied her up, and he said, "Fool, I have got you, I shall take you to the sky god in exchange for his stories." And he went off home with her.

Now Ananse spoke to his mother, Ya Nsia, the sixth child, saying, "Rise up, let us go, for I am taking you along with the fairy to go and give you to the sky god in exchange for his stories." He lifted them up, and went off there to where the sky god was. Arrived there he said, "Sky god, here is a fairy and my old woman whom I spoke about, here she is, too." Now the sky god called his elders, the Kontire and Akwam chiefs, the Adonten, the Gyase, the Oyoko, Ankobea, and Kyidom. And he put the matter before them, saying, "Very great kings have come, and were not able to buy the sky god's stories, but

Kwaku Ananse the spider has been able to pay the price: I have received from him Osebo the leopard; I have received from him Onini the python; and of his own accord, Ananse has added his own mother to the lot; all these things lie here." He said, "Sing his praise." "Eee!" they shouted. The sky god said, "Kwaku Ananse, from today and going on forever, I take my sky god's stories and I present them to you, kose! kose! kose! my blessing, blessing, blessing! No more shall we call them the stories of the sky god, but we shall call them spider stories."

This, my story, which I have related, if it be sweet, or if it be not sweet, take some elsewhere, and let some come back to me.[9]

The Tasks of the Trickster ▪ ▪ ▪
CREEK

Rabbit was discontented. He went to Esarketummesee (Hisakita imisi), the Life Controller, and said:

"I am unhappy. The other animals are better provided than I am for offense. When I am attacked I can only run."

Esarketummesee said: "Go and bring yonder Rattlesnake to me." The Snake was coiled and ready to strike. The Rabbit approached him and said:

"Esarketummesee has ordered me to take your measure, and, if you will get out of your coil, I will see how long you are."

The Rattlesnake felt flattered at this and stretched himself at full length. But Rabbit had provided a stick and a string, and quickly tying the stick to the snake near his head and tail he took him and ran away to Esarketummesee.

"Well done," said he. "Now, go and bring yonder swarm of Gnats which you see flying in the air."

Rabbit ran to the place and sat under the swarm and while the king of the Gnats was playing ball with his young men Rabbit said to him, "You have a large band, and Esarketummesee has sent me to count them. If you will enter this bag I will count as they go in." Rabbit saw that they all followed their king, as the bees follow their queen.

The king felt flattered at this and entered Rabbit's bag, all his young men following him, whereupon Rabbit tied the bag and ran away to Esarketummesee, where he threw it down.

Then Esarketummesee said to Rabbit, "See what you have done by using the faculties I gave you. Go and use the powers I have bestowed upon you and you will fulfill the destiny I designed for you."[10]

A Tug of War ▪ ▪ ▪
FAN (CONGO)

Tortoise considered himself a great personage. He went about calling

232

attention to his greatness. He said to people, "We three, Elephant, Hippopotamus, and I, are the greatest, and we are equal in power and authority."

Thus he boasted, and his boasts came to the ears of Elephant and Hippopotamus. They listened and then they laughed. "Pooh, that's nothing. He is a small person of no account, and his boasting can only be ignored."

The talebearer returned to Tortoise telling him what the two great ones had said. Tortoise grew very vexed indeed. "So, they despise me, do they? Well, I will just show them my power. I am equal to them, and they will know it before long! They will yet address me as Friend." And he set off.

He found Elephant in the forest, lying down; and his trunk was eight miles long, his ears as big as a house, and his four feet large beyond measure. Tortoise approached him and boldly called out, "Friend, I have come! Rise and greet me. Your Friend is here."

Elephant looked about astonished. Then spying Tortoise he rose up and asked indignantly, "Tortoise, small person, whom do you address as Friend?"

"You. I call you Friend. And are you not, Elephant?"

"Most certainly I am not," replied the Elephant in anger. "Besides, you have been going about and saying certain things about your great power—that it is equal to mine. How do you come to talk in such a way?"

Tortoise then said, "Elephant, don't get angry. Listen to me. True, I addressed you as Friend and said we were equal. You think that because you are of such a great size, you can surpass me, just because I am small? Let us have a test. Tomorrow morning we will have a tug-of-war."

Said Elephant, "What is the use of that? I can mash you with one foot."

"Be patient. At least try the test." And when Elephant unwillingly consented, Tortoise added, "When we tug, if one pulls over the other, he shall be considered greater, and if neither overpulls, then we are equal, and will call each other Friend."

Then Tortoise cut a very long vine and brought one end to Elephant. "This end is yours. I will go off with my end to a certain spot; and we will begin to tug, and neither of us will stop to eat or sleep, until one pulls the other over, or the vine breaks." And he went off with the other end of the vine and hid it on the outskirts of the town where Hippopotamus lived.

Hippopotamus was bathing in the river and Tortoise shouted to him, "Friend, I have come! You! Come ashore! I am visiting you!"

There was a great splashing as Hippopotamus came to shore, bellowing angrily, "You are going to get it now! Whom do you call Friend?"

"Why, you, of course. There is no one else here, is there?" answered Tortoise. "But do not be so quick to fight. I do not fear your size. I say we are equals, and if you doubt me, let us have a trial. Tomorrow morning we will have a tug-of-war. He who shall overcome the other, shall be the superior. But if neither is found superior, then we are equals and will call each other Friend." Hippopotamus thought the plan was absurd, but finally he consented.

Tortoise then brought his end of the vine to Hippopotamus and said, "This end is yours. And now I go. Tomorrow when you feel a pull on the vine, know that I am ready at the other end. Then you begin to tug, and we will not eat or sleep until the test is ended."

In the morning, Tortoise went to the middle of the vine and shook it. Elephant immediately grabbed his end, Hippopotamus caught up his end, and the tugging began. Each pulled at the vine mightily and it remained taut. At times it was pulled in one direction, and then in the other, but neither was overpulling the other.

Tortoise watched the quivering vine, laughing in his heart. Then he went away to seek for food, leaving the two at their tug, and hungry. He ate his bellyful of mushrooms and then went comfortably to sleep.

Late in the afternoon he rose and said, "I will go and see whether those fools are still pulling." When he went there the vine was still stretched taut, with neither of them winning. At last, Tortoise nicked the vine with his knife. The vine parted, and at their ends Elephant and Hippopotamus, so suddenly released, fell with a great crash back onto the ground.

Tortoise started off with one end of the broken vine. He came on Elephant looking doleful and rubbing a sore leg. Elephant said, "Tortoise, I did not know you were so strong. When the vine broke I fell over and hurt my leg. Yes, we are really equals. Strength is not because the body is large. We will call each other Friend."

Most pleased with this victory over Elephant, Tortoise then went off to visit Hippopotamus, who looked sick and was rubbing his head. Hippopotamus said, "So, Tortoise, we are equal. We pulled and pulled and despite my great size I could not surpass you. When the vine broke I fell and hurt my head. Indeed, strength has no greatness of body. We will call each other Friend."

After that, whenever they three and others met in council, the three sat together on the highest seats. And always they addressed each other as Friend.

Do you think they were really equal?[11]

A Tug of War ▪ ▪ ▪
CREEK (TASKIGI)

One day Rabbit and Tie-snake met. Rabbit had heard that Tie-snake was the strongest beast there was, so he made up his mind that he could fool him. He went to where Tie-snake had his den and told him that he had heard that he was the strongest puller in the world, but that he wanted to challenge him to a contest. "Why, nothing in the world will compare with me in pulling," said Tie-snake. But Rabbit was determined to hold a contest with him. Well, after a while Tie-snake agreed. Rabbit then gave him four days to prepare, and appointed the day.

Then Rabbit went to where another Tie-snake had his den, and told him

234

that he had heard it said that he was the strongest puller in the world, and challenged him to a contest. "Why, you are too small, you can't pull much," said this Tie-snake. But Rabbit urged and urged, and at last this Tie-snake agreed to have a contest with him. So he appointed four days later for the trial, and left him.

Now, Rabbit went to the river where the contest was to be held and fixed a big grapevine across it with an end resting on each bank. This was the way they had of doing the pulling, one on each side of the river trying to pull the other into the water.

On the fourth morning Rabbit took his place in the brush along the river bank, and soon saw the Tie-snakes come to the place agreed upon, and they took hold of the ends of the grapevine and were ready to commence. Rabbit gave a whoop, which was the signal to begin, and the Tie-snakes began pulling. Each one thought that Rabbit was on the other end, but he was pitting them against each other. Now, they kept on pulling nearly all day, and at night they gave it up and went home. The next day Rabbit went to see the first Tie-snake, and the snake said, "Well, I am surprised! Who would ever think that such a little animal could pull like that! I never pulled so hard in my life! Well, you certainly are stout!" Then he went to see the other Tie-snake, and he told Rabbit that he was very strong, but that nobody would ever suspect it by looking at him.

Now, by winning the contest with the Tie-snakes, Rabbit won also the privilege of going to the river to get his water, instead of having to go to wells for it.[12]

Tar-Baby ■ ■ ■
BAKONGO (CONGO)

It was during an almost rainless "hot season," when all who had no wells were beginning to feel the pangs of thirst, that the rabbit and the antelope formed a partnership to dig a deep well so that they could never be in want of water.

"Let us finish our food," said the antelope, "and be off to our work."

"Nay," said the rabbit; "had we not better keep the food for later on, when we are tired and hungry after our work?"

"Very well, hide the food, rabbit; and let us get to work, I am very thirsty."

They arrived at the place where they purposed having the well, and worked hard for a short time.

"Listen!" said the rabbit; "they are calling me to go back to town."

"Nay, I do not hear them."

"Yes, they are certainly calling me, and I must be off. My wife is about to present me with some children, and I must name them."

"Go then, dear rabbit, but come back as soon as you can."

The rabbit ran off to where he had hidden the food, and ate some of it, and then went back to his work.

"Well!" said the antelope. "What have you called your little one?"

"Uncompleted one," said the rabbit.

"A strange name," said the antelope.

Then they worked for a while.

"Again they are calling me," cried the rabbit. "I must be off, so please excuse me. Cannot you hear them calling me?"

"No," said the antelope. "I hear nothing."

Away ran the rabbit, leaving the poor antelope to do all the work, while he ate some more of the food that really belonged to them both. When he had had enough, he hid the food again, and ran back to the well.

"And what have you called your last, rabbit?"

"Half-completed one."

"What a funny little fellow you are! But come, get on with the digging; see how hard I have worked."

Then they worked hard for quite a long time. "Listen, now!" said the rabbit. "Surely you heard them calling me this time!"

"Nay, dear rabbit, I can hear nothing; but go, and get back quickly."

Away ran the rabbit, and this time he finished the food before going back to his work.

"Well, little one, what have you called your third child?"

"Completed," answered the rabbit. Then they worked hard and as night was setting in returned to their village.

"I am terribly tired, rabbit; run and get the food, or I shall faint."

The rabbit went to look for the food, and then calling out to the antelope, told him that some horrid cat must have been there, as the food was all gone, and the pot quite clean. The antelope groaned, and went hungry to bed.

The next day the naughty little rabbit played the antelope the same trick. And the next day he again tricked the antelope. And the next, and the next, until at last the antelope accused the rabbit of stealing the food. Then the rabbit got angry, and dared him to take casca, a purge or emetic.

"Let us both take it," said the antelope, "and let him whose tail is the first to become wet be considered the guilty one."

So they took the casca and went to bed. And as the medicine began to take effect upon the rabbit, he cried out to the antelope:

"See, your tail is wet!"

"Nay, it is not!"

"Yes, it is!"

"No, but yours is, dear rabbit; see there!"

Then the rabbit feared greatly, and tried to run away. But the antelope said: "Fear not, rabbit; I will do you no harm. Only you must promise not to drink of the water of my well, and to leave my company forever."

Accordingly the rabbit left him and went his way.

Some time after this, a bird told the antelope that the rabbit used to drink the water of the well every day. Then the antelope was greatly enraged, and determined to kill the rabbit. So the antelope laid a trap for the silly little rabbit. He cut a piece of wood and shaped it into the figure of an animal about the size of the rabbit; and then he placed this figure firmly in the ground near to the well, and smeared it all over with birdlime.

The rabbit went as usual to drink the waters of the well, and was much annoyed to find an animal there, as he thought, drinking the water also.

"And what may you be doing here, sir?" said the rabbit to the figure.

The figure answered not.

Then the rabbit, thinking that it was afraid of him, went close up to it, and again asked what he was doing there.

But the figure made no answer.

"What!" said the rabbit. "Do you mean to insult me? Answer me at once, or I will strike you."

The figure answered not.

Then the little rabbit lifted up his right hand, and smacked the figure in the face. His hand stuck to the figure.

"What's the matter?" said the rabbit. "Let my hand go, sir, at once, or I will hit you again."

The figure held fast to the rabbit's right hand. Then the rabbit hit the figure a swinging blow with his left. The left hand stuck to the figure also.

"What can be the matter with you, sir? You are excessively silly. Let my hands go at once, or I will kick you."

And the rabbit kicked the figure with his right foot; but his right foot stuck there. Then he got into a great rage, and kicked the figure with his left. And his left leg stuck to the figure also. Then, overcome with rage, he bumped the figure with his head and stomach, but these parts also stuck to the figure. Then the rabbit cried with impotent rage. The antelope, just about this time, came along to drink water; and when he saw the rabbit fearlessly fastened to the figure, he laughed at him, and then killed him.[13]

Tar-Baby ■ ■ ■
BILOXI

The Rabbit and the Frenchman were two friends. The Rabbit aided the Frenchman, agreeing to work a piece of land on shares. The first season they planted potatoes. The Rabbit, having been told to select his share of the crop, chose the potato vines, and devoured them all. The next season they planted corn. This year the Rabbit said, "I will eat the roots." So he pulled up all the corn by the roots, but he found nothing to satisfy his hunger. Then the Frenchman said, "Let us dig a well." But the Rabbit did not wish to work any longer with his friend. Said he to the Frenchman, "If you wish to dig a well, I shall not help you." "Oho," said the Frenchman, "you shall not drink any of the water from the well." "That does not matter," replied the Rabbit, "I am accustomed to licking the dew from the ground." The Frenchman, suspecting mischief, made a tar-baby, which he stood up close to the well. The Rabbit approached the well, carrying a long piece of cane and a tin bucket. On reaching the well he addressed the tar-baby, who remained silent: "Friend, what is the matter? Are you angry?" said the Rabbit. Still the tar-baby said nothing. So the Rabbit hit him with one forepaw, which stuck there. "Let me go or I will hit you on the other side," exclaimed the Rabbit. And when he found that the tar-baby paid no attention to him, he hit him with his other forepaw, which stuck to the tar-baby. "I will kick you," said the Rabbit. But when he kicked the tar-baby, the hind foot stuck. "I will kick you with the other foot," said the Rabbit. And when he did so, that foot, too, stuck to the tar-baby. Then the Rabbit resembled a ball, because his feet were sticking to the tar-baby, and he could neither stand nor recline.

Just at this time the Frenchman approached. He tied the legs of the Rabbit together, laid him down and scolded him. Then the Rabbit pretended to be in great fear of a brier patch. "As you are in such fear of a brier patch," said the Frenchman, "I will throw you into one." "Oh, no," replied the Rabbit. "I will throw you into the brier patch," responded the Frenchman. "I am much afraid of it," said the Rabbit. "As you are in such dread of it," said the Frenchman, "I will throw you into it." So he seized the Rabbit, and threw him into the brier patch. The Rabbit fell at some distance from the Frenchman. But instead of being injured, he sprang up and ran off laughing at the trick which he had played on the Frenchman.[14]

Racing a Trickster ■ ■ ■
IBO (NIGERIA)

A frog challenged a deer to a race. Before the day appointed for the contest, the frog entered into a league with all his companions and arranged that they should station themelves at regular intervals along the course, and that each should wait in readiness to answer the calls of the deer as he raced along toward the goal. The race started. The deer thought to outstrip the frog with ease, and soon called back in mocking tones to ask where the frog was. To his surprise the answer, "Here I am," came from the opposite direction to what he expected. He raced along once more and repeated the challenge. Again a voice answered from in front of him, and once more he was deceived and thought he was being left behind in the race. The strategy was repeated all along the course until the deer fell down exhausted and died.[15]

Racing a Trickster ▪ ▪ ▪
CREEK (TASKIGI)

Turtle had heard that Rabbit was the swiftest runner. So one day he went to Rabbit, and said, "I understand that you are the fastest runner. I want to run a race with you."

Rabbit said, "What! You run a race with me? Why, look at your legs. You can't run at all!"

But Turtle said that he could, and he would not be satisfied until Rabbit agreed to have a race with him. The Turtle set the day for the race, and set the fourth day from that time. He said, "When you see me with a white feather on my head, you will know that it is I and not some other turtle." Then the Turtle went and got three more of his friends and put a white feather on the head of each. Now, the course over which they were to race was chosen by Rabbit. It was where there were four hollows and four hills. They were going to start on top of the first hill and race for the top of the last. Now, when the fourth day came around, Turtle placed one of his friends in each of the hollows. When all was ready Rabbit whooped to start, and they started. When Rabbit got to the top of the first hill he saw a turtle with a white feather going up the other hill ahead of him. And when he got to the top of that one he saw a turtle with a white feather going up the next. And so on till the last ridge. When he reached the goal, there was Turtle ahead of him.

"Well!" said Rabbit, "You are a great runner! Who would think that you could run with such short legs!"[16]

The debate over the African source of Southeastern Native American tales is an old one, for as soon as Southern Afro-American lore began to be collected and published in the late nineteenth century, the parallels were obvious. When Mooney published his classic Cherokee collection in 1900 he briefly asserted the Native American priority and made an unkept promise to prove it in a later essay. The conclusion of the debate had to wait until there were adequate collections and indexes from Africa to permit full comparison. It was Dundes who settled the general question in a brief essay in 1969. Having demonstrated that Africa was the source of some of the Southeastern narratives, he went a step farther and asserted an answer to the other major problem: was trickster Rabbit African or North American? He found for Africa.[17]

If that assertion could be proved, it would be a conclusion of great importance, for it would demonstrate that peoples not only can borrow motifs and narratives from alien groups, but also can borrow major mythic figures without any substantial change in the social system, such as absorbing or merging with the other society. Proving that viewpoint, however, seems impossible. There is a "Hare" which is the trickster for some African tribes, but there is also the Hare who is a culture hero–trickster–transformer for the central Algonkin and Siouan tribes.[18] Since our comparative studies have shown repeatedly that some portion of the Creeks has been in close contact with those peoples, judging by narrative affiliations, there is reason to believe that they knew the Rabbit trickster of the Eastern Woodlands. Then, too, the northern Rabbit is also a major mythic character whose trickster episodes are often found in the most solemn mythic contexts, and the same phenomenon occurs in the Southeast. Simplicity suggests an alternate view of the origin of Rabbit: the Southeast, as a melting-pot of traditions, had several tricksters, one of the most important of whom was the Rabbit of northern fame. The addition of tales and motifs from Africa increased the body of trickster tales, many of which were adapted by giving the trickster the identity of Rabbit—a tendency increased by the discovery that the Africans, too, knew the Rabbit. Thus Africa led to the creation of an illusion, that there was a single important trickster in the Southeast, whereas Rabbit may earlier have been but one among several.

This scenario has the virtue of explaining the Southeastern adoption of African trickster tales with a minimum reconstruction of the mythic world-view. The fact that the Southeastern tribes changed the identity of the African tricksters (e.g., Ananse the spider disappears completely) while keeping the tales, suggests that the pre-existent Rabbit was stronger than any alien figure; the materials coming from those tribes who knew Hare, of course, required very little alteration. The consequence of this view is that incorporation of African sources led to an intensification of the central Woodlands Rabbit in the Southeast, a process requiring minimal restructuring of the world-view.

The Africans brought more than just trickster stories into the lore of the Southeast. Here is a set of texts embodying a clear structural problem: how are we to account for the anomalous bat? Is it a four-legged animal or a bird? While it is possible that such a category problem was thought about independently, African influence seems likely. If so, then the way the Southeasterners adapted the story is instructive.

The War Between Birds and Animals ■ ■ ■
IBO (NIGERIA)

Once upon a time there was a war between the animals and birds. A serious debate took place as to which party the bat would join, and he, being a wily creature, kept his own counsel. When the birds were in the ascendant he threw in his lot with them. For forty years they kept the animals in subjection. At last the lion and the tiger, in despair of overthrowing their oppressors, advised that measures should be taken to bring about peace. This counsel was derisively rejected by the other animals, who were of opinion that fortune was, at last, about to favor them, so hostilities were resumed. A watch was now set upon the bat's movements, and it was discovered that he was holding himself aloof, at that time, from both parties. The fox was sent to arrest him and he was brought before the leaders of the animals. He was charged with playing a double game and an explanation was demanded. His defense was that he had followed the advice of his wife, who had persuaded him to hold himself in readiness to join whichever party prevailed, with the view of ultimately receiving a share of the spoils.

He was chided severely for his double-dealing and thrown into prison to await his trial at the conclusion of the war. For ten years longer the struggle continued and finally it ended in the complete defeat of the birds.

The bat was summoned before the council and, finding the case too hard for him, he engaged a clever lawyer to plead his case. The advocate contended that his client had a perfect right to side with either party, according to his inclination. He based his opinion on the anatomy of the bat. Though not a bird yet he was equipped with wings and, being able to fly, he insisted that when the bat was in the air he was not trespassing; all must admit that he was in his rightful sphere. On the other hand he was covered with fur, he had teeth and long ears, whereas the birds had none of these characteristics. All things considered there seemed no doubt that the bat possessed qualities which made it admissible for him to be termed either an animal, or a bird, or both.[19]

The War Between the Animals and Birds ■ ■ ■
CREEK

The birds challenged the four-footed animals to a great ball play. It was agreed that all creatures which had teeth should be on one side and all those which had feathers should go on the other side with the birds.

The day was fixed and all the arrangements were made; the ground was prepared, the poles erected, and the balls conjured by the medicine men.

When the animals came, all that had teeth went on one side and the birds on the other. At last the Bat came. He went with the animals having teeth, but they said:

"No, you have wings, you must go with the birds."

He went to the birds and they said: "No, you have teeth, you must go with the animals." So they drove him away, saying: "You are so little you could do no good."

He went to the animals and begged that they would permit him to play with them. They finally said, "You are too small to help us, but as you have teeth we will let you remain on our side."

The play began and it soon appeared that the birds were winning, as they could catch to ball in the air, where the four-footed animals could not reach it. The Crane was the best player. The animals were in despair, as none of them could fly. The little Bat now flew into the air and caught the ball as the Crane was flapping slowly along. Again and again the Bat caught the ball, and he won the game for the four-footed animals.

They agreed that though he was so small he should always be classed with the animals having teeth.[20]

In Nigeria a major institution is the court in which legal argumentation is done by proverbs and reason. While they also had the council of "beloved men" with a rhetoric of its own, the Creeks adapted the story to its important institution, the ball-play. While it was entertaining and a great athletic sport, it is clear that it bore greater meaning. We know that when town played town, the "color" of the victor—its status as a red (war) or white (peace) town— changed. There are ritual indications that the game was also a battle with mythical meaning. Some have interpreted the prehistoric engravings of the Southeastern Ceremonial Complex as indicating that in earlier times human decapitation followed the game. It is that significant institution of the Southeast which became the setting for the problem of the anomalous Bat. The Cherokee included the flying squirrel and had the anomalous features of both created in order to add them to the teams in the ballplay.

All told, the amalgamation of African and Native American folklore is one of the more interesting topics in Southeastern studies, for the processes of transmission involved can shed much light on the dynamics of acculturation. The subject awaits careful study by a student of all three culture groups: African, Afro-American, and Native American.

Epilogue

If you set out to read the legend texts, your venture is ended. The texts given in this volume are by no means all that exist, but they are intended to be a representative sample. If you wish to read more, ample bibliographic notes have been included to aid you in your quest.

For those who have grown interested in the constant theme of geographic distribution that has run through this volume, it is time to draw the threads together. As should be clear by now even to the most casual reader, the loss of lore and the adaptation process in the Southeast have been devastating to any definitive study of the Native American world-view of that region. Nonetheless, several patterns have emerged from our tedious tracing of the affinities of legends and motifs.

New World. Some of the materials are so widespread that there is no dispute that they should be accepted as ancient lore, perhaps from the dawn of human habitation of the New World.

Circumpolar. Some of the narratives display distribution in the northern reaches of the continent and seem to be related to hunting cultures. Estimating age is difficult, but that those materials probably are pre-agrarian is likely, which would put them at 500 B.C. or earlier.

Circum-Caribbean. To our astonishment, more than a few motifs and composite legends find close relationships in Central and South America. Since there are archaeological and linguistic reasons for suspecting Caribbean intrusions into the Southeast, it perhaps should not be so surprising to find these folkloric affinities. Nevertheless, modern political boundaries weigh more heavily in our minds than they should, and the narratives correct that prejudice.

Eastern Woodlands. A few motifs and recognizable oicotypes seem to be found throughout the Eastern Woodlands, with little distribution elsewhere. In the light of what we know of prehistoric and historic movements of peoples throughout the region, that is not a surprising fact, for there has been ample movement and trading to create folkloric similarities, particularly when the various tribes were in basic agreement on cosmology and world-view.

Plains Group. For those who think of the Creeks as the stable core of the Southeastern peoples, the discovery that a significant number of legends and oicotypes relate them to the central Algonkin, Plains Siouans, and Caddoans may be surprising. Without any way of proving it, I have come to think of this cluster as the "Mississippian Group." I think some portion of the Creeks was living in proximity to those peoples in a time of formation of a superculture, and that they began to move into the Southeast perhaps around 1000 A.D. If we do not see some sort of radiation of peoples and traditions from some more central area, such as the Mississippi Valley, then we are left with the problem of explaining why there are such similarities between so widely separated groups as Creeks and, say, Mandan. This is not a minor supposition, and it seems impossible to prove, but it helps explain some of the peculiar affinities of Creek lore as well as the sense of a "superculture" in which some Southeastern tribes participated.

Southwest. There are more indications of relation between the Southeast and the Southwest than have been indicated in this collection. The problem of interpreting that relationship lies in the question of whether it was direct or whether there was a common ancestor in MesoAmerica. This is an endless debate, not likely to be solved by examination of the folklore.

African. Finally, there are materials that entered the Southeast from Africa. Euro-Americans were no more adept at picking up African lore than Native American legends, but the latter absorbed a sizeable body of narratives from Africans and adapted it to their own uses.

Ultimately, the Southeast cannot be viewed as a discrete region in Native American studies, for the folklore, even the little that was collected so late, reveals it to have been an eclectic area from long before the arrival of Europeans and Africans. The body of materials will continue to reside in our libraries waiting for students with new insights and techniques of analysis which will force those legends to give up their treasures of cultural understanding. Despite the difficulties of studying the Southeastern peoples, attention to the old Southeast is not wasted energy, for it would be hard to identify a region whose checkered history is more important to an understanding of the cultural processes that have resulted in modern America.

Frontispiece
Map of approximate locations "at the time of contact." That means that the Timucua location, for example, is 1540, while the Mandan area is as of 1750. Adapted from Driver 1961.

Chapter 1. Preliminary Reflections
1. Hudson 1976.
2. Mooney 1900; Swanton 1929.
3. Hudson 1976.
4. Haas 1947.
5. Thompson 1929.
6. Aarne and Thompson 1958.
7. Thompson 1956–60.

Chapter 2. The Native American Southeast
1. Phillips and Brown 1984.
2. Tuggle 1973.
3. Speck 1934:x.
4. Swanton 1911:357.
5. Gatschet 1884.
6. Gatschet 1893.
7. Dorsey and Swanton 1912.
8. Dorsey 1893b:48.
9. Dorsey and Swanton 1911.
10. Mooney 1900.
11. Dorsey 1905:5.
12. Dorsey 1904b, 1904c, 1904d, 1905, 1906.
13. Speck 1907:103.
14. Speck 1909:5.
15. Swanton 1907:285.
16. Bushnell 1909:29f.
17. Bushnell 1910.
18. Swanton 1911, 1913, 1922, 1928a, 1928b, 1931.
19. Swanton 1929.
20. Martin 1977:x.
21. Swanton 1929:1.
22. Swanton 1917.
23. Speck 1934:x.
24. Speck 1934:x. See Swanton 1918.
25. Speck 1934:xi.
26. Kilpatrick and Kilpatrick 1966:385.
27. Wagner 1931:viii.
28. Martin 1977:x.
29. Densmore 1937; Martin 1977:x.
30. Haas 1947:404.
31. Haas 1947:403f.
32. Howard 1959.
33. Lombardi 1984.
34. Le Page DuPratz (Histoire de La Louisiane 2:313) in Swanton 1911.
35. Swanton 1911:171.
36. Swanton 1928a:367.
37. Milfort (Memoire 47f) in Swanton 1928a:455.

38. Mooney 1900:229f.
39. Radin 1945.
40. Dorsey 1895:131.
41. Hodgson 1823:278.
42. Bushnell 1910.
43. Swanton 1928a:521.
44. Swanton 1928a:63.
45. Swanton 1929:1.
46. Dorsey 1889:190.
47. Dorsey 1888:120.
48. Chamberlain 1891:195.
49. Bergen 1896:54.
50. Swanton 1928a:490.
51. Dorsey 1904d:xxiif.
52. Mooney 1900:229f, 232.
53. Speck 1909:138.
54. Swanton 1928d:491.
55. Hultkrantz 1981.
56. Walker 1983; Swanton 1928a:487.

Chapter 3. The Above World

1. Witthoft and Hunter 1957.
2. Waring and Holder 1945; Howard 1968; Swanton 1928c.
3. Swanton 1928c; Haas 1942.
4. Engraving of the Timucua solar worship by Theodore DeBry in 1591, after LeMoyne. "Solemnities at Consecrating the Skin of a Stag to the Sun." Fundaburk 1958: Engraving 35.
5. Swanton 1911.
6. Several incidents of such "retainer sacrifices" were observed among the Natchez by the French.
7. DuPratz (Histoire de La Louisiane II:340f), quoted in Swanton 1911:171f.
8. Gatschet 1893:281.
9. Swanton 1929:84.
10. Haas 1942:531. For the full text in Tunica, see Haas 1950:20–23.
11. Many Native American groups had linguistic ways of indicating when they were speaking of a given animal and when they were referring to the "type" animal of a species in the primal times before the present order. Early collectors adopted a convention to express this difference, so that an "otter" is not quite the same as the "Ancient of Otters."
12. Dorsey and Swanton 1912:110f.
13. Swanton 1911:357; letter from Martin Duralde to William Dunbar, ca. 1810.
14. Mooney 1900:252ff.
15. Mooney 1900:256f.
16. Thompson 1929:273f.
17. Dorsey and Swanton 1912:112.
18. White-Bread to G.A. Dorsey, 1903–05, one of 530 Caddo remaining in 1903, in western Oklahoma. Dorsey 1905:7–13.
19. Swanton 1929:123.
20. Mooney 1900:240ff.
21. Drawings adapted from Phillips and Brown 1984: Pl. 246. These spider gorgets (left to right) were found in: Union County, Illinois; Perry County, Missouri; Madison County, Illinois; and Fulton County, Illinois. Others are known from as far away as Florida.

22. Swanton 1929:102f; equivalents are Swanton 1929: Hitchiti 25, Koasati 53, Creek 43 and 44, and Yuchi 144.
23. Benjamin Paul to Swanton, in Swanton 191:358.
24. Swanton 1929:122.
25. Mooney and Olbrechts 1932:24; Hudson 1976.
26. Cross and sun circles on shell gorgets. The cross stands for fire and was figured in the Creek four-log ceremonial fire, while the circles and scallops represent the sun. Left to right: Stallings Island, Georgia; Moundville and Limestone Counties, Alabama. Adapted from Fundaburk and Foreman 1957: Plates 32, 41, and 43.
27. This appears to be an inventory of the paraphernalia involved in ritual smoking.
28. From prehistoric times on, both ceramic and stone pipes were made in effigy form. Several frog pipes have been found in various archaeological contexts. See Fundaburk and Foreman 1957:103.
29. This is, of course, a post-European substitution or addition. The original form may have referred to "Stoneclad" remembered by the Cherokee and Iroquois.
30. This is probably a reference to ritual magic and possibly to the motif "Contest in magic" (D1701.1).
31. The directional winds now become associated with animals and birds. The connection may be through the seasons—each wind and animal being considered appropriate to a particular season.
32. Speck 1909:147f.
33. Note that if these two designs are roughly equivalent, then the crested bird, frequently identified as a pileated woodpecker, the lightning eye-design, thunder, men, and directions are revealed as aspects of the same figure. It is difficult not to speculate that these much-discussed SCC designs are related to the Thunderbird concept, an artistic form of which is not otherwise found in the Southeast.
34. Thompson 1929:292.
35. Benjamin Paul to Swanton, in Swanton 1911:359.
36. Swanton 1929:154. Equivalent texts are Koasati (Swanton 1929:193) and Hitchiti (Swanton 1929:90).
37. Kilpatrick and Kilpatrick 1966b:391f. Informants: Morgan Calhoun, half-brother of Will West Long; they were Olbrecht's major informants. Collector: Frans Olbrechts. Big Cove, North Carolina, February 1927. Other texts: Mooney 1900:315f, 317, Kilpatrick and Kilpatrick 1964:71–76.
38. Southeastern tribes kept the areas around their houses clear of grass so as to reduce insects and snakes. Europeans learned the practice from them, and the custom is still found in the rural South.
39. Hunting was a ritual activity, because success as a hunter was dependent on relations with the animal powers. Fasting was an important preparation for the encounter.
40. Feathers were important in ritual regalia, and eagle feathers were worn only by those who had caught eagles. This reference is probably to a known set of feathers kept for ritual purposes. (See the conclusion of the text.)
41. Swanton 1929:246f. See also Hitchiti (Swanton 1929:90), Alabama (Swanton 1929:154), and Koasati (Swanton 1929:193).
42. Thompson 1929:318.
43. Skinner 1911:140. Informant not identified. Collected by Skinner at Menomini reservation in northern Wisconsin, summer of 1910.
44. Coleman et al. 1962:102. For other specialized accounts of thunderbirds, see McClintock 1941:15:164–68, 224–27; 16:16–18. Skinner 1914:71f. Eells 1889:329–36. Chamberlain 1890:51–54.
45. Thunderbirds with lightning-eye designs. From Spiro, Oklahoma, and Moundville, Alabama. (Phillips and Brown 1984: Pl. 85, p. 199.)

247

46. Swanton 1911:354.
47. Swanton 1929:8f. Another text, 9f.
48. "Nephew" and "uncle," but the English terms don't communicate what is meant by that relationship. In the Southeast the tribes were matrilineal; descent was traced through the mother and included family, clan, and phratry membership. In matrilineal societies the father-son relationship of the Euro-American world existed between the child and mother's brother. Thus Thunder was virtually adopting the man.
49. Kilpatrick and Kilpatrick 1966a:391f. See also Mooney 1900:300f; Kilpatrick and Kilpatrick 1964:50–56; Swanton 1929:7–9.
50. Inf: unidentified. Dorsey 1905:30.

Chapter 4. The Under World

1. Swanton 1929:32f, "Creek 1."
2. Swanton 1929:34, "Creek 8."
3. Swanton 1929:30, "Creek 6."
4. Swanton 1928a:492.
5. Archaeologists may find intriguing this reference to a custom of sending a bowl as an ambassadorial gift, for it suggests a reason other than trade for the presence of "exotic" ceramics at sites in the Southeast.
6. This is a good example of Native American structuring. Whereas Europeans tend to organize things by threes, the Native American tradition emphasizes fours. Time and again in oral narrative people attempt actions four times before succeeding. It is almost an unconscious structural principle.
7. Collected by W.O. Tuggle in Oklahoma. Swanton 1929:34ff.
8. Swanton 1929: Creek 34, Hitchiti 98, Alabama 147; Mooney 1900:#73, 83, 85, 87; Dorsey and Swanton 1912:#18.
9. Tuggle 1973:176. V.J. Knight has pointed out that this same merging of history and mythology is also recorded for the Creek War: Nunez 1958:149; and Debo 1941:81f.
10. Methvin 1927.
11. Swanton 1929:97. Also Natchez (Swanton 1929:245) and Cherokee (Mooney 1900:#53).
12. Inf: Jackson Lewis. Swanton 1928a:492f.
13. Inf: George Clinton. Wagner 1931:200f.
14. Mooney 1900: passim.
15. Swanton 1928a:494.
16. Swanton 1929:176f. For more Creek lore, see Gatschet 1899:259. Other texts are Koasati (Swanton 1929:172), Alabama (Swanton 1929:126), Natchez (Swanton 1929:234), and Shawnee (Gatschet 1899:256f).
17. See Thompson 1929: Note 179 for bibliography; this is "Whale-boat" (R2145).
18. Bowers 1950; Beckwith 1938; Swanton 1907.
19. Horned serpents from Spiro, Oklahoma, Moundville, Alabama, and Walls, Mississippi. (Phillips and Brown 1984: 199).
20. Swanton 1928a:53.
21. Swanton 1928a:69.
22. These are puns on the names of the towns.
23. Swanton 1928a:70f. Similar texts, but with the water serpent marrying the woman, include Iroquois, Menomini, Zuni, Hopi, Tunica, and Caddo; see Wycoco-Moore 1951:#571.
24. Eyman 1962.
25. Gatschet 1899:255–60. Howard 1960. Michelson 1935:197–99.
26. English 1922:151–56.

27. Phillips and Brown 1984:140–43, 200. Pictured are three of the renditions of the underwater panther ("Piasa"). One is from Moundville, Alabama, and two are from Spiro, Oklahoma. (Phillips and Brown 1984: 196, Pl. 228, Pl. 223).
28. Swanton 1929:#14.
29. Swanton 1922:241.
30. Inf.: Ispahihtca from Kasihta. Collected by Gatschet in Oklahoma, 1880s. Swanton 1928a:61.
31. Writer: Minnie Walter Myers, 1898, in WPA 1938:287f. For more on this Euro-American use of a Native American legend, see Porter 1946 and Anderson 1963:37–43.
32. Inf: Wing. Dorsey 1905:18f. This is the motif "Deluge" (A1010).
33. Rands 1954:79ff.
34. Conzemius 1932:130ff.
35. Rands 1954:81.
36. Conzemius 1932:169.
37. Ibid.
38. Paredes 1970 has an excellent introduction, but see Radin 1944 and Foster 1948 for discussions of problems in the collection of Mexican folktales.
39. Roth 1915:184.
40. Roth 1915:184ff.
41. Steward 1948:267.
42. Roth 1915:148.
43. Frazer 1923:102; for other texts see Farabee 1918:110ff; Farabee 1924:83ff; Brett 1880:106ff, 127ff; Ogilvie 1940:64ff.
44. Roth 1915:378.
45. Steward 1948:320, 347, 382, 462, 539.
46. Arikara (Dorsey 1904b:#21, 22); Mandan (Maximilian 2:185; Bowers 1950:199); Hidatsa (Maximilian 2:230; Bowers 1965:360); Gros Ventre (Kroeber 1908:116); Blackfoot (Wissler and Duvall 1908).
47. Lowie 1909:#25a–c.
48. Lowie 1918:214ff; Simms 1903:296ff.
49. See Bowers 1950:Ch. 6; Beckwith 1938:117ff.
50. Gaschet 1899:258. See also Dorsey 1893:233.
51. Ponca (Dorsey 1890:322); Skidi Pawnee (Dorsey 1904d:293); Caddo (Dorsey 1905:65); Apache (Goddard 1919:64ff; 135ff).
52. Hopi: Voth 1905:48ff; Nequatewa 1936:85ff; Waters 1963:82ff; Courlander 1971:67ff. Zuni: Benedict 1935:1:10ff; Cushing 1896:429; Stevenson 1905:61. Sia: Stevenson 1889:35f.
53. Tyler 1964:244ff.
54. Design from "The Hollywood Beaker" from the Hollywood site on the Savannah River in Georgia. (Phillips and Brown 1984:194.)

Chapter 5. The Middle World
1. Speck 1907:103.
2. Speck 1907:144.
3. Speck 1907:145f. Infs. not identified. "Primeval water" is Motif A810; "Earth-diver" is A812.
4. Wagner 1931:3–13. Inf. Maxey Simms. Another text, almost identical, is found in Speck 1909.
5. Mooney 1900:239
6. Swanton 1928a:487.
7. Reichard 1922.
8. Count 1949:55.

9. Rooth 1957.
10. Benjamin Paul to Swanton, in Swanton 1911:357f.
11. Motif A2211.1.
12. Halbert 1899:230f.
13. Inf: Big Jack of Hilibi. Swanton 1928a:488.
14. Kongas 1960:151–180.
15. Swanton 1929:121. Other deluge texts are Natchez (Swanton 1929:214; Swanton 1911:176ff; Swanton 1922:316); Cherokee (Mooney 1900:#14); Choctaw (Bushnell 1910:#6; Swanton 1931:202ff); Caddo (Dorsey 1905:18f); Tunica (Haas 1950:); Yuchi (Wagner 1931:100ff); Biloxi (Dorsey and Swanton 1912).
16. Stiggins 1959:44.
17. Schoolcraft 1851:1:267f; Swanton 1922:191. Other Alabama texts:Swanton 1922:192.
18. Inf: Pistonatubee (b. 1815), Newton County, Miss., ca. 1898. Halbert 1904:268f. Includes Choctaw text. Other Choctaw texts: Halbert 1899:229f; Alfred Wright (*Missionary Herald* 1828:215), in Gatschet 1884:106f; Du Pratz 295; Bushnell 1910:526f; Romans 1775:38f, 47f.
19. Wheeler-Voegelin and Moore 1957:74.
20. Wheeler-Voegelin and Moore 1957:67.
21. Gatschet 1884:1:244–51.
22. Pennington 1931:192–98.
23. This pole is an important feature of all the Muskhogean migration texts, and in some it indicates the direction of march by leaning during the night.
24. The Tukabahchee claim these important medicines were given to them by four men. The Busk, or Green Corn fesival, was the major ritual of the year for all of the Southeastern peoples, as far as is known.
25. The reference is to a taboo concerning menstruation. In order to avoid "polluting" the sacred fire and thus weakening the medicine power of the tribe, women made a separate fire for the duration of their menstrual period.
26. The names of the nations vary from text to text, probably reflecting current understandings of relationships between peoples. Here it is Kasihta which receives priority, followed by Chickasaws, Alabama, and Abihka (Upper Creek); this is, of course, a Kasihta informant. The Choctaw are here ignored, but they link themselves in their version with the Chickasaw.
27. The Gatschet text added an "also" after the reference to the eagle, but the original reveals that whether the King of Birds is the same as the eagle, is obscure. Gatschet chose to see them as two birds, but the text itself does not warrant that conclusion. The latter portion describes the red/white dualism of war and peace, a belief used metaphorically later on in references to a "white path" and the "red arrows." The eagle-impersonation describes the method of sending ambassadors to each other.
28. This is probably a reference to the Choctaw, who lived in the vicinity of Okaloosa Creek and were known to the Soto chroniclers as Calusa.
29. Coosa was the ancient "mother-town" of the Upper Creeks. Soto seems to have seen them at the peak of their power in 1540 on the upper Coosa River, but by the late eighteenth century the talwa existed mostly as a memory.
30. This legend apparently accounts for a totem or possibly a war bundle which was carried on war forays.
31. This may be an early variant of the "local flood" legend known in separate form, which was discussed in the preceding chapter.
32. The custom of skull deformation was practiced prehistorically over much of the Southeast, and the Choctaw are known to have continued it into historic times.
33. Swanton noted that Tomochichi was chief of the Yamacraw tribe, settled where Savannah now stands when Oglethorpe established his colony. Cf. Swanton 1922:108f.

34. Black drink was a strong tea made of the leaves of *Ilex cassina*. Ingestion of large amounts followed by vomiting was a ritual that purified the individual and prepared him for powerful activity. It was therefore universally used in the Southeast as a customary beginning of councils and hunting or war expeditions. See Hudson 1979.

35. The red and white metaphors are again used to refer to the war-seeking attitude and its opposite. Behind the metaphor is the social organization of the Muskhogeans and others who used the system, because each talwa was designated as a red or white town, and there was a dual political system within each talwa. The white council was in control until they declared war, then the alternate warrior hierarchy ruled until the war was declared done. All of this is referred to here by the red/white symbolism. In addition there is an allusion to the custom of burying the hatchet beneath one of the cabins or sheds ("bed") that comprise the Creek "square grounds" or "council center" to declare peace, or a shift from red to white.

36. Gatschet 1884:1:244–51. See also Brinton 1870. Other emergence/migration texts are in Swanton 1928a: Hitchiti (52), Coweta (52f), Tukabahchee (65f) and two more from Kasihta (54f). There are seven more Creek migration texts without the emergence motif—in Swanton 1928a:40–74.

37. Inf.: Rev. Peter Folsom, "a Choctaw from the nation west, who was employed in 1882 by the Baptists of Mississippi to labor as a missionary among the Mississippi Choctaws. Mr. Folsom stated that soon after finishing his education in Kentucky, one day in 1833, he visited Nanih Waiya with his father and while at the mound his father related to him the migration legend of his people." Halbert 1899:228f. Other Choctaw accounts appear in Claiborne 1880. Two Chickasaw texts are found in Warren at the turn of the century. See Swanton 1928b:174–80. A Tunica text is contained in Haas 1950, and the lengthy Caddo version is in Dorsey 1905.

Chapter 6. The Tribes of People

1. Speck 1907:146ff. Inf. unknown. Fieldwork in 1904/05.
2. Bushnell 1909:32. Other texts are in Swanton 1929: Alabama (126), Hitchiti (91), Koasati (193).
3. Swanton 1929:98f. Other texts in Mooney (#83, 85), Swanton 1929: Creek (34), Alabama (147).
4. Bushnell 1909:32f. Swanton 1929: Alabama 151 (two texts).
5. Swanton 1929:149f; another text, 150; Koasati (27).
6. Early European accounts tell amazing stories about the supernatural abilities of seers to locate people and objects.
7. Swanton 1929:124f. Koasati:185f.
8. "Bayou" is a Choctaw word for creek or estuary which through French adoption has become a familiar place name in the Southeast.
9. Bushnell 1910.
10. Dorsey and Swanton 1912:37. Swanton 1929: Hitchiti (90), Creek (36).
11. Swanton 1907:287f; Benjamin Paul to Swanton in Swanton 1911:359.
12. Extracted from a lengthy creation legend. Dorsey 1905:10f. Other texts: Cherokee (Mooney 1900:240ff; see Chapter 7); Creek (Swanton 1929:6); Biloxi (Dorsey and Swanton 1911:54).
13. Hultkrantz 1961:55.
14. Hultkrantz 1961:57.
15. This motif is "Impounded water" (A1111).
16. Swanton 1929:123f.
17. Swanton 1929:168.
18. Swanton 1929:102. Other texts: Creek (Swanton 1929:42); Alabama (Swanton 1929:157); Koasati (Swanton 1929:201); Natchez (Swanton 1929:253).

19. Mooney 1900:290f.
20. Roth 1915:334ff. Two Warao versions.
21. Levi-Strauss 1969:35, 206.
22. Mooney 1900:#5.
23. Levi-Strauss 1969:205; 1973:87.
24. Speck 1909:140.
25. Stewart R. Shaffer, Albion Mich., to James H. Howard in 1954. Howard 1959:134–38. Other texts: Creek (Gatschet 1884:1:248; Swanton 1929:39); Cherokee (Mooney 1900:311, 319, 326). Also noted for the Menomini, Micmac, Wyandot, Sarcee, Saulteaux and Creek, Dakota, Apache.
26. Dorsey 1888:237; Dorsey 1895:130.
27. Speck 1909:110.
28. Gaschet 1888:237. The motif is "Dwarfs" (F495).
29. Inf: Ahojeobe (Emil John), St. Tammany Parish, La. Bushnell 1910:30f.
30. Inf: Ahojeobe at Bayou Lacomb, March 1909. Bushnell 1910:31.
31. Bushnell 1910:32.
32. Inf.: Mrs. Margaret Wiley Brown (died in 1922), North Carolina. Speck 1934:27.
33. Inf: Molly Sequoyah, Big Cove, N.C. 1945. Witthoft and Hadlock 1946:415.
34. Names and informant, "Nancy Brave," are pseudonyms, for it is considered dangerous to talk about the Little People. Tahlequah, Oklahoma, 1979. Lombardi 1984.
35. Speck 1907:150.
36. Speck 1907:145.
37. Speck 143.
38. Wagner 1931:157f.
39. Inf: Jackson Lewis. Swanton 1922:173.
40. Inf: "one of the oldest women among the Alabama living in Texas." Swanton 1922:192.
41. Hitchcock 1842:125ff. Inf: Tukabahchee Micco, Oklahoma.
42. Wagner 154f; Inf. Maxey Simms.
43. Infs.: "Odumata and other principal men." Bowditch 1819. Quoted in McLoughlin 1976:334.
44. Inf. Chief Neamathla. Recorded by William P. Duval. Florida, 1823–24. McKenney and Hall 1838:2:38f.
45. Hitchcock 1842:126f. Inf: Tukabahchee Micco, Oklahoma. Other texts: Swanton 1929:74, 75 (Creek); Swanton 1929:75n (Seminole).
46. Dorsey and Swanton 1912:32f; collecting by Gatschet (1886) and J.O. Dorsey (1892) at Lecompte, La. Infs.: Bankston Johnson, Betsey Joe, daughter Maria.

Chapter 7. The Plant World
1. Speck 1909:146f. The Hitchiti text is Swanton 1929:87. There are three Creek texts: Swanton 29:19f.
2. Hawkins 1848:81f.
3. Haas 1950:69.
4. Halbert 1899:230f.
5. Schoolcraft 1851:1:311.
6. Speck 1934:23f.
7. Williams 1827:86. For another text, see Wolley 1902:42.
8. Brown 1940:20f.
9. Mooney 1893:959.
10. Inf: Jackson Lewis. Swanton 1929:9f. Other texts: Creek (Swanton 1929:13f); Koasati (Swanton 1929:168); Seminole (Marriott 1968:137ff.
11. Curtin and Hewitt 1918:280, 636ff; Parker 1923:205ff.
12. Curtin and Hewitt 1918:637.

13. Cushing 1920:101f; Benedict 1935:1:20ff, 2:1ff, 20ff; Parsons 1917:316f. Dorsey 1904b:#42 (Arikara).
14. Mooney 1888:98.
15. Explanations of natural phenomena abound in Native American lore, but an early scholar, by comparing many different texts, concluded that these "etiological elements" are extremely variable and cannot be used as a way of typing legends. They appear to be attached loosely to any legend and vary from tribe to tribe and teller to teller. Waterman 1914.
16. This wheel is a widespread feature, and it always matches the implement used locally in a game. In the Southeast the form was a ground stone disk called a "chunkstone" for playing chunky. The night direction was west, where the sun disappears at dusk.
17. Mooney 1888:98–105. Baillou 1961:100f; Kilpatrick and Kilpatrick 1964:132; Kilpatrick and Kilpatrick 1966a:189, 391; Traveller Bird 1974:29. Illustrated is a shell gorget from Tennessee in the "spaghetti style" of that area for which there are many examples. This is the only one on which the thunder figure is doubled. (Fundaburk and Foreman 1957: Pl. 45).
18. Swanton 1929:11ff. Other texts: Creek (Swanton 1929:13ff, 15ff); Natchez (Swanton 1929:230, 230ff); Seminole (Greenlee 1945:141).
19. Hale 1888:178.
20. Parker 1923:64.
21. Hewitt 1903:460ff
22. Parker 1923:413.
23. Brown 1940:22.
24. Brown 1890:214; Mechling 1914:87f; Nicolar 1893:58ff; Speck 1935:75.
25. Brown 1890:214.
26. Roth 1915:134. See p. 133 for a slightly different text from the neighboring Warao.
27. Hatt 1954:853–914.

Chapter 8. The Twins
1. This appears to be an embellishment based on "Tar-Baby," a trickster legend introduced into the Southeast by African slaves (see Chapter 12). Regardless of the accretion, the motif is "Burr-woman" (G311), a widely known Native American incident.
2. This incident may have a double meaning. The Choctaw burial practices involved a priestly specialist with very long fingernails. The "bone-picker" removed the decayed flesh from scaffolded bodies and cleaned the bones for reburial in a bundle. The Alabama, part of the Creeks in the historic period, followed Choctaw customs, and it may be that this "Long Finger-nails" is a Creek jibe at a Choctaw custom they did not share.
3. Swanton 1929:4–7. The Natchez have two texts, one identical to the Cherokee, but omitting the maize legends, and one similar to the Creek (Swanton 1929:222ff, 227ff). The Alabama and Koasati have elements which appear in the Creek text, but the origin episodes are missing; the boys simply appear as brothers (Swanton 1929:133, 181f).
4. Dorsey 1905:31–36. Inf.: Wing.
5. Radin 1950:359–419.
6. Rand 1894:62, Curtin and Hewitt 1918:#34, Radin 1915:81, Skinner and Satterlee 1915:332ff.
7. Skinner 1925:427, Dorsey 1890:215, Lasley 1902:176.
8. Reichard 1922:269–307.
9. Sumner 1951:73f.
10. Motif is "Dreadnaughts" (Z210).
11. Hudson 1976:148.

12. Roth 1915:133ff.
13. Metraux 1946:114–23.

Chapter 9. The Wonderful Garments
1. Inf: Big Jack of Hilibi, Oklahoma. Swanton 1929:14f. Also in Swanton 1929:Creek (10ff, 15ff, 17ff); Natchez (230ff, 234ff). Major motifs are: "Bloodclot" (L113), "Magic headdress" (D1079.4), and "Magic flute" (D1223.1). Additional motifs are "Magic objects acquired by trickery" (D838), "Fatal imitation" (J2401), and "Unsuccessful imitation of magic production of food" (J2411.3).
2. Swanton 1929:178ff.
3. Swanton 1929:134f, 136f.
4. Swanton 1929:230ff, 234ff.
5. Dorsey 1890:48ff; Skinner 1925:#5; Dorsey 1904d:80ff.
6. Dorsey 1890:604ff
7. Inf: Fox, in Oklahoma. Dorsey 1904c:178–84.
8. Thompson 1929:327
9. Swanton 1929:166. See Thompson 1965.
10. "The Old Woman Who Never Dies" was sometimes called Grandmother, and her connection with the corn has already been noted. Will and Hyde, summarizing an account by Maximilian, state that '[h]er residence was for a long time on the west side of the Missouri, some 10 miles below the Little Missouri River, on the banks of a little slough known as the Short Missouri. A single large house-ring here is pointed out as the site of her home, and the high bottom there is said to have been the Grandmother's field. According to the traditions, she became impatient at the too frequent visits of the Hidatsas and moved into the west.' The location is evidently the same as that given in connection with this legend, identifying 'Granny' as the Old Woman Who Never Dies." Densmore 1923:80 (Densmore's note).
11. Inf: Ben Benson. Densmore 1923:80ff.
12. Fuller studies of the Grandmother figure can be found in Hatt 1949; Hultkrantz 1957; Lankford 1975; Prentice 1986:239–66. In this last otherwise admirable study, the author too quickly concluded that "[i]n the Southeast the grandmother motif does not appear to occur..." (249)

Chapter 10. The Bead- Spitter/Marooned Hero
1. Rabbit is the Muskhogean trickster. (See Chapter 12.)
2. In the Eastern Woodlands beads assumed cultural importance at least by Mississippian times. They served as status indicators and ritual regalia. They were strung in strands and sewn onto belts, where, as "wampum," they served as mnemonic devices and ambassadorial gifts. In historic times they became a form of money, but that role may have been prehistoric, as well. Since most beads werc shell, they were in short supply. From the beginning of their widespread use shells were a part of the international trade network. Possession of shells by inland people indicated success in that network. It is no wonder that the young women might fantasize about such a husband.
3. This motif of the sifter test is found in the Southeast in various contexts. It seems to be another connection between the Southeast and South America. (Roth 1915.)
4. Swanton 1929:2ff.
5. A sapia was a crystal or stone of power frequently given to selected persons by plants. It gave the possessor power in hunting and war, and sometimes medicine.
6. This is apparently a Muskhogean symbol of subordination, for strings of dog excrement were used that way in one of the migration legend texts. See Swanton 1928a:58. This may also be a reference to a now lost dance practice.

7. Motif is "Jewels from spittle," D1001, D1456. The Seneca apparently equated the ability to spit beads with shamanistic power. A related practice, "shooting" initiates with shells, was a part of the Ojibwa Midewiwin. The Seneca have four texts of the "Wonderful Garments" legend (see Chapter 9), in which the garments are accompanied by the ability to spit shells. (Curtin and Hewitt 1918:127ff, 139ff, 262ff, 501ff.) They do not have the "Bead-spitter" legend itself.

8. Swanton 1929:172. The Alabama text is almost identical in detail, including the continuation into the marooned hero legend: Swanton 1929:126f.

9. Insertion of anachronistic details is a common feature of oral tradition everywhere. Since narratives inevitably reflect the ethnographic reality of the tellers, it is more surprising that so many archaic details persist.

10. Here in the last paragraph of the text Riggs seems to have made an error in translation which causes the introduction of a new character, "Sharp-Grass." If, however, as seems possible from the Dakota text, the word "sharp-grass" was intended to modify "knife," the passage makes sense.

11. Riggs 1893:148f. Dakota text included. Inf: Michel Renville. The illustration is a shell gorget from Castalian Springs, Tennessee. (Phillips and Brown 1984: 180).

12. Inf. not given. Skinner and Satterlee 1915:408ff.

13. Skinner 1925.

14. Dorsey and Kroeber 1903:272ff. The Gros Ventre text is similar, for Loon kills Shell-spitter after the Sun-dance. Kroeber 1908:108f.

15. Dorsey 1895:130.

16. Inf.: Wing. Dorsey 1905:67f. Other texts are from the Hare, Loucheux, Achomawi, Southern Ute, Ojibwa, Seneca, Huron, Apache, and Navaho.

17. Dorsey and Swanton 1912:99–107. A somewhat similar version has been collected from the Dakota, raising the question of whether the Biloxi have here preserved a bit of their Siouan heritage. See Riggs 1893:139ff.

18. Riggs 1893:138.

19. Inf. unidentified. Dorsey 1905:26f.

20. Swanton 1929:175–77. Other texts are Alabama (126–28) and Koasati (172–74). The "Whale-boat" motif is inserted in a different Natchez legend (238f).

21. Distribution of Potiphar's wife includes Eskimo, Sahaptin, Tsimshian, Haida, Omaha, Arapaho, Dakota, Blackfoot, Gros Ventre, Assiniboin, Cree, Ojibwa, Kickapoo, Naskapi, Seneca and Biloxi, roughly the distribution of Marooned egg-gatherer. The Whale-boat appears to be concentrated in the Northeast, but it seems likely that the three should be considered a complex which was known generally over the northern part of North America.

Chapter 11. Other Adventures
1. Bushnell 1909:35.
2. Swanton 1911:358.
3. Hultkrantz 1957.
4. This is "Rising and falling sky" (F791), in which the sky vault is envisioned as a dome which rocks at the edge of the Middle World. Getting through to the outside of the dome required precise timing, as the death of one adventurer testifies. See J.O. Dorsey 1904:64.
5. This is "Magic pot" (D1171.1), and "Inexhaustible food supply" (D1031), in which a little food expands to satisfy all. A widely known and used theme, as might be expected among people for whom hunger is a present danger.
6. Inf: Charles M. Thompson (Sun-Kee), chief of Alabama, Livingston, Texas, died 1935. Densmore 1937:276f.

7. Swanton 1929:139f, 140f, 141.
8. Heard 1937:276f.
9. Martin 1946:67ff. Martin 1977:24ff.
10. Hultkrantz 1957:230.
11. Hultkrantz 1957:54.
12. Speck 1909:144ff. Other texts: Alabama (Swanton 1929:141f, 142f); Koasati (Swanton 1929:189f); Cherokee (Mooney 1900:#5). For the many non-Southeastern texts, consult Hultkrantz 1957.
13. Haas 1950:77–82. Text in Tunica included. Related texts include the Alabama, Koasati, and Yuchi. (Speck 1909:149.) In the Alabama and Koasati texts the Cannibal-woman's nose is cut off for use as a pipe. The Alabama brothers who break a looking taboo are turned into a wildcat, a crow, a chicken hawk, and two unspecified. (Swanton 1929:129ff.) The Cherokee brothers turn into a wildcat, a panther, an owl, a crow, and their sister became a partridge. (Swanton 1929:169f.)
14. Pisatuntema (Emma), Heleema (Louisa), and John at Bayou Lacombe, St. Tammany Parish, La., in 1908–09 to Bushnell. Bushnell 1909:34f.
15. Swanton 1929:186ff.
16. Swanton 1929:133. Other texts: Alabama (Swanton 1929:131f); Koasati (Swanton 1929:182, 183); Creek (Swanton 1929:20). This is a widespread legend which has been studied by Waterman 1914:1–54. "Obstacle flight" is Motif D672.
17. Inf.: Moses Owl, Birdtown, North Carolina. Collected in 1945 by John Witthoft and Wendell S. Hadlock. Witthoft and Hadlock 1946:419.

Chapter 12. Tricksters
1. For the classic study of the Eastern Woodlands trickster, see Radin 1957.
2. Dorsey 1905:106f.
3. Swanton 1929:111f. Other texts: Creek (Swanton 1929:55f); Cherokee (Mooney 1900:#43); Alabama (Swanton 1929:162); Koasati (Swanton 1929:210); Yuchi (Speck 1909:153); Natchez (Swanton 1929:254); Biloxi; and Caddo.
4. Bushnell 1909:32. Other texts: Taskigi (Speck 1907:156); Hitchiti (Swanton 1929:#21); Biloxi (Dorsey and Swanton 1912:68f). This is "Death through foolish imitation" (J2400.1), a motif well known everywhere in North America, with the weakest showing in the Plains and the Southeast.
5. Swanton 1929:208.
6. Swanton 1929:241f. One other Southeastern text is Cherokee (Mooney 1900:293).
7. Speck 1907:154f.
8. Dundes 1969.
9. Radin and Sweeney 1952.
10. This is Motif H1154.6. Swanton 1929:60f. Other texts in Swanton 1929: Creek (58f, 59f), Hitchiti (104f), Natchez (233f); Tunica (Haas 1950:101ff). In the latter the measuring of Rattlesnake is made a concluding episode of the Orphan myth.
11. Jablow 1961.
12. Speck 1907:156f. Other texts are in Swanton 1929: Creek (48f, 49, 49f, 50, 50f, 51f, 52f), Hitchiti (105ff). This is Motif K22. Despite the fact that this is an African tale, it has been entered in the Tale Type Index as Aarne-Thompson 291.
13. Dennet 1898. Reprinted in Feldman 1963:141–44.
14. Dorsey 1893:48f. Collected in central Louisiana, January–February 1892. Other texts: Yuchi (Speck 1909:152f), Cherokee (Mooney 1900:#21), Taskigi (Speck 1907:149f), Creek (Swanton 1929:68), Hitchiti (Swanton 1929:161), Natchez (Swanton 1929:258), Alabama (Swanton 1929:161), and Koasati (Swanton 1929:208f). The tar-baby is indexed as Aarne-Thompson 175, and it is known from both Africa, Europe, and, of course, Afro-Americans.

15. Basden 1921. Reprinted in Feldman 1963:140f.
16. Speck 1907:155f. Other texts are: Cherokee (Mooney 1900:#20), Creek (Swanton 1929:53, 53, 54, 54, 54f), Hitchiti (Swanton 1929:101f), Natchez (Swanton 1929:252), Alabama (Swanton 1929:157f), Koasati (Swanton 1929:201); Catawba (Speck 1934:13); Yuchi (Wagner 1931:36). This tale is indexed as Aarne-Thompson 1074, and it is known from Africa, Europe, and Afro-America.
17. Dundes 1969:207ff.
18. See Dorsey 1892.
19. Basden 1921. Reprinted in Feldman 1963:214f.
20. Collected by Tuggle. Swanton 1929:23. Another text is Cherokee (Mooney 1900:286f). Found in Africa and Europe, this is Aarne-Thompson 222A and motif B261.1.

AA—*American Anthropologist*
BAEAR—*Bureau of American Ethnology Annual Report*
BAEB—*Bureau of American Ethnology Bulletin*
JAF—*Journal of American Folklore*

Aarne, Anti, and Stith Thompson.
    1958   The types of the folktale. Helsinki: *Folklore Fellows Communications* 74.
Anderson, John Q.
    1963   A burlesque of the legend of "The Singing River." *Louisiana Studies* 2:37–43.
de Baillou, Clement.
    1961   A contribution to the mythology of the Cherokee. *Ethnohistory* 8.
Basden, G.T.
    1921   *Among the Ibos of Nigeria.* London: Seeley Service and Co., Ltd.
Beckwith, Martha W.
    1938   Mandan-Hidatsa myths and ceremonies. *American Folklore Society Memoir* 32.
Benedict, Ruth.
    1935   *Zuni Mythology* (2 vols.) Columbia University Contributions to Anthropology.
Bergen, Mrs. F.D.
    1896   Note. *JAF* 9:54.
Bowditch, T.E.
    1819   *Mission from Cape Coast Castle to Ashantee.* London.
Bowers, Alfred.
    1950   *Mandan Social and Ceremonial Organization.* Chicago: University of Chicago Press.
    1965   Hidatsa social and ceremonial organization. *BAEB* 194.
Brett, W.H.
    1880   *Legends and Myths of the Aboriginal Indians of British Guiana.* London.
D.G. Brinton.
    1870   *National Legend of the Chahta-Muskokee Tribes.* Morrisiana, New York.
Brown, D.M.
    1940   Wisconsin Indian corn origin myths. *Wisconsin Archeologist* 21:19ff.
Brown, Mrs. W. Wallace.
    1890   Wa-ba-ba-nal, or Northern Lights: A Wabanaki legend. *JAF* 3:214.
Bushnell, David I.
    1909   The Choctaw of Bayou Lacomb, St. Tammany Parish, Louisiana. *BAEB* 48.
    1910   Myths of the Louisiana Choctaw. *AA* 12:526–37.
Chamberlain, A.F.
    1890   The Thunder-bird amongst the Algonkins. *AA* 3:51–54.
    1891   Nanibozhu amongst the Otchipwe, Mississagas, and other Algonkian tales. *JAF* 4:193ff.
Claiborne, J.F.H.
    1880   *Mississippi as a Province, Territory and State* (reprint). Baton Rouge: Louisiana State University Press, 1964.
Clarke, Kenneth W.
    1958   A motif-index of the folktales of culture-area V, West Africa. Indiana University: Unpub. Ph.D. dissertation.
Clements, William M. and Frances M. Malpezzi.

1984   *Native American Folklore, 1879-1979: An Annotated Bibliography.* Athens, Ohio: Swallow Press.

Coleman, Bernard, Sr., Ellen Frogner, and Estelle Eich.
1962   *Ojibwa Myths and Legends.* Minneapolis.

Conzemius, E.
1932   Ethnographical survey of the Miskito and Sumu Indians of Honduras and Nicaragua. *BAEB* 106.

Count, Earl.
1949   The Earth-diver and the rival Twins: A clue to time correlation in North-Eurasiatic and North American mythology. In *Indian Tribes of Aboriginal America* (Sol Tax, ed.). 29th International Congress of Americanists.

Courlander, Harold.
1971   *The Fourth World of the Hopis.* New York: Fawcett.

Curtin, Jeremiah, and J.N.B. Hewitt.
1918   Seneca fictions, legends and myths. *BAEAR* 32.

Cushing, F.W.
1896   Outlines of Zuni creation myths. *BAEAR* 13.
1920   Zuni Bread Stuffs. *Heye Foundation Notes and Monographs* 8.

Debo, Angie.
1941   *Road to Disappearance.* Norman, Oklahoma: University of Oklahoma Press.

Dennet, R.E.
1898   Notes on the folklore of the fjort. *Publications of the Folklore Society 41.* London.

Densmore, Frances.
1923   Mandan and Hidatsa music. *BAEB* 80.
1937   The Alabama Indians and their music. In "Straight Texas" (Mody Boatright, ed.). *Publications of the Texas Folklore Society* 13:276f.

Dorsey, George A.
1904a   Traditions of the Osage. *Field Museum* 7.
1904b   Traditions of the Arikara. *Carnegie Institution* 17.
1904c   The mythology of the Wichita. *Carnegie Institution* 21.
1904d   Traditions of the Skidi Pawnee. *American Folklore Society Memoir* 8.
1905   Traditions of the Caddo. *Carnegie Institution* 41
1906   The Pawnee: Mythology, part 1. *Carnegie Institution* 59.

Dorsey, G.A., and A.L. Kroeber.
1903   Arapaho traditions. *FCM Anthro Publications* 5.

Dorsey, G.A., and John R. Swanton.
1912   The Biloxi and Ofo languages. *BAEB* 47.

Dorsey, J.O.
1888   Notes and queries. *JAF* 1:237.
1889   Omaha folk-lore Notes. *JAF* 2:190.
1890   The Dhegiha language. *Smithsonian Institution Contributions to North American Ethnology* 6.
1892   Nanibozhu in Siouan mythology. *JAF* 5:293-304.
1893a   Notes and queries. *JAF* 6:233.
1893b   Two Biloxi tales. *JAF* 6:48f.
1895   Kwapa folk-lore. *JAF* 8:130.
1904   Rising and falling sky in Siouan mythology. *AA* 6:64.

Driver, Harold E.
1961   *Indian Tribes of North America.* Chicago: University of Chicago Press.

Dundes, Alan.
1969   African tales among the North American Indians. *SFQ* 29:207ff.

Eells, Myron.
    1889   The thunder bird. *AA* 2:329–36.
English, Tom.
    1922   The Piasa petroglyph: The Devourer from the Bluffs. *Art and Archaeology*
              14:151–56.
Eyman, Frances.
    1962   An unusual Winnebago war club and an American water monster. *Expedition*
              5:4:31–35.
Farabee, W.C.
    1918   The Central Arawak. *University of Pennsylvania Museum Anthropological*
              Publication 9.
    1924   The Central Caribs. *University of Pennsylvania Museum Anthropological*
              Publication 10.
Feldman, Susan.
    1963   *African Myths and Tales.* New York: Dell.
Foster, G.M.
    1948   The current status of Mexican-Indian folklore studies. *JAF* 61:368ff.
Frazer, J.G.
    1923   *Folk-Lore in the Old Testament.* New York: Tudor.
Fundaburk, E.L., and M.D.F. Foreman.
    1957   *Sun Circles and Human Hands.* Luverne, Alabama.
Gatschet, Albert S.
    1884   *A Migration Legend of the Creek Indians* (2 vols.).Philadelphia.
    1888   Notes and queries. *JAF* 1:237.
    1893   Some mythic stories of the Yuchi Indians. *AA* (OS) 6:279–82.
    1899   Water monsters of American Aborigines. *JAF* 12:255–60.
Goddard, P.E.
    1920   Myths and tales of the San Carlos Apache and White Mountain Apache.
              AMNH Anthropological Paper 24.
Greenlee, R.F.
    1945   Folktales of the Florida Seminole. *JAF* 58:138ff.
Haas, Mary R.
    1942   The solar deity of the Tunica. *Publications of the Michigan Academy of Science,*
              Arts, and Literature 28:531–35.
    1947   Southeastern Indian folklore. *JAF* 60:403f.
    1950   *Tunica Texts.* Berkeley: University of California Press.
Halbert, Henry S.
    1899   Nanih Waiya, the sacred mound of the Choctaws. *Publications of Mississippi*
              Historical Society 2:230f.
    1901   The Choctaw creation legend. *Publications of the Mississippi Historical Society*
              4:268f.
Hale, Horatio.
    1888   Huron folk-lore. *JAF* 1:177ff.
Hatt, Gudmund.
    1954   The Corn Mother in America and in Indonesia. *Anthropos* 46:853–914.
Hawkins, Benjamin.
    1848   A sketch of the Creek country, in 1798 and –99. *Georgia Historical Society*
              Collections 3:1:81f.
Heard, Elma.
    1937   Two tales from the Alabamas. In "Straight Texas" (Mody Boatright,ed.). *PTFS*
              13:276f.

Hewitt, J.N.B.
    1903   Iroquoian cosmology. *BAEAR* 21.
Hitchcock, E.A.
    1842   A traveler in Indian territory. Cedar Rapids, Iowa. Reprint 1930.
Hodgson, Adam.
    1823   Remarks During a Journey Through North America. New York.
Howard, James H.
    1959   Altamaha Cherokee folklore and customs. *JAF* 72:134–38.
    1960   When they worship the underwater panther: A Prairie Potawatomi bundle ceremony. *SWJA* 16.
    1968   The Southeastern Ceremonial Complex and its interpretation. Columbia: *Missouri Archaeological Society Memoir* 6.
Hudson, Charles.
    1976   *The Southeastern Indians.* Knoxville: University of Tennessee Press.
    1979   *The Black Drink.* Athens: University of Georgia Press.
Hultkrantz, Ake.
    1957   The North American Indian Orpheus tradition. Stockholm: *Ethnographic Museum Publication* 2.
    1961   (ed.) The supernatural owners of nature. *Ethnografiska Studien.*
    1981   Myths in Native American religions. In *Belief and Worship in Native North America.* Syracuse: Syracuse University Press, 3–19.
Jablow, A.
    1961   *Yes and No, the Intimate Folklore of Africa.* New York: Horizon Press.
Kilpatrick, J.F., and Anna Gritts Kilpatrick.
    1964   *Friends of Thunder: Folktales of the Oklahoma Cherokees.* Dallas: SMU Press.
    1966   The Wahnenauhi manuscript. *BAEB* 196.
    1966   Eastern Cherokee folktales: Reconstructed from the field notes of Frans M. Olbrechts. *BAEB* 196:391f.
Kongas, Elli Kaija.
    1960   The Earth-diver (Th. A812). *Ethnohistory* 7:151–180.
Kroeber, A.L.
    1908   Gros Ventre myths and tales. *American Museum of Natural History Anthropological Papers* 1.
Lankford, George E.
    1975   The tree and the frog: An exploration in stratigraphic folklore. Indiana University: Unpub. Ph.D. dissertation.
Lasley, Mary.
    1902   Sac and Fox tales. *JAF* 15:170ff.
Levi-Strauss, Claude.
    1969   *The Raw and the Cooked.* New York: Harper and Row.
Lombardi, Betty J.
    1984   Comments on the Little People Stories collected from the Cherokee Indians of Northeastern Oklahoma. *Mid-America Folklore* 12:1:32–39.
Lorant, Stephen.
    1947   *The New World.* New York.
Lowie, Robert H.
    1909   *The Assiniboine.* American Museum of Natural History Anthropological Paper 4.
    1918   Myths and traditions of the Crow Indians. *American Museum of Natural History Anthropological Papers* 25.
Marriott, Alice.
    1968   American Indian Mythology. New York: Mentor.

Martin, Howard N.
    1946   Folktales of the Alabama-Coushatta Indians. In Mexican border ballads and other lore. (Mody C. Boatright, ed.) *Publications of the Texas Folklore Society* No. 21:67ff.
    1977   *Myths and Folktales of the Alabama-Coushatta Indians of Texas.* Austin: Encino Press.

McClintock, Walter.
    1941   The thunderbird myth. *The Masterkey* 15:164–68, 224–27; 16:16–18.

McKenney, Thomas L., and James Hall.
    1838   *History of the Indian Tribes of North America* (2 vols.). Philadelphia.

McLoughlin, William G.
    1976   A note on African sources of American Indian racial myths. *JAF* 89:334.

Mechling, W.H.
    1914   Malecite tales. Ottawa: *Geological Survey of Canada* 49.

Methvin, J.J.
    1927   Legend of the Tie-snakes. *Chronicles of Oklahoma* 5:391–96.

Metraux, Alfred.
    1946   Twin heroes in South American mythology. *JAF* 59:114–23.

Michelson, Truman.
    1935   The Menomini hairy serpent and the hairy fish. *JAF* 48:197–99.

Mooney, James.
    1888   Myths of the Cherokees. *JAF* 1:98.
    1893   The ghost-dance religion. *BAEAR* 14.
    1900   Myths of the Cherokees. *BAEAR* 19:2.

Mooney, James, and Frans M. Olbrechts.
    1932   The Swimmer manuscript: Cherokee sacred formulas and medicinal prescriptions. *BAEB* 99.

Nequatewa, E.
    1936   Truth of a Hopi and other clan stories of Shungopovi. Flagstaff: *Museum of Northern Arizona Bulletin* 8.

Nicolar, J.
    1893   *Life and Traditions of the Red Man.* New York.

Nunez,
    1958   *Ethnohistory* 5:2:

Ogilvie, John.
    1940   Creation myths of the Wapisiana and Taruma, British Guiana. *Folk-lore* 51.

Paredes, Americo, ed.
    1970   *Folktales of Mexico.* Chicago: University of Chicago Press.

Parker, A.C.
    1923   Seneca myths and folktales. *Buffalo Historical Society Publication* 27.

Parsons, E.C.
    1917   Notes on Zuni. *AAA Memoir* 4.

Pennington, Edgar L.
    1931   Some ancient Georgia Indian lore. *Georgia Historical Quarterly* 15:192–98.

Phillips, Philip, and James A. Brown.
    1984   *Pre-Columbian Shell Engravings from the Spiro Mound at Spiro, Oklahoma* (6 vols. in two). Cambridge: Peabody Museum of Archaeology and Ethnology, Harvard University.

Porter, Kenneth W.
    1946   A legend of the Biloxi. *JAF* 59:168–73.

Prentice, Guy.
    1986   An analysis of the symbolism expressed by the Birger Figurine. *American Antiquity* 51:239–66.

Radin, Paul.
    1915   The Winnebago myth of the twins. *Southwestern Anthropological Papers* 1:40ff.
    1945   *Road of Life and Death.* New York: Pantheon.
    1950   The basic myth of the North American Indians. *Eranos Jahrbuch* 17:359–419.
    1956   *The Trickster.* New York: Schocken Books.

Radin, Paul, and Sweeney, J.
    1952   *African Folktales and Sculpture.* New York: Bollingen Foundation.

Rand, S.T.
    1894   *Legends of the Micmacs.* Wellesley College Philological Publications.

Rands, Robert.
    1954   Horned serpent stories. *JAF* 67:79ff.

Reichard, Gladys.
    1922   Literary types and dissemination of myths. *JAF* 34:269–307.

Riggs, Stephen.
    1893   Dakota grammar, texts, and ethnography. *Contributions to North American Ethnology* 9.

Romans, Bernard.
    1775   *A Concise Natural History of East and West Florida* (Vol. 1). London.

Rooth, Anna Birgitta.
    1957   The creation myths of the North American Indians. *Anthropos* 52:497–508.

Roth, W.E.
    1915   An inquiry into the animism and folklore of the Guiana Indians. *BAEAR* 30.

Schoolcraft, H.R.
    1851–60   *Historical and Statistical Information Respecting the History, Condition, and Prospects of the Indian Tribes of the United States* (6 vols.). Philadelphia.

Simms, S.C.
    1903   Traditions of the Crows. Chicago: *Field Museum Publication* 2.

Skinner, Alanson.
    1888   Note. *JAF* 1:120.
    1911   The Menomini game of lacrosse. *American Museum Journal* 11:138–41.
    1914   The Algonkin and the thunderbird. *American Museum Journal* 14:71f.
    1925   Traditions of the Iowa Indians. *JAF* 38:27ff.

Skinner, Alanson, and S. Satterlee.
    1915   Menomini folklore. *American Museum of Natural History Anthropological Papers* 13:408ff.

Speck, Frank G.
    1907   The Creek Indians of Taskigi town. *American Anthropological Society Memoirs* 2:2.
    1909   Ethnology of the Yuchi Indians. *Anthropology Publication of University of Pennsylvania Museum,* No. 1.
    1934   *Catawba Texts.* New York: Columbia University Press.
    1935   Penobscot tales and religious beliefs. *JAF* 48.

Stevenson, M.C.
    1889   The Sia. *BAEAR* 11.
    1905   The Zuni Indians. *BAEAR* 23.

Steward, Julian H.
    1948   The Circum-Caribbean Tribes. In Handbook of South American Indians 4. *BAEB* 143.

Stiggins, George.
 1959 *Ethnohistory* 6:44.
Sumner, M.L.
 1951 Lodge-Boy and Thrown-Away: An analytic study of an American Indian Folktale. Stanford University: Unpub. M.A. thesis.
Swanton, John R.
 1907 Mythology of the Indians of Louisiana and the Texas coast. *JAF* 20:285ff.
 1911 Indian tribes of the Lower Mississippi Valley and adjacent coast of the Gulf of Mexico. *BAEB* 43.
 1913 Animal stories from the Indians of the Muskhogean stock. *JAF* 26:193–218.
 1917 Some Chitimacha myths and beliefs. *JAF* 30:474–78.
 1918 Catawba notes. *Journal of the Washington Academy of Sciences* 8.
 1922 Early history of the Creek Indians and their neighbors. *BAEB* 73.
 1928a Social organization and social usages of the Indians of the Creek Confederacy. *BAEAR* 42.
 1928b Social and religious beliefs of the Chickasaw Indians. *BAEAR* 44.
 1928c Sun worship in the Southeast. *AA* 30:206–13.
 1929 Myths and tales of the Southeastern Indians. *BAEB* 88.
 1931 Source material for the social and ceremonial life of the Choctaw Indians. *BAEB* 103.
 1942 Source material on the history and ethnology of the Caddo Indians. *BAEB* 132.
Thompson, Stith.
 1929 *Tales of the North American Indians.* Bloomington: Indiana University Press. (Reprint 1965.)
 1956–60 *Motif Index of World Literature* (6 vols.). Bloomington: Indiana University Press.
 1965 Star-Husband. In *The Study of Folklore,* Alan Dundes, ed. Prentice-Hall.
Traveller Bird.
 1974 *The Path to Snowbird Mountain.* North Carolina.
Tuggle, W.O.
 1973 *Shem, Ham and Japeth: The Papers of W.O. Tuggle.* Athens: University of Georgia Press.
Tyler, Hamilton A.
 1964 *Pueblo Gods and Myths.* Norman: University of Oklahoma Press.
Voth, H.R.
 1905 Traditions of the Hopi. *Field Museum Publication* 8.
Wagner, Gunter.
 1931 Yuchi tales. *Publications of the American Ethnological Society* 13.
Waring, A.J., and Preston Holder.
 1945 A prehistoric ceremonial complex in the Southeastern United States. *AA* 47:1ff.
Wassen, S.H.
 1949 Contributions to Cuna ethnography. Stockholm: *Etnologiska Studier* 16.
Waterman, T.T.
 1914 The explanatory element in the folk-tales of the North American Indians. *JAF* 27:1ff.
Waters, Frank.
 1963 *The Book of the Hopi.* New York: Ballentine.
Wheeler-Voegelin, Erminie, and Remedios W. Moore.
 1957 The emergence myth in Native North America. In *Studies in Folklore,* Edson Richmond, ed. Bloomington: Indiana University Press.

Wied, Prince Maximilian zu.
  1976   *People of the First Man: Life among the Plains Indians in their Final Days of Glory: The Firsthand Account of Prince Maximilian's Expedition up the Missouri River, 1833–34* (ed. Davis Thomas and Karin Ronnefeldt). New York: E.P. Dutton.
Will, G.F., and G.E. Hyde.
  1917   *Corn Among the Indians of the Upper Missouri.* St. Louis: W.H. Miner Co.
Williams, Roger.
  1827   A key into the language of America (1643). *Collections of the Rhode Island Historical Society* 1.
Wissler, Clark, and D.C. Duvall.
  1908   Mythology of the Blackfoot Indians. *American Museum of Natural History Anthropological Papers* 2.
Witthoft, John, and Wendell S. Hadlock.
  1946   Cherokee-Iroquois little people. *JAF* 59:413–22.
Witthoft, John, and William A. Hunter.
  1955   The seventeenth-century origins of the Shawnee. *Ethnohistory* 2:42–57.
Wolley, T.
  1902   *Two Years' Journal of a Sojourn in New York.* New York.
Works Progress Administration.
  1938   *Mississippi: A Guide to the Magnolia State.*
Wycoco, Remedios S.
  1951   The types of the North American Indian folktale. Indiana University: Unpub. Ph.D. dissertation.

Multicultural Books and Audiobooks
from August House

Thirty-three Multicultural Tales to Tell
Pleasant DeSpain
Hardback / ISBN 0-87483-265-9
Paperback / ISBN 0-87483-266-7
Audiobook / ISBN 0-87483-345-0

Wisdom Tales From Around the World
Fifty gems of wisdom from world folklore
Heather Forest
Hardback / ISBN 0-87483-478-3
Paperback / ISBN 0-87483-479-1

Wonder Tales From Around the World
Heather Forest
Hardback / ISBN 0-87483-421-X
Paperback / ISBN 0-87483-422-8
Audiobook / ISBN 0-87483-427-9

Of Kings and Fools
Stories of the French Tradition in North American
Michael Parent and Julien Olivier
Paperback / ISBN 0-87483-481-3

Cajun Folktales
J.J. Reneaux
Hardback / ISBN 0-87483-283-7
Paperback / ISBN 0-87483-282-9

August House Publishers P.O. Box 3223 Little Rock, AR 72203
800-284-8784 / order@augusthouse.com